Davy Crockett
Day by Day:

A Popular Culture and
Historical Calendar

by William R. Chemerka

Dedication

To Gary L. Foreman and Carolyn Raine-Foreman, two memorable and generous people who have shared Crockett's story with me and many others.

Davy Crockett Day by Day
© 2019. William R. Chemerka. All rights reserved.

All illustrations are copyright of their respective owners, and are also reproduced here in the spirit of publicity. Whilst we have made every effort to acknowledge specific credits whenever possible, we apologize for any omissions, and will undertake every effort to make any appropriate changes in future editions of this book if necessary.

No part of this book may be reproduced in any form or by any means, electronic, mechanical, digital, photocopying or recording, except for the inclusion in a review, without permission in writing from the publisher.

Published in the USA by:
BearManor Media
P O Box 71426
Albany, Georgia 31708
www.bearmanormedia.com

Printed in the United States of America
ISBN   978-1-62933-424-0 (Paperback)
         978-1-62933-425-7 (Hardcover)

Cover design by Mike Boldt and Darlene Swanson
Book and cover design by Darlene Swanson • www.van-garde.com

Contents

	Acknowledgments vii	
	Author's Introduction. xi	
Section One:	The David Crockett of History 1	
Section Two:	The Davy Crockett of Popular Culture 63	
Section Three:	The Crockett Calendar 207	
	Epilogue 273	
Appendix A:	David Crockett Biography, Collection of the U.S. House of Representatives. 277	
Appendix B:	David Crockett's Legislative Career.. 279	
Appendix C:	*Davy Crockett; Or, Be Sure You're Right, Then Go Ahead* cast.. 283	
Appendix D:	Topps *Walt Disney's Davy Crockett* picture cards, 1956.. 285	
Appendix E:	Western Writers of America's "All-Time Greatest Western TV Series, Movies and Miniseries" 2009 poll winners. 289	
Appendix F:	*Billboard* magazine's Top Singles of the Year, 1955 . . 291	
Appendix G:	*The Crockett Chronicle's* Top Ten Best Davy Crockett Movie Lines. 293	
	Bibliography 295	
	Index 309	

Acknowledgments

I am very grateful for the friendships I have made during my association with the life and legend of Davy Crockett. I'm fortunate that my wife, Debbie, has shared many of my adventures along the Crockett trail.

Once again, the talented Mike Boldt created a BearManor Media book cover for me. This imaginative cover depicts the David Crockett of history, as exemplified by a portrait attributed to Chester Harding in 1834. The accompanying calendar page reflects the month of Crockett's birth in 1786. The illustration of Fess Parker as Walt Disney's *Davy Crockett, King of the Wild Frontier*, drawn by the accomplished artist and historian Gary S. Zaboly, displays the memorable backwoods hero of popular culture. The other calendar page is the month when "Davy Crockett, Indian Fighter," the first episode of Walt Disney's *Davy Crockett* TV trilogy, aired in 1954. Gary provided additional illustrations in this book, some of which had appeared in other published works, including *The Crockett Chronicle*, and *The Alamo Journal*, two periodicals on which I served as editor and publisher.

I appreciate the friendship of Gary L. Foreman and Carolyn Raine-Foreman, to whom this humble book is dedicated. Over the years, we have worked together in films, documentaries, and living history events, and followed Crockett's path in Tennessee and Texas. Gary helped organize activities at the Witte Museum in San Antonio, Texas on August 17, 1986, which coincided with the bicentennial of Crockett's birth. Thanks, Gary, for allowing me to portray Crockett at the memorable event. The Foremans' Native Sun production company also created the wonderful History Channel documentary *Boone & Crockett: The Hunter Heroes* in 2001.

Thanks to Charles Martin Brazil who allowed me to use some of his creative images in this book.

Over the years, I have enjoyed working with many historians and researchers on such projects and events as The History Channel's *Live from Austin: The Story of Davy Crockett* in 2002; "The Crockett Symposium" at the Bob Bullock Texas History Museum in Austin in 2002; the "Davy Crockett" panel at the Western Writers of America conference in Knoxville, Tennessee in 2009; and numerous library and historical society programs.

I appreciate David Dewhurst, the former State of Texas Land Commissioner, for acknowledging my "contributions to the preservation of Texas history and the adoption of David Crockett's Land Grant File" in a presentation made by him on July 24, 2002.

A salute of gratitude to Joy Bland, Tim Massey, Vicky Henry, Carolyn Cotton, Frances John, and other members of the Direct Descendants and Kin of David Crockett. And thanks to Jim and Julie Simmons who secured one of those large "Crockett For Congress" campaign signs for me during the 1996 Direct Descendants and Kin of David Crockett reunion in Tennessee.

Thanks to Jasen Emmons, Director of Curatorial Affairs at Seattle's Museum of Pop Culture, who a decade ago, as Senior Curator at Seattle's Experience Music Project, helped organize and display some of the items from my Davy Crockett collection in *Disney: The Music Behind the Magic,* the national touring exhibit, in 2007-2009.

I am grateful to Ray Herbeck, Jr. Executive Producer of *Alamo... The Price of Freedom,* who allowed me to deliver the lines, "Crockett, North Wall! Crockett!," in the 1988 IMAX film, which allowed me to gain membership in the Screen Actors Guild.

Thanks to all of the guests from many states who attended the Davy Crockett Birthday Parties that Debbie and I hosted at our homes from 1990 to 2000. And thanks to Tom and Nancy Feely, and Murray and Heidi Weissmann for continuing to host them in the years that followed.

Mary Wilson of the Supremes, who recorded "The Ballad of Davy Crockett" many years ago, was scheduled to appear at a nearby concert in 2018. I asked her bass player, Dave Lowrey, a good friend of mine, if I could meet her after the show. Thanks to him, Debbie and I had the pleasure to sing the lyrical line "Davy, Davy Crockett, king of the wild frontier" with her. Of course, thank you, Mary Wilson.

I appreciate Elizabeth Gerberding LeBlanc, the talented harpist at Victoria & Albert's restaurant at Walt Disney World's Grand Floridian Resort, for always playing "The Ballad of Davy Crockett" in its most elegant form whenever Debbie and I dine there.

Denmark's Gert Petersen is one of the world's best Crockett researchers and he gladly shared some of his information with me. Gert and I maintain "Friend" memberships in the Direct Descendants and Kin of David Crockett. Gert also provides the most detailed information about Crockett's various Tennessee homes and properties on Facebook's The Historic David Crockett Homepage.

Thanks also to Joseph Musso, William Groneman III, Kate Nichols, Lenny Hekel, Jeff Bearden, Bill Earle, Robert L. Durham, Corwyn Edwards, John Kilbride, Pat Lederer, Robert Jahn, Nancy Boldt, Pastor Rodriguez, Tim Niesen, Jerry Laing, Alan Kude, Jim McCrain, Dean Shostak, Howard Bender, Don Vicaro, Paul DeVito, Mo Jones, Joe Rainone, Texas-Bob Reinhardt, Jerry Caine, Neil Abelsma, Larry Brenneman, John Hinnant, James R. Bolyston, Allen J. Wiener, Joe Swann, Jim Clayborn, Tim McCurry, Mark Sceurman, Paul Hutton, Robert Weil, David Zucker, Rich Markey, Manley F. Cobia, Phil Riordan, Eli Parker, Ashley Parker Snider, and Chuck Bargiel.

I appreciate the assistance provided by Sally Baker, Manager and Curator of the Crockett Tavern Museum in Morristown, Tennessee; Patricia Osborne and Sean McKay of the David Crockett Birthplace State Park in Limestone, Tennessee; and the staffs of the Daughters of the Republic of Texas Library Collection in San Antonio, Texas; the Morristown-Hamblen Library in Morristown, Tennessee; and the Morris County Library in Whippany, New Jersey.

And a tip of the coonskin cap to the late Fess Parker, who started me on this Crockett journey so many years ago. I am grateful for his friendship and appreciate the opportunity to have been able to write his authorized biography, *Fess Parker: TV's Frontier Hero*.

Finally, thanks again to Ben Ohmart and the staff at BearManor Media.

Author's Introduction

There has never been an American celebrity quite like David ("Davy") Crockett of Tennessee—frontier adventurer, flintlock sharpshooter, bear hunter, Creek War veteran, justice of the peace, militia commander, state legislator, congressman, author, Alamo defender. Legend.

George Washington may have thrown a Spanish milled dollar (or was it a small piece of slate?) across the Rappahannock River (or was it the wider Potomac?), but he never rode a giant pet alligator up Niagara Falls like Davy Crockett did. Benjamin Franklin's kite string fibers reacted to lighting during an experiment in a thunderstorm but, unlike Crockett, the enterprising Philadelphian never grabbed a lightning bolt and streaked away on it. Well, at least that's what some of the 19th century Crockett almanacs claimed.

Besides the fictional exploits and exaggerated tall tales of the Crockett almanacs, which were published from 1835 to 1856, there were enough real adventures in Crockett's life to distinguish him from so many others. His popular reputation was characterized in many ways. In 1834, Edward L. Carey and Abraham Hart, Crockett's publishers, called him the "Son the West," and in the years that followed various authors described him as "the very model of the trans-Appalachian frontiersman," "an immortal part of the national mythology," "the essence of the backwoods," and "one of America's greatest frontier heroes." Like other prominent individuals, he had his critics, and they called him everything from "the western Ourang Outang," and "rude and ridiculous" to one of the "Smart Alecks of the canebrakes."

Nevertheless, he was one of a kind, a self-made independent man who followed in no one's footsteps. When he was elected to public office, he sought to represent those without a political voice, particularly the poor farmers of Tennessee and the southeastern Native American tribes who were devastated by war, an awkward peace treaty, and legislation that eventually forced them off their lands on the infamous "Trail of Tears."

Famous in his own lifetime, Crockett transcended his own popularity when he died at the Alamo in 1836. Since then his legend has grown considerably. "Everybody, young and old, has heard of David Crockett, and some of his printed sayings are matters of every day reference," stated the March 16, 1863 edition of the *Indiana State Sentinel*. Forty-one years later, Council Bluffs, Iowa's *Daily Nonpareil* noted that "there is no name deserving of higher veneration than that of David Crockett."

Greater accolades were given to him in the 20th century. The Walt Disney *Davy Crockett* TV series of 1954-1955, and the popular song "The Ballad of Davy Crockett," helped launch an international popular culture phenomenon: the Davy Crockett Craze. It was the most extraordinary expression of the ongoing Crockett legend, but it simply followed peoples' continuous interest in the famous backwoodsman. In *Davy Crockett: The Man, The Legend, the Legacy, 1788-1986*, essayist Margaret King incorrectly stated that "Disney's version revived him from near-obscurity and enlarged substantially a minor American hero." The pages which follow counter the idea that Crockett was a "minor hero" who existed in "near obscurity."

Crockett's real-life adventures and legendary exploits have been constantly acknowledged, memorialized, and celebrated in prose and poetry, film and television, music and art, newspapers and periodicals, and in outrageous myths. This book provides a chronicle of those assorted manifestations in three major sections: The first highlights Crockett's life, the second traces his legend, and the third provides a 366-day calendar, which notes various aspects of both the David Crockett of history and the Davy Crockett of popular culture. The calendar's entries state actual moments from Crockett's life, newspaper accounts of his years in Congress, reports about his thirteen days of glory at the Alamo, and comments about the many actors who played him on stage, radio, recordings, film, and television. Also included are references about the tall tales that were featured in the Crockett almanacs, fictionalized and embellished events created by numerous writers, and excerpts from his autobiography, *A Narrative of the Life of David Crockett of the State of Tennessee.*

The line between the real man and the legendary character has not always been clear, and that's why Crockett remains such an interesting character. It is not surprising to understand that Crockett's life and legend have been shaped and altered as much by professional historians and writers as by whimsical tunesmiths and poets.

In any event, it is time to "Go Ahead!"

SECTION ONE

The David Crockett of History

*I leave this rule for others when I am dead,
Be always sure you're right—Then Go Ahead!*
— David Crockett, 1834

Following the American War for Independence, a "new society had been established, differing in essentials from the colonial society of the coast. It was a democratic self-sufficing, primitive agricultural society, which individualism was more pronounced than the community life of the lowlands. It was a region of hard work and poverty, not of wealth and leisure."[1] And David Crockett was its native son.

John Crockett, a veteran of the Revolutionary War, who participated in the Battle of Kings Mountain in 1780, and his wife, Rebecca, had six sons and three daughters. Their fifth son, David, was born on August 17, 1786, in their log cabin home on leased land, which was located at the mouth of Limestone Creek at the Nolichucky River in what is now eastern Tennessee, lands which were also occupied by the Creeks. Like other pioneers, John Crockett cleared the land, built his home, raised livestock, and hunted. Conflicts soon developed between the native peoples and the new settlers. "By the

Creeks, my grandfather and grandmother Crockett were both murdered, in their own house, and on the very ground where Rogersville, in Hawkins county, now stands," stated Crockett.[2]

The Crocketts were poor like so many other struggling frontier farming families. Whenever prospects seemed brighter or if conditions became increasingly more difficult, they moved and started all over again. Crockett recalled that around 1792 his family moved "about ten miles above Greeneville," which was close to the home of Rebecca's brother, John Hawkins. Two years later, they moved about sixteen miles away to Cove Creek where John Crockett and an associate, Thomas Galbreath, built a mill, hoping that it would provide a modest source of income. Neighboring farmers, rather than grinding flour at home by hand, would now have it done more easily at the mill. However, a flood destroyed the structure. "Away went their mill, shot, lock, and barrel," recalled young David. "I remember the water rose so high, that it got into the house we lived in, and my father moved us out of it, to keep us from being drowned."[3]

When Crockett was ten years old his family moved again. In 1796, his father opened a tavern on the road from Abingdon, Virginia to Knoxville, but it was not successful.[4] "I began to make up my acquaintance with hard times, and a plenty of them," noted the youngster.

The "hard times" became more obvious to David when he turned twelve. John Crockett's debts became so burdensome that he loaned his son out as a laborer to John Siler, a stranger, who was driving cattle to Virginia. Young Crockett made the demanding 400-mile journey on foot. Upon arriving at a destination near Natural Bridge, Siler, whom Crockett called the "old Dutchman," paid the young Tennessean and persuaded him to remain. Crockett stayed with Siler for another month but left him when he met a group of wagoners who were headed back to Tennessee. Fearful of Siler's wrath, Crockett agreed to meet the teamsters the following dawn at a tavern, which was located seven miles away. He had a restless night. "For though I was a wild boy, yet I dearly loved my father and mother, and their images appeared so deeply fixed in my mind, that I could not sleep for thinking of them," he remembered.[5] He awoke several hours before dawn and quietly left Siler's place during a snow storm. He estimated eight inches of snow had already fallen by the time he began his walk towards the road, which was located about a half mile away. Once Crockett reached the road, he continued towards the tavern. By the time he reached the wagoners, the snow had piled as high as his knees.

Crockett was appreciative of the wagoners, but their slow ride only made him more impatient to get home. During an overnight stay at the house of John Cole near Roanoke, Crockett explained to the others that he wanted to leave for home the following morning. He believed that he could cover more ground on foot than traveling with the wagons. "But home, poor as it was, again rushed on my memory, and it seemed ten times as dear to me as it ever had before," said Crockett. "The reason was, that my parents were there; and there my anxious little heart panted to be."[6] Shortly after he began his walk, a man with a drove of horses caught up to him and allowed Crockett to ride one of them, which took him to within fifteen miles of his father's tavern. Once the man turned on another road, Crockett left him and walked the remaining distance. It had been a long and arduous journey, but Crockett finally reached home. Unfortunately, he would not remain there for long.

In the autumn of 1799, thirteen-year-old David Crockett went to school for the first time. But after only four days in Benjamin

Kitchen's "little country school," Crockett got into a fight with an older boy. Fearful that Kitchen would whip him upon his return, Crockett stayed away from the school; however, he left home each morning so that his father thought he was going to school. John Crockett soon found out. "My father told me, in a very angry manner, that he would whip me an eternal sight worse than the master, if I didn't start immediately to school," said Crockett, who promptly ran away from home.[7]

He traveled several miles to the home of Jesse Cheek who was about to depart with a drove of cattle. Crockett joined him on the journey which ended in Front Royal, Virginia. The roughhouse community, which was located about seventy-five miles from Washington City, was also known as "Helltown" because of its brawling tavern clientele.

Crockett fell in with Adam Myers, another wagoner, who was headed to Gerrardstown, Virginia [now West Virginia]. Upon arrival at the Berkeley County community, the teenage runaway secured employment working on John Gray's farm at a wage of twenty-five cents a day. Upon Myers' return, Crockett left Gray and joined the teamster in several round trips to Baltimore, which almost led to a trans-Atlantic adventure.

He was fascinated by the tall ships in Baltimore's harbor. "I had never seen any such things before, and, indeed, I didn't believe there were any such things in all nature," he said.[8] Crockett walked aboard one ship and was approached by its captain who offered him an opportunity to sail to London. The teenager was enthused by the offer to sail the Atlantic. Crockett promptly asked Myers for his pay and extra clothes, but the teamster refused and threatened to bring him back to Tennessee. Several days later, he fled the wagoner. Without money and his few possessions, Crockett missed his opportunity to sail.

Fortunately, Crockett was befriended by Henry Myers, another wagoner, who later confronted Adam Myers about the young man's money and clothes. Threatened, Adam Myers agreed to pay Crockett when they both returned to Tennessee. However, after a few days, Crockett decided to travel on his own. Henry Myers and a few other teamsters gave Crockett three dollars and wished him well on his travels.

By the time he reached Christiansburg in Montgomery County, Virginia, his money had run out.[9] He labored a month for James Caldwell, and worked a year and a half for Elijah Griffith, a hatter. "I, however, set in again, and worked about as I could catch employment, until I got a little money, and some clothing; and once more cut out for home," he said.[10] He survived a treacherous canoe ride and trekked several miles through the woods, wearing frozen clothes, until he reached his brother's house in Sullivan County, Tennessee. He remained with his brother for a few weeks before continuing his journey home.

Crockett hadn't been home in over two years, and his family did not know whether he was dead or alive. "I had been gone so long, and had grown so much, that the family did not at first know me," he recalled. "The joy of my sisters and my mother, and, indeed, all of the family, was such that it humbled me, and made me sorry that I hadn't submitted to a hundred whippings, sooner than cause as much affliction as they had suffered on my account."[11]

One thing hadn't changed during Crockett's departure: his father's indebtedness. The sixteen-year-old was soon sent to work for a man named Abraham Wilson to whom John Crockett owed thirty-six dollars. After working six months to pay off Wilson, Crockett went to work for another six months to pay off yet another of his father's debts, a forty-dollar note held by John Canady, whom he called Kennedy in his autobiography years later.

Upon completion of his assigned labor, Crockett returned to Canady, who he called "an honest old Quaker," as a paid worker. Canady became more than just an employer: he became a second father to Crockett, providing the young man with a sense of morality, purpose, and direction. Furthermore, he helped curb Crockett's self-proclaimed "wild boy" frontier conduct, courtesy of a "Quaker doctrine [that was] far more effective in controlling behavior and encouraging hard work than other social and religious orders."[12]

Crockett was focused on his employment until two months later when Canady's half-niece, Amy Sumner, visited. He promptly fell in love. "For when I would think of saying anything to her, my heart would begin to flutter like a duck in a puddle; and if I tried to outdo it and speak, it would get right smack in my throat, and choak (sic) me like a cold potato," he lamented. But the one-sided romance quickly came to an end when she told him that she was engaged to her cousin. Crockett took the news hard. "The news was worse to me than war, pestilence, or famine," he remembered.[13]

Crockett came to the conclusion that his romantic failures were based upon his lack of a proper education. "I began now to think that all my misfortunes growed out of my want of learning," he said. "I had never been to school but four days."[14] Crockett worked out an agreement with Canady's married son, Charles, who ran a small school: he would attend class four days a week and would work two days to pay for the schooling. Crockett expected to be better prepared for his next romantic encounter.

Crockett began a courtship with Margaret Elder. "I still continued paying my respects to her, until I got to love her as bad as I had the Quaker's niece," said Crockett.[15] After nearly a year of seeing each other, the nineteen-year-old secured a marriage license on October 21, 1805.[16] But on the eve of the scheduled wedding, he received unpleasant news from his betrothed's sister. "She then burst into tears, and told me her sister was going to deceive me; and that she was to be married to another man the next day," he recalled. "This was as sudden to me as a clap of thunder [on] a bright sunshiny day." The girl urged Crockett to fight for her sister and "break off the match," but he said that his "heart was bruised" and "could go no further."[17]

Crockett reacted to his "down-spirited situation" by hunting. Alone, he took his flintlock rifle, powder horn, and shot pouch, and entered the forest primeval, which provided him an opportunity to concentrate on something other than his romantic failures. Fortunately, his romantic fortunes soon changed.

At a reaping frolic, Crockett met Mary Polly Finley, to whom he was immediately attracted. "She looked sweeter than sugar," he recalled. Their courtship quickly developed into a serious relationship, although her mother was initially not fond of Crockett. The couple secured a marriage license and were wed on August 16, 1806, a day before Crockett's twentieth birthday; Polly was nineteen.

They rented a farm in Finley Gap in East Tennessee. The next year Polly gave birth to John Wesley; William was born in 1809. "I was better at increasing my family than my fortune," he noted. In the early autumn of 1811, after exploring an area in south-central Tennessee, Crockett and his family moved to Lincoln County, just north of Lynchburg. "It was here that I began to distinguish myself as a hunter, and to lay the foundation for all my future greatness," said Crockett. He moved yet again in 1812 to Bean Creek in Franklin County, Tennessee, where he rented land from Francis "Glaspie" (who had purchased it from Robert Bean), and called his new homestead "Kentuck."[18]

During the winter of 1811-1812, several devastating earthquakes shook the region and created large cracks in the earth. For Crockett, the earthquakes altered hunting grounds which allowed bears to move about more freely without being seen on the surface. Years later, Crockett remarked that a "bear got down in one of the cracks, that the earthquakes had made in the ground, about four feet deep."[19] The New Madrid earthquakes, as they are now called, were concentrated in southeast Missouri, but tremors were felt as far away as New England. The rumblings of earthquakes would soon be replaced by artillery explosions and musket volleys from a foreign foe. By the time Polly gave birth to her third child, Margaret, in November, the United States was at war again with Great Britain.

In the years following the Revolutionary War, Great Britain and France waged war against each other. The American merchant fleet was caught up in the conflict when the European rivals harassed foreign ships on the high seas. Under the pretext of searching American ships for cargoes sent to France and for seeking the return of deserters from the Royal Navy, British warships disrupted shipping and impressed Yankee sailors who were forcibly removed from their vessels. "British ships have continually violated the American flag on the great highway of nations," stated President James Madison in his war message to Congress on June 1, 1812. The diplomatic saber rattling over Atlantic Ocean disputes seemed too distant a concern for the Crocketts and other frontier families, but the nation's fourth president explained an additional threat Great Britain posed to American settlers. "In this warfare, both women and children are killed and the Indians use brutal fighting methods," said Madison. "It is difficult to account for the activity among tribes in constant communication with British traders and garrisons without connecting their hostility with that influence."[20]

On June 18, 1812, the United States declared war against Great Britain. The conflict marked the emergence of a new generation of American leaders, military commanders, and diplomats who followed the legacies of George Washington, Nathaniel Greene, Daniel Morgan, Alexander Hamilton, Benjamin Franklin, and so many others who were no longer alive.

For over a year, Tennessee was far removed from the War of 1812. Most of the battles had been fought along the Canadian border, especially around the eastern Great Lakes at such places as Fort Dearborn, Sackets Harbor, Brownstown, and Ogdensburg. The fighting soon shifted south.

The war exacerbated tensions among the Creeks. Many had embraced aspects of white society, but the Red Stick faction of the Creeks (named after the red painted war clubs they carried) opposed the influence of the expanding frontier settlements. The Creeks also waged war against each other. On July 27, 1813, a group of Red Stick warriors, which had been supplied with ammunition from Spain, a British ally, was traveling back from Pensacola when they were attacked by an American force at Burnt Corn Creek, in what is now southern Alabama. On August 30, the Creeks retaliated by attacking Fort Mims, which was located about 40 miles north of Mobile, Alabama. Nearly one thousand warriors killed or captured approximately five hundred militiamen and noncombatants. "For when I heard of the mischief which was done to the fort, I instantly felt like going, and I had none of the dread of dying that I expected to feel," said Crockett, who enlisted on September 24, 1813, for a ninety-day term of service in Capt. Francis Jones' Company of Tennessee Volunteer Mounted Riflemen, which was part of Col. Newton Cannon's regiment.[21] "The time arrived; I took a parting farewell of my wife and little boys, mounted my horse, and set sail, to join my company," said Crockett."[22]

Volunteers poured in from the backwoods, established settlements, and frontier towns. "At last we mustered about thirteen hundred strong, all mounted volunteers, and all determined to fight, judging from myself, for I felt wolfish all over," said Crockett, who was soon approached by Maj. John H. Gibson to join an expedition into Creek territory. "He came to my captain, and asked for two of his best woodsmen, and such as were best with a rifle. The captain pointed me out to him."[23] The man Gibson saw "was about six feet high, weighed about two hundred pounds, had no surplus flesh, broad shouldered, stood erect, was a man of great physical strength, of fine appearance, his cheeks mantled with a rosy hue."[24]

Crockett and George Russell, the other handpicked rifleman, and three additional volunteers were ordered into the woods; Gibson and six other men took another path into the wilderness. Crockett and his squad located a group of Creeks, and quickly reported to Col. John Coffee's headquarters near what is now Huntsville, Alabama. However, Coffee, who would soon be promoted to brigadier general, was reluctant to accept Crockett's report without confirmation, which he received a day later when Gibson arrived. Crockett was livid. "When I made my report, it wasn't believed, because I was no officer: I was no great man, but just a poor soldier," said Crockett. "But when the same thing was reported by Major Gibson!! why, then, it was all true as preaching, and the colonel believed every word."[25] The incident reinforced Crockett's growing belief that pioneer people were held in contempt by those in authority, especially high-ranking military officers.

Coffee promptly informed Gen. Andrew Jackson, who was camped with his army about forty miles away. Jackson, the rugged commander known as "Old Hickory," arrived at Coffee's new headquarters along the Tennessee River on October 10, 1813. Following his arrival, Crockett was engaged in several operations against the Creeks, but supplies began to run low, and half-rations were issued. Many of the volunteers survived by eating handfuls of parched corn. As a result of the dwindling camp provisions, Crockett was authorized to hunt, and thanks to his skills, he soon provided deer and wild hog meat for the troops.

Jackson planned a major offensive against the Creeks at Tallusahatchee, in what is now Calhoun County, Alabama. On November 3, Jackson divided his force into two divisions and attacked the Creek village. Musket volleys, rifle shots, darting arrows, and hand-to-hand fighting filled the battleground. One Creek woman, who sat in the doorway of a house, supported a bow with her feet and released an arrow which struck one of Crockett's comrades, who quickly died. The soldiers and volunteers were enraged and fired at her. She had "at least twenty balls blown through her," recalled Crockett. "We now shot them like dogs; and then set the house on fire, and burned it up with the forty-six warriors in it."[26] Nearly two hundred Creeks were killed; Jackson's forces suffered fewer than four dozen casualties.

Thirty miles to the south, a sizable Creek force besieged Fort Talladega. Six days later, on November 9, Jackson's army advanced against over a thousand Native American warriors. "They had encamped near the fort, and had informed the friendly Indians who were in it, that if they didn't come out, and fight with them against the whites, they would take their fort and all their ammunition and provision," said Crockett.[27]

The inhabitants of the fort held out as Jackson's force battled the Creeks. "They fought with guns, and also with their bows and arrows, but at length they made their escape through part of our line, which was made up of drafted militia, which broke ranks, and they passed," recalled Crockett. "We lost fifteen of our men, as brave fellows as ever lived or died."[28] Approximately three hundred Creek warriors were killed.

Crockett's enlistment expired on Christmas eve, and he departed Jackson's ranks for home. His dedicated military pay, which included an extra payment for his horse, totaled $65.65, although for some reason his actual pay totaled six cents less.

While Crockett remained at home with his family, the Creek War continued until March 27, 1814, when Jackson was victorious at the Battle of Horseshoe Bend in the Alabama Territory. Although some Creeks remained on the warpath, the southeastern-based tribe ceded nearly two-thirds of its lands, nearly 36,000 square miles, to the United States on August 9, 1814, in the Treaty of Fort Jackson.[29]

Despite the suppression of the Creeks, the War of 1812 continued. In the summer of 1814, Great Britain invaded the Chesapeake region of the United States and soon gained control of the young nation's capital. On August 24, British forces set fire to many of the federal government's buildings, including the White House.

A month later a combined British land and sea assault against Baltimore was stopped at Fort McHenry. Two weeks later, on September 28, 1814, Crockett reenlisted.

Crockett and nearly two hundred other volunteers marched to Pensacola on November 8, and joined Jackson's army, which had witnessed the departure of the British fleet a day earlier. Jackson subsequently moved on to New Orleans where the British were planning to attack. Crockett, serving in Maj. Uriah Blue's regiment, marched to Fort Montgomery, which was located about a mile and a half away from Fort Mims. "We had about one thousand men, and as part of that number, one hundred and eighty-six Chickasaw and Choctaw Indians with us," said Crockett, who later went on a scouting mission with some of the indigenous allies.[30] The animosity among the various tribes became clear when two Creeks were decapitated and scalped by the Chickasaw and Choctaw scouts. The inter-tribal hostility was a violation of Treaty of Fort Jackson, but nothing was done to the scouts.[31]

The patrol continued its Florida operations along the Escambia River and the Chocktawhatchee River for weeks, but its twenty-day ration supply was soon exhausted. "I remember well, that I had not myself tasted bread but twice in nineteen days," said Crockett. "As the army marched, I hunted every day, and would kill every hawk, bird, and squirrel that I could find."[32] He also traded some black powder and lead rifle balls to some friendly Creeks in exchange for corn.

Crockett and his comrades in arms were unaware that Jackson had won a brilliant victory against the British at New Orleans on January 8, 1815, two weeks after peace was negotiated in Ghent, Belgium. Prisoners, occupied lands, and ships were returned. Although the issue of impressment was not completely resolved in the treaty, the British ended its practice against American shipping.

Crockett and the rest of his comrades in arms began their long march back to Tennessee.

On March 27, 1815, Crockett ended his second volunteer tour of service with the rank of fourth sergeant, although another service record identifies his rank as third sergeant. "This closed my career as a warrior, and I am glad of it, for I like life now a heap better than I did then; and am glad all over that I lived to see these times, which I should not have done if I had kept fooling along in war, and got used up in it," he said.[33] Crockett was out of the army, but something he had said during his service remained with the men in ranks, at least according to one writer's recollection. Capt. William Moore, who at one time was Crockett's company commander, went to see Gen. Jackson about problems the young officer was having with his young recruits. Crockett accompanied Moore and remembered Jackson telling the officer, "Captain, don't make any orders without needing them, and then execute them, no matter what it costs." When the two returned to camp, some of the soldiers wanted to know what happened. Crockett responded with a laugh and said that "the General told the Captain to be sure he is right and then go ahead," [and] the next day [Moore said that] Crockett's words were in the mouth of every soldier in the regiment."[34]

The new year looked promising. The war was over and Crockett was home with his family, but tragedy struck. "Death, that cruel leveler of all distinctions—to whom the prayers and tears of husbands, and of even helpless infancy, are addressed in vain—entered my humble cottage, and tore from my children an affectionate good mother, and from me a tender and loving wife," said Crockett, who asked his younger brother's family to live with him a while.[35] Crockett, though, acknowledged that he "must have another wife."

Davy Crockett at the End of the Creek War. **Illustration by Gary S. Zaboly.**

By the time he was elected a lieutenant in the 32nd Regiment of the Tennessee State Militia, he was courting Elizabeth Patton, a twenty-six-year-old widow whose husband had died during the Creek War. "She had two small children, a son and a daughter, [George, born in 1810, and Margaret Ann, born in 1813] and both quite small, like my own," he said. "I began to think, that as both we were in the same situation, it might be that we could do something for each other; and I began to hint a little around the matter, as we were once in a while together."[36] The courtship, however, was seemingly based more on Crockett's need to provide a mother for his children than to fulfill his own romantic void. The pair were married on May 22, 1815, Elizabeth's twenty-seventh birthday, and on September 16, 1816, Elizabeth gave birth to Robert Patton Crockett. Rebecca Elvira Crockett was born on December 15, 1818, and Matilda Crockett was born on August 2, 1821.

Always adventurous, he left his home at the Rattle Snake Spring branch of Beans Creek and joined three neighbors in a lengthy backwoods trek during the autumn of 1815. After crossing the Tennessee River, one of them was bitten by a venomous snake and was left behind to recuperate at the home of a Crockett acquaintance. Crockett and the others went on. One day, just before dawn, their horses walked away. Crockett promptly went after them, since he could hear the small bells that had been placed on them. But the steeds were elusive. Despite an all-day search through swamps and creeks, Crockett finally gave up his quest due to physical concerns. "The next morning I was so sore and fatigued, that I felt like I couldn't walk any more," he said. "I now began to feel mighty sick, and had a dreadful headache."[37] His conditioned worsened. Initially found by two Indians who took him to a nearby woman's house, Crockett was subsequently located by his two hunting companions who carried him to the home of Jesse Jones. Crockett seemed to be suffering from malaria and remained at the house for two weeks. Crockett, who recalled that he was "speechless for five days," was given a powerful concoction of Batesman's drops, a solution of camphor, opium, and catechu, an Acacia tree extract.

Crockett, though severely weakened, eventually recovered and made it home. "When I got there, it was to the utter astonishment of my wife; for she supposed I was dead," he said.[38] Crockett believed that the area where they lived was "sickly," so he set out the next year to look for land at Shoal Creek, which was about eighty miles away. Upon his arrival there, he seemed to suffer a relapse of malaria, but it did not prevent him from settling there.

Shoal Creek, located northeast of modern Lawrenceburg, developed quickly, and the county of Lawrence was created in October 1817. On November 25, 1817, the Tennessee General Assembly authorized the creation of twelve justices of the peace for the area. Crockett, known to his neighbors as a veteran of the Creek War and an accomplished hunter, was appointed to one of the positions. "When a man owed a debt, and wouldn't pay it, I and my constable ordered our warrant, and then he would take the man, and bring him before me for trial," said Crockett, who was later elected the colonel of the 57th Regiment of Militia in Lawrence County on March 27, 1818.[39] As time passed, he was frequently referred to as Colonel Crockett.

In 1819, Crockett acquired a new parcel of land that was situated close to what was to become Lawrenceburg. He moved his family there and was appointed to a five-man commission which was authorized to select the location of the new community.[40] The next year, a majority of the commissioners decided to establish the town on the Military Road on Shoal Creek, but Crockett voted against the decision and later resigned from the commission on January 1, 1821. Crockett and his family moved again, this time at Crowson Creek, which was his final home in Lawrence County.

Crockett had a new goal: he decided to run for a position in the Tennessee General Assembly. Such a move, of course, would involve campaigning and "speechifying." Although a brave Creek War veteran and a fearless backwoods hunter, Crockett felt uncomfortable delivering a public address. "The thought of having to make a speech made my knees feel mighty weak, and set my heart to fluttering," he confessed. However, he quickly developed a successful campaign strategy: speak for a short time, "tell some laughable story, and quit."[41] Crockett's simplistic, from-the-heart strategy, which utilized strategic boasting with doses of self-deprecating humor, captivated crowds. Sometimes he would end his presentation with a special invitation. "I took care to remark that I was as dry as a powder horn, and that I thought it was time for us to wet our whistles a little; and so I put off to the liquor stand, and was followed by a greater part of the crowd," he said. Among candidates on the stump, Crockett enjoyed speaking last. "These big candidates spoke nearly all day, and when they quit, the people were worn out with fatigue, which afforded me a good apology for not discussing the government,"[42] he said. It worked. He was elected to the House of Representatives in Tennessee's Fourteenth General Assembly, and traveled to Murfreesboro for the opening of the first session on September 17, 1821.

He was named to the Committee of Propositions and Grievances, which soon resolved that Western district land owners be exempt from a so-called double tax payment. Crockett's first vote soon followed when he cast an affirmative ballot for a resolution which named a replacement for a vacant U.S. Senate seat.

Crockett's backwoods status as a member of the General Assembly was not respected by all. In 1822, a critic called him "the gentleman from the cane," a sarcastic expression which cast a dispersion on his poor canebrake residency. However, rather than criticizing the derogatory characterization, Crockett embraced the title and continued to emphasize his humble background to the voting public.

Crockett's main legislative concern was protecting the rights of the poor squatters who had moved onto government-owned lands. The squatters had made improvements on the lands by clearing the woods, building homes, and raising crops and livestock, but were too poor to purchase the property. Crockett not only represented the frontier farmers, he identified with them. Like most of his constituents, he was not in the best of financial situations, but he had high hopes for a newly-built enterprise consisting of a grist mill, gunpowder mill, and distillery. However, a damaging flood destroyed the mills, which continued his streak of misfortunes. Crockett was soon on the move again.

In September 1822, he settled his family near the Rutherford Fork of the Obion River in Carroll County, which was later designated as part of Gibson County. He established a farm and completed his term in the General Assembly. "I attended it, and served out my time, and then returned, and took my family and what plunder I had, and moved to where I built my cabin, and made my [crop]," he said.[43]

He ran for a new term against Dr. William Butler, an educated man who was married to one of Andrew Jackson's nieces. On the campaign trail, Crockett characterized Butler as an eastern elitist, one who supposedly could not relate to the backwoods constituency. Crockett helped his own cause when he offered select voters drinks from his liquor bottle and "chaws" of tobacco. Word quickly spread about his generosity on the stump. Crockett won reelection and returned to Murfreesboro on September 15, 1823, where he represented the counties of Carroll, Henderson, Humphreys, Madison, and Perry in the Fifteenth General Assembly. Crockett became an active member of the legislative body, and he learned much about the nature of politics, spirited debating, diplomacy, and the art of compromise.

As in the previous session of the General Assembly, Crockett championed the rights of poor farmers and squatters; however, he was unsuccessful securing legislation that would protect them against wealthier political factions and speculators. Years later, on the national stage, he would fight again for the impoverished agrarians.

Although initially supportive of Andrew Jackson, Crockett's political split with his former Creek War commander developed when the frontier legislator cast a vote for Col. John Williams, the incumbent Tennessee Senator, instead of Jackson, in a U.S. Senate election. "I thought the colonel had honestly discharged his duty, and even the mighty name of Jackson couldn't make me vote against him," said Crockett. "But voting against the old chief was found a mighty up-hill business."[44] Jackson won the Senate seat, but "Old Hickory" had his sights on the nation's highest office. Crockett's permanent split with Jackson was still several political seasons away.

In the 1824 presidential election, Jackson won more electoral votes than any of his three opponents, but his plurality was not enough to win. A subsequent runoff vote in the House of Representatives on February 9, 1825, resulted in a victory for John Quincy Adams, who became the nation's sixth chief executive. Jackson resigned from the Senate, returned to Tennessee, and vowed to come back. Crockett also entered the national political arena in 1825 when he challenged Col. Adam Alexander, a supporter of Jackson and a pro-tariff advocate, in the election for Tennessee's

Ninth District in Congress. During the campaign, Crockett reminded farmers and squatters that revenue generated from foreign imports would do little to improve their lives; Alexander countered his claims. "For it was that year that cotton brought twenty-five dollars a hundred; and so Colonel Alexander would get up and tell the people, it was all the good effect of this tariff law; that it had raised the price of their cotton, and that it would raise the price of everything else they made to sell," said Crockett.[45] Alexander rode western Tennessee's tide of relatively good economic times and won by a vote of 2,866 to 2,599. Like Jackson, Crockett vowed to win in the next election.

An historical nostalgia movement, inspired by the Marquis de Lafayette's return visit in 1824, pervaded the nation at the same time Crockett was becoming more active in politics. The famous Frenchman's tour of the United States reminded citizens of the founders' contributions and the role played by veterans of the American Revolution. The movement manifested itself in a number of important ways: Historical associations were formed, the Washington National Monument Society dedicated itself to raise funds to build a towering obelisk to the nation's first Constitutional president, and the Revolutionary War Pension Act was amended. Despite this national celebration of the past, a new group of political leaders was emerging with distinct visions of the future. And Crockett was among them.

For a while, America's period of harmonious nostalgia shrouded the growing antagonisms that were developing in the nation, especially those between the northern and southern states. The Panic of 1819, the Missouri Compromise, the fight over the National Bank, the conflict over the future of Indian lands in the Southeast, the

Nullification Crisis, and the pervasiveness of the so-called "peculiar institution" created tensions and exacerbated sectional antagonisms.

Despite his legislative duties in Tennessee's General Assembly, Crockett still had responsibilities at home, although his wife, Elizabeth, carried the entire domestic load in his absence. Tending the farm and raising the children, three of whom were under the age of nine years old, were quite enough for any couple to handle, let alone one parent on the frontier. When he wasn't in Murfreesboro, he was frequently away from home for one reason or another. During the winter of 1825-1826, he claimed to have killed 105 bears. Soon thereafter, he was off on a river journey, bringing two boatloads of approximately 30,000 wooden barrel staves to New Orleans. Crockett and his crew were not the most experienced river travelers, and the group was soon challenged when their boats crashed into a piece of large drift timber and started to sink. Momentarily caught below deck, Crockett managed to escape by climbing through a small window. Crockett and his mates spent the night on the drift timber, but were rescued the next morning. They were later brought to Memphis where Crockett was clothed by postmaster Marcus B. Winchester, who urged him to run again for congress.

By the early summer of 1827, Crockett was back on the campaign trail, challenging Col. Adam Alexander, the incumbent, and newcomer Col. William Arnold. Once again, Crockett was broke, but Winchester bankrolled him. Alexander and Arnold treated the Congressional race as a two-man campaign, and most of the time they ignored Crockett, who benefited from being out of the national spotlight during a two-year recession. Crockett split the vote and won with 5,868 votes; Alexander totaled 3,646 votes, and Arnold tallied 2,417 votes. For Crockett, it was an important achievement. In less than five years, the backwoodsman had gone from being a town commissioner to a member of the United States House of Representatives.

The Twentieth Congress of the United States convened with the Honorable David Crockett representing Tennessee's Ninth District as a Jacksonian, the party affiliation of the other eight Tennessee congressmen. To the Washington elite, Crockett was an uneducated backwoodsman who seemed to represent the unpleasant underside of democracy. To be sure, he lacked the college educations which half his fellow Tennessee representatives possessed, and his limited experience as a justice of the peace paled in comparison to the formal legal backgrounds of other Tennessee congressmen. Others, however, found his humble frontier upbringing and interpretation of the world around him rather amusing. Moreover, like Andrew Jackson, Crockett signaled a developing shift of political power from the eastern seaboard to the West. Later, Jackson's victory in the election of 1828 marked for the first time that the nation's chief executive was born in a state that didn't border the Atlantic. And once again, That same year, Crockett moved his family to a tract of land in what is now Gibson County.

Cognizant of the struggle of the squatters, Crockett focused his efforts on the Tennessee Vacant Land Bill, which was designed to allow the state to sell unclaimed federal land within its borders and use some of the funds to build public schools. Fellow Tennessee congressman James Knox Polk, who represented the Sixth District, argued that the state would benefit if the land could be sold at the highest price, but Crockett questioned the impact of the bill on the squatters who could not afford to purchase the real estate. Furthermore, Crockett thought that the cash-less farmers would lose their land to speculators. In any event, the House of Representatives tabled the bill, and the political harmony which had once existed among the Tennessee delegation began to deteriorate.

Crockett proposed a revision to Polk's bill which would benefit the squatters by giving them direct title to their improved lands (capping the real estate amount at 160 acres), but the amendment was rejected by the rest of the Tennessee delegation. Crockett went public in December 1828, arguing for his position and indirectly criticizing Polk and the other Tennessee representatives. The split between Crockett and the Polk-led Tennesseans, who were in the political camp of Andrew Jackson, widened. Pryor Lea, who represented Tennessee's Second District, became Crockett's most vocal critic. Both men became engaged in a series of heated attacks in newspapers and circulars; in fact, the two seemed to be heading towards a physical confrontation that recalled the fatal meeting between Alexander Hamilton and Aaron Burr. The bill and Crockett's amendment were tabled on January 13, 1829, and were not revived during the session. Although Crockett was unable to secure the legislation, the poor citizens in his district appreciated the honest way he represented them. Crockett expected that his effort, not his legislative failure, would generate votes in the next election.

Crockett's opponents not only criticized him on policy matters but increasingly condemned him as a backwoods buffoon, uneducated and illiterate, and incapable of being a gentleman. Increasingly, false information was provided to newspapers in which Crockett was accused of a number of improper behaviors, including awkward dining deportment in the presence of President Adams. Some publications immediately came to his defense. On January 22, 1829, North Carolina's *Raleigh Star* stated: "Personally, we know him not, but from the character of the subjoined language [a letter written by Crockett on January 3, 1829, condemning the accusations], we take him to be a man of good sense, and proper feeling." Nevertheless, Crockett said enough on the campaign trail to substantiate his critics' claims. One statement describes his reaction to a claim made against him: "Friends, fellow-citizens, brothers and sisters: They accuse me of being a drunkard, it's a damned eternal lie—for whiskey can't make me drunk."[46] Crockett, though, was more competent and astute than his critics realized, and he easily won reelection in 1829, when he received 6,773 votes to Col. Adam Alexander's 3,641 ballots. An interesting post-election comment in New York's *Commercial Advertiser* on September 8, 1829, provided an example of a larger-than-life personality in the making: "Col. David Crockett, who looked a wild cat to death, swam the Mississippi towing a steam boat, and did a great many other feats…has been re-elected to Congress from the Western District of Tennessee, by a majority of 3,000 votes."

When he returned to Washington City, Andrew Jackson resided at the White House. The comradeship that they had originally enjoyed ended. "I was willing to go with General Jackson in everything that I believed was honest and right; but further than this, I wouldn't go for him, or any other man in the whole creation; that I would sooner be honestly and politically [damned], than hypocritically immortalized," he said.[47] The Hero of New Orleans had pro-Jacksonian majorities in both houses of Congress; however, Crockett later become the only anti-Jacksonian in the Tennessee delegation.

As a member of the Twenty-first Congress, Crockett attempted to revive his land bill. He managed to write compromise legislation that would seemingly benefit both Tennessee (the state would have control over selling the land) and the squatters (they would be able to purchase their improved lands for 12½ cents an acre). Crockett didn't want the farmers to pay anything for the land, but the bill at least offered them a less expensive way of securing legal title to the land. The Tennessee delegation supported it, but the bill failed because the seaboard states were opposed to it. For Crockett and the poor farmers, the land bill was a major political failure.

Crockett's failed attempts to assist the poor farmers did not go unnoticed. In the July 6, 1831 issue of the *Nashville Whig*, he was praised for his "pertinacious efforts to obtain for those needy but hardy families, who have made clearings on the public lands in the western district of Tennessee, the pre-emption rights to those lands, or to have them granted directly their industrious and enterprising occupants, for a small price, instead of giving the lands to the state of Tennessee, and leaving the state to sell them to the occupants, as was the wish of the rest of the delegation of that state."

Crockett sat for his first portrait in the early 1830s. The unknown artist, who has sometimes been incorrectly identified as Rembrandt Peale, depicted Crockett with a serious look and wearing the clothes of a gentleman. Extant reproductions of the work are quite dark, with only Crockett's face and parts of his shirt as identifiable elements. Only four years after that seating, Crockett became a popular subject for some of America's best artists.

Besides his endeavors on behalf of the struggling frontier farmers, Crockett criticized government institutions which favored the upper socio-economic classes. For example, he viewed the United States Military Academy at West Point as an elitist aristocratic institution which benefited rich appointees, and he spoke out against its existence. For Crockett, locally elected militia officers were preferred over government trained officers. Obviously, his efforts to reform or eliminate the Academy were unsuccessful.

He also voted against other Jackson-supported measures which reinforced his isolation from his Tennessee Congressional peers and the President. Nothing represented the divide more than Crockett's position on the Indian Removal Act, which proposed moving many of the Southeastern tribes from their homelands to designated areas west of the Mississippi River. On May 19, 1830, Crockett addressed his fellow members of the House of Representatives and explained that the Indians were not being treated fairly. If tribes had to be moved, he reasoned, they would have to willingly agree to it. To some, Crockett's opposition was difficult to understand. His grandparents had been killed by Creeks, and he had fought in the Creek War, but Crockett thought the proposed legislation was morally wrong. "I voted against this Indian bill, and my conscience yet tells me that I gave a good and honest vote, and one that I believe will not make me ashamed in the day of judgment," he said.[48] Crockett's vote was one of 97 cast against the bill; 102 voted for it. The Senate had already voted for the legislation by a vote of 28 to 19. Jackson signed the bill on May 24, 1830. The infamous "Trail of Tears" would follow.

Although the bill had become law, Crockett continued to criticize Jackson and those in Congress who supported the legislation. In a sixteen-page February 28, 1831 circular addressed to the "Citizens and Voters of the Ninth Congressional District," Crockett attacked the Jacksonians for wasteful spending and their positions against poor squatters and Native Americans. "You know that I am a poor man; and that I am a plain man, I have served you long enough in peace, to enable you to judge whether I am honest or not—I have never deceived you—I will never deceive you," stated Crockett. "I have fought with you in war, and you know whether I love my country, and ought to be trusted, I thank you for what you have done for me and I hope that you will not forsake me to gratify those who are my enemies and yours."[49]

On April 25, 1831, Crockett's public profile was elevated when James Kirke Paulding's play, *The Lion of the West*, opened in New York City. The play's fictional title character, Nimrod Wildfire, played by James Hackett, was a brave and boastful backwoodsman who was costumed in primitive clothing and a fur-skin cap, but the staged characterization was a parody of Crockett. "I'm half horse, half alligator, a touch of the airth-quake, with a sprinkling of the steamboat!" boasted Wildfire.

Paulding, who had originally written the play as an entry into a contest sponsored by Hackett the year before, did not initially base the Wildfire character on Crockett. However, Paulding combined elements of backwoods brags and tall tales with Crockett's growing notoriety to create the finished character. The play was later revised by John Augustus Stone before the production began its tour later in 1831. At first, Crockett was not amused by Hackett's depiction, but as the play's popularity grew, he began to embrace it, especially when a new antagonist, Mrs. Amelia Wallope, an English lady who frowned on American manners, was introduced. The female character was a satirical treatment of Frances Trollope, the author of *Domestic Manners of the Americans*, a two-volume title published in London in 1832, which contained observations about the author's sojourns in the United States, particularly in Tennessee and Ohio. Above all, Trollope frowned upon the crudeness of stateside behavior. Audience members saw Wildfire as Crockett and Wallope as the Eastern establishment. Theater patrons championed the uncouth, rough and tumble character and Crockett.[50]

Crockett's name was given to a race horse for the first time in

1831. As the years passed, many horses carried the famous frontiersman's name; however, none of the steeds ever became a major winner at any American track. Still, the horses contributed to Crockett's growing level of celebrity.

When Crockett returned to the campaign trail, his principled stands were promptly challenged by his political opponents who, in turn, were countered by his supporters. The July 6, 1831 issue of the *Nashville Whig* noted that "this plain spoken, unsophisticated individual, of whom everybody has heard, and whose peculiarities have been the subject of much exaggeration, being a candidate for re-election to Congress, and having a competitor for the honor, is consequently warmly assailed in some of the newspapers of his district." The campaign would be his most challenging yet.

The Jacksonians mobilized against Crockett in the next Congressional election. The heated race, in which candidate William Fitzgerald pulled a pistol on Crockett at one event, featured anti-Crockett articles in Madison County's influential *Jackson Gazette*. Crockett remained independent and true to his convictions, and he received nearly 8,000 votes, over a thousand more than he tallied in the previous election, but the Jackson political machine was too powerful for him to overcome; Fitzgerald received 8,534 votes.

Crockett returned home in 1831 where he faced more debts, legal suits, and unpaid tax bills. He sold some of his acreage and accepted several local government jobs to help pay off his debts. He moved to yet another nearby parcel of land, which he leased from Atlas Jones for six years. Crockett planned "to build cabins, a smokehouse, corn cribs, and stables."[51]

Jackson was reelected in 1832, but "Old Hickory" was criticized over a number of issues, from his opposition to the Second National

Bank and his stand against nullification to his alleged abuse of the veto. Jackson's Democrat Party controlled the Senate but a coalition of National Republicans and anti-Jacksonians held a majority in the House. In less than two years, the opposition forces would merge into a new political party, the Whigs, who were opposed to the policies of "King Andrew I."

Crockett was eager to return to Congress, and he mounted a new campaign for Tennessee's new Twelfth District in 1833. However, he faced a difficult task: William Fitzgerald, a Jackson supporter, was the incumbent, and the new gerrymandered district included Madison County, a Jackson stronghold. Although Crockett faced constant criticism from the pro-Jackson press, his popularity was elevated thanks to some works of fiction. The Major Jack Downing letters, fictional tales of cracker barrel wisdom and frontier philosophy about a Maine wilderness character written by Seba Smith, were printed in newspapers and embraced by the public. Clearly, Downing was not real, but to many readers he made the frontier and its people seem more approachable and entertaining. Crockett benefited from comparisons with him. A year later, in Washington, Crockett met Smith, and the pair dined together.

In 1833, Crockett's identity received a boost when the *Davy Crockett*, a steam locomotive designed by John B. Jervis, and built under the supervision of Robert Stephenson, began carrying passengers and freight on the Saratoga and Schenectady Railroad in New York State. Actor John C. Mossie elevated the Tennessean's popularity when he began an extensive stage tour in which he performed improvisational imitations of noteworthy Americans, including congressman Henry Clay of Kentucky and Crockett.

That same year, James Strange French wrote *Life and Adventures of Colonel Crockett of West Tennessee.* The book, which over the years had been mistakenly attributed to Matthew St. Claire Clarke, utilized actual observations of Crockett ("a finely proportioned man, about six feet high, aged, from appearance, forty-five") and borrowed lines from James Kirke Paulding's popular play, *The Lion of the West*, which featured the Crockett-like Nimrod Wildfire. Paulding included a boastful passage which came to be associated with Crockett forever: "I'm that same David Crockett, fresh from the backwoods, half-horse, half-alligator, a little touched with snapping turtle." At first, Crockett was critical of the satirical work but soon realized the positive impact it had on his recognition factor. The book was so popular that it spawned a new edition: *Sketches and Eccentricities of Colonel David Crockett of West Tennessee.* Unlike any other candidate, Crockett had become a genuine celebrity, aided by French's book, Paulding's play, and the race horse and steam locomotive which were named after him.

In the election, Crockett defeated Fitzgerald 3,985 to 3,812. He headed back to Washington City and the Twenty-third Congress where he aligned himself with a strong anti-Jackson faction led in the United States Senate by Henry Clay of Kentucky, Daniel Webster of Massachusetts, and John C. Calhoun of South Carolina. "We have had some opportunity of knowing the calibre of many members of congress for 25 or 30 years past, and have met with many, very many, far less capable of ascertaining truth than col. C.," reported the September 7, 1833 edition of the *Niles' Daily Register.* "Whether right or wrong, the vote is his own."

An image of Crockett appeared in print for the first time when a characterization of him appeared in the October 16, 1833 issue of *Galaxy of Comicalities,* a satirical periodical published by Lesher and Shelly of Philadelphia. Accompanying an article titled "Crockett

Teaching a Landlord how to Grin," an illustration depicted a distorted cartoon-like Crockett pulling a man's mouth apart.

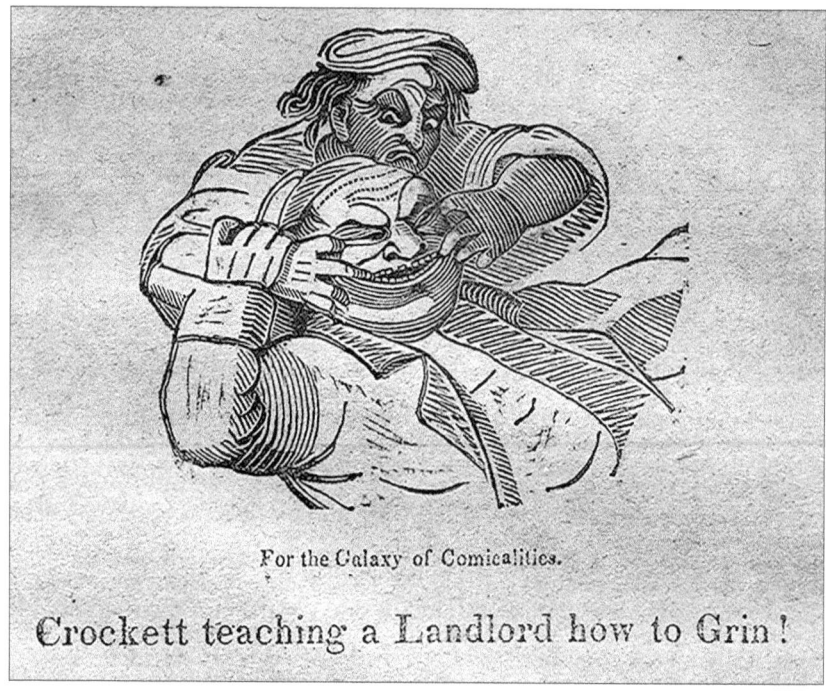

The first printed image of Crockett. *Galaxy of Comicalities* (1833).

Crockett's celebrity status was acknowledged when he attended a performance of *The Lion of the West,* which starred James Hackett, in Washington on December 12, 1833. "A whole box was assigned to the Colonel, and the Colonel bowed and Nimrod Wildfire bowed, both at each for a long time, as if old acquaintances, while the Theatre rang with cheers of the multitude assembled," reported the *Portland Advertiser* twelve days later.

In an effort to exploit the increasing national interest in him, Crockett decided to write his autobiography. The book would be more than just a life story: it was designed to showcase and promote a rising figure in American politics. Coincidentally, a Mississippi delegation expressed its support for Crockett if he ever decided to run for President. Crockett was pleased. On December 1, 1833, he penned a lengthy letter to the Mississippi convention. "How thankful I am for your pitching on me for the presidency," wrote Crockett. "But I am sorry, I don't want the office right now—I'm after another thing. I'm a very candid man, and when my mind is fixed upon a matter, you might as well try to stop gunpowder half blown up, as to stop me. I can't agree to be President."[52]

In February 1834, Crockett's publishers, Edward L. Carey and Abraham Hart of Philadelphia, announced the forthcoming release from a "genuine Son of the West." Crockett, cognizant of the literate audience that awaited his book, provided an explanation of his writing style in the preface. As for spelling, Crockett said, "That's not my trade." Grammar? "I hadn't time to learn it, and make no pretensions to it." The title page included his motto: "Be always sure you're right—then go ahead!" The *Narrative* was filled with hunting tales, romantic encounters, Creek War exploits, and political anecdotes that detailed his battles against Jackson and his followers. "Look at my neck, you will not find there any collar, with the engraving MY DOG, Andrew Jackson," stated Crockett on the last page of his book. With assistance from Kentucky's Thomas Chilton, who provided some "little alterations" to the text, *A Narrative of the Life of David Crockett of Tennessee* became an immediate best seller; as a matter of fact, the publishers had to issue subsequent editions before the year was out.

Crockett's autobiography was the not the first or the most famous of self-penned efforts written by famous political figures in American history; in fact, Benjamin Franklin's collection of assorted recollections, *The Life and Essays of Benjamin Franklin,* was the first, although it was not published until after his death. Franklin, the quintessential American Renaissance man, had an extraordinary life of amazing accomplishments which spanned ten decades; Crockett was only forty-seven when his *Narrative* was published. However, both books shared some commonalities. Like Franklin's autobiography, Crockett's book emphasized personal achievements, political observations, joyous anecdotes, and a spirited sense of optimism. Since Crockett owned a copy of Franklin's work, it may have influenced the style and structure of the *Narrative.* The success of Crockett's book was remarkable, and only three years later, Carey and Hart printed the *Narrative's* twenty-fourth edition.

Using his book as a self-promotional tool, Crockett told a friend that in the spring he intended to tour the northeastern states "merely for curiosity." The sojourn would provide him with a chance to not only satisfy the public's interest to see him in person, but it gave the embryonic Whigs an opportunity to assess his possibilities in the next national election. The anti-Jacksonians were also looking ahead for a single champion who could challenge the victor of Horseshoe Bend and New Orleans in 1836.

On April 25, 1834, Crockett began his tour in Baltimore, a hotbed of anti-Jackson sentiment. He surprised many with his appearance; he was not someone who looked as if had just emerged from a hunting expedition in the backwoods, and he was clearly not the off-stage embodiment of Nimrod Wildfire. "Colonel Crockett is an uncommonly fine looking man, to use the current Yankee phraseology," noted Hallowell, Maine's *American Advocate.* "His face has an exceedingly amiable expression, and his features are prominent and striking. He wears his hair, which is black (with a light shade of brown), parted from the centre line of his head, combed back from his temples, and ending in a slight natural curl at the neck—not unlike the simple manner of many of the clergy. The stories that have been told of him are ridiculous and wanton exaggerations."[53] At each stop, Crockett delivered a speech, told some anecdotal tales, and charmed the crowd. Crockettmania had begun.

After sailing past historic Fort McHenry in Baltimore harbor, he traveled through Delaware on his first train ride, a seventeen-mile journey that took forty-five minutes. At New Castle, Delaware, he boarded a steamboat and arrived in Philadelphia where the Young Whig association informed him that the membership would present him with a custom-made rifle in a few months. He attended a performance of *Jim Crow*, the black-face minstrel show starring Thomas D. Rice, at the Walnut Theater. "After the play, Mr. Rice made his appearance on the stage, and bowed very respectfully to Colonel Crockett, who returned the compliment by rising," reported the *Philadelphia Inquirer* on April 28.

Although Crockett wore the clothes of a gentleman on the tour, in the eyes of those who lived in the growing urban and industrial centers of the east coast, he was the symbol of the untamed west, a rugged man of the woods who represented an America that seemingly no longer existed. Crowds flocked to him with curious fascination.

The Tennessee congressman crossed the Delaware River, took a train ride across New Jersey on the Camden and Amboy Railroad, and arrived in Manhattan to cheering crowds. Crockett returned to New Jersey on May 2, and participated in a rifle frolic. "I witnessed shooting by Davy Crockett of Kentucky fame," recalled Gus Maxwell Hinchman in Munsell's *History of Morris County, New*

Jersey. "He was then in Congress; a plain sensible man, and by no means the rough character he was frequently described as being. The only thing remarkable in his apparel was the cameo breast pin with the head of Washington, about three inches in diameter. His poise when shooting exhibited familiarity with the rifle. He shot well on that occasion, but complained that the gun was different from those he had been accustomed to use."[54] Crockett returned to New York and boarded a steamboat to Boston where his tour continued.

Crockett wearing the Washington cameo pin.
Illustration by Joseph Musso.

Enthusiastic crowds greeted him in Boston, although Crockett thought that some may have been disappointed when they didn't see an actual half-horse, half-alligator personality show up. The city's *Evening Transcript* noted that in one speech Crockett "expressed his gratitude for the unexpected honors which had been paid to him." While in Boston, performer John C. Mossie invited Crockett to view a show at Concert Hall where the actor imitated him again. Crockett also traveled to Lowell, Massachusetts where he marveled at the "clock-work" efficiency of the mills, the quality of the finished fabrics, and the impressive labor skills displayed by the predominantly female work force which toiled long hours during a six-day work week.

During this time, Crockett sat for a few portrait artists, including Boston's Chester Harding who depicted the frontier congressman with a solid build, ruddy complexion, and dark hair, parted down the middle. In his finished canvas, Crockett wears the clothes of a gentleman but the garments appear as if they had been in use for some time.[55] Washington artist John Gadsby Chapman depicted Crockett in a full-body pose carrying a rifle, wearing buckskins, and accompanied by hunting dogs. Crockett holds a broad-brimmed hat in his right hand, his arm extended out and up. Over the years, the image would be copied in other illustrations and in statue designs.

A painting by Samuel Stillman Osgood received Crockett's endorsement. "I have no hesitation in saying that it is the most perfect likeness I ever saw," wrote Crockett, about the painting which was completed in the spring of 1834.[56] Engravings and lithographs of the Osgood image with the Crockett quote about the work's accuracy were printed and circulated. Other artistic creations were crafted by Albert Newsam, James Hamilton Shegogue, and Anthony Lewis DeRose.

John G. Chapman's image of Crockett.
Illustration by Gary S. Zaboly.

Samuel S. Osgood's image of Crockett. Illustration by Gary S. Zaboly.

The tour ended in May, but two months later Crockett returned to Philadelphia on July 1, where he was presented with a fine rifle made by gunsmith Richard Constable. "It is a percussion cap rifle with an octagonal barrel and a stock of curly maple," said Mary Elizabeth Crockett Holderness, who later owned the weapon. "Along the top of the barrel in inlaid letters of gold are the words

'Presented By The Young Men of Philadelphia To The Hon. David Crockett.' Down near the end of the barrel, near the sight, are the words 'Go Ahead' and an arrow all in gold. The fittings are of silver. The trigger guard has an alligator engraved on it. The patch box has engraved on it a raccoon at a reed-surrounded pond."[57] He also received a silver tomahawk, a knife, canisters of DuPont black powder, and boxes of percussion caps.

On July 4, Crockett delivered a speech at the Music Fund Hall which was enthusiastically received. "The Honorable member from Tennessee presented himself before his delighted auditors, and his usual unaffected and good humored manner, contributed to the gratification of the day," reported the *American Daily Advertiser*. He later made a speech at the Hermitage where he was once again received with joyous pandemonium. Crockett's popularity seemingly reached its highest point in Philadelphia. His appearance in the City of Brotherly Love was the perfect match of patriotism and nostalgia, and he represented both elements in grand style. His association with the Whigs, who challenged "King Andrew I," underscored his connection to the nation's past when the American colonists stood against the tyranny of King George III.

Crockett, though, was not the manipulated mouthpiece of the Whigs; his anti-Jackson stance began long before the Whigs became a political party. However, thanks to the extensive newspaper coverage of the tour, the Whigs benefited from Crockett's travels because his anti-Jackson message was spread beyond the places where he made appearances and delivered speeches. The next presidential election was only two years away, and the Whigs would need much more national support if they expected to defeat the next Democratic candidate.

Crockett's growing popularity was exemplified in ways that he was probably not even aware of. For example, the flatboat *Davy Crockett* began its operation on the Mississippi in 1834, and the stern-wheeler steamboat *David Crockett,* which was based in Charleston harbor, began its passenger and cargo service, too. These transportation vehicles were among the first items named after him, but they would not be the last.

On July 12, 1834, Crockett continued his attacks against Jackson in Cincinnati. "We see ourselves arrived at a crisis when one man can hold the sword in his hand and the power in that, and bid defiance to Congress and the nation," said Crockett. "That man is Andrew, the first king of this country."[58] Newspapers printed the speech, and noted that Crockett was greeted with "loud and long continued cheering." His presence was so memorable that a likeness of him was placed in the city's wax museum.

Of course, the Jacksonians did not sit idly by as Crockett charmed the crowds. Philadelphia's *Daily Pennsylvanian* printed a mock toast directed at him: "Colonel David Crockett: The idol of the Whigs of '34, a party claiming all the intelligence of our country." The *Alexandria Gazette* reprinted a characterization of Crockett as "the western Ourang Outang," and New York's *Monroe Democrat* described him as "that grinning traitor of a Crockett."

Crockett remained independent—perhaps too independent, since he never mastered the art of compromise—and served only to benefit his struggling constituency, not himself. In fact, his Congressional salary ($8 per day) and his book royalties did not generate enough income to adequately support him and his family. Crockett's financial problems continued, but Nicholas Biddle, President of the Second Bank of the United States, renewed a personal note and worked out a repayment schedule for the Tennessean.

Crockett looked ahead with confidence to his reelection campaign in 1835. The positive momentum which emanated from his autobiography and the northeastern tour was strengthened with the printing of the first Crockett almanac, *Davy Crockett's Almanack of Wild Sports of the West, And Life in the Backwoods.* Produced by Nashville's Snag and Sawyer, the almanac contained such fundamental information as sunrise and sunset times, and weather predictions, but it also was filled with such tall tales as "Hunting the Wolf," "Fight with a Whooping Crane," and "Fight Between an Alligator and a Bear." Compared to future almanacs which were filled with outrageous stories of super-human, wild, science fiction-like behaviors (for example, Crockett unfreezes the sun, swallows a bolt of lightning, and drinks the Gulf of Mexico), the 1835 publication's contents were rather restrained. Crockett's "sharp wit, his unwavering patriotism, his 'everyman' Americanism and his tall tales were the basis for the almanacs," which "significantly paved the way for future humorists, artists, and publishers."[59]

The almanac's contents typified the exaggerated absurdities of American humor, which set itself apart its European counterparts. With the passing of each year, the Crockett of the almanacs became even more of a larger-than-life character as he accomplished an assortment of fantastic deeds. Filled with boastful brags, which reflected the restless optimism of other pioneer folks, the almanacs became symbolic of America's Manifest Destiny as the nation continued its inexorable expansion from sea to shining sea.

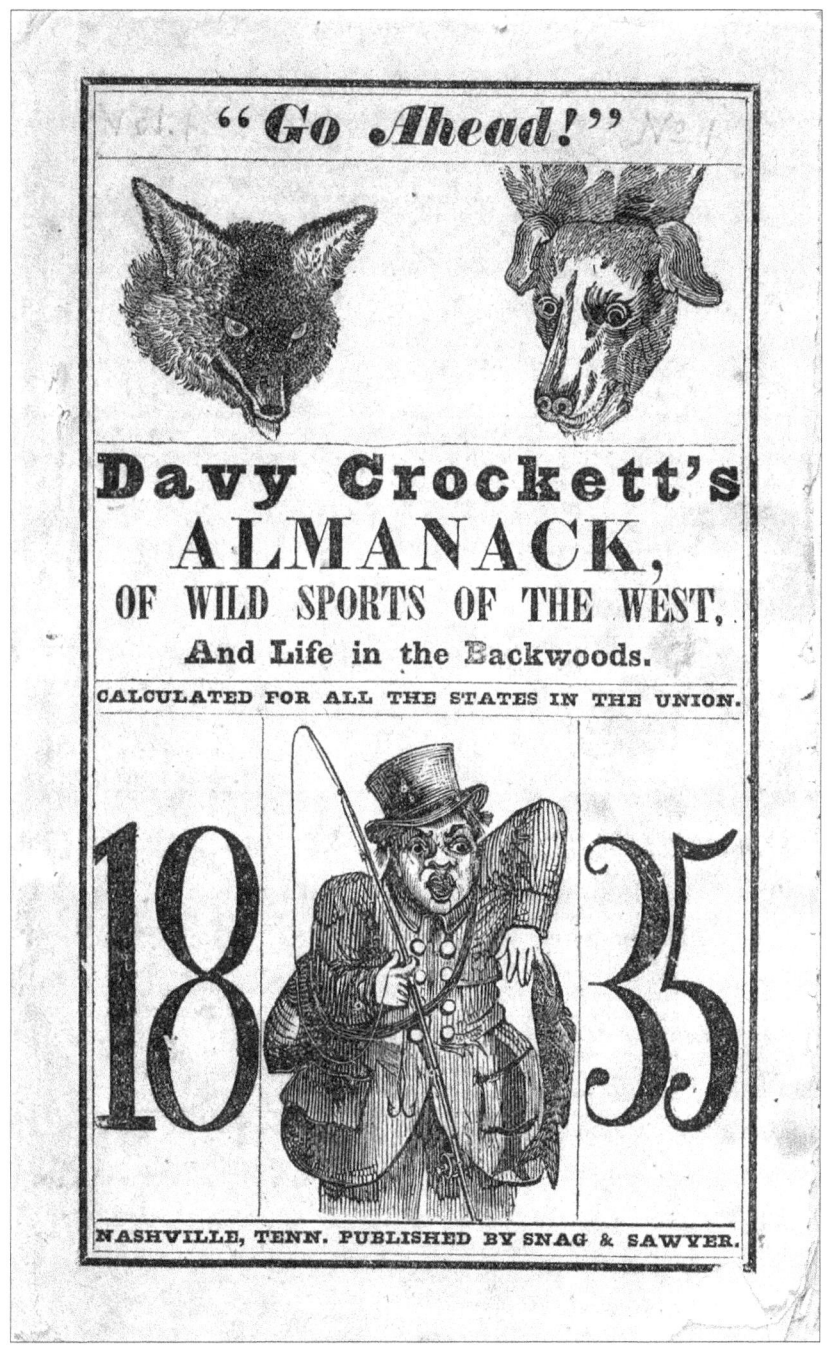

Crockett Almanack 1835.

The annuals also promoted a host of "shemale" characters, including Sally Ann Thunder Ann Whirlwind Crockett, Crockett's wife, who were also capable of memorable superhuman feats.[60] These wild women of the west reminded readers that both men and women could be resourceful enough to survive on the frontier. Elizabeth Patton Crockett could attest to that.

Since the almanacs were held for a year by their owners, the Crockett legend was constantly renewed and reinforced with every reading. Furthermore, many of the almanacs were held long after their respective years had concluded, and the tall tales and illustrations remained as sources of entertainment.

The release of two ghost-written books published by Carey and Hart, *An Account of Col. Crockett's Tour to the North and Down East* (written by Crockett and William Clark) and *The Life of Martin Van Buren* (written by Georgia congressman Augustin Smith Clayton), and the publication of "The Crockett Victory March," a musical composition, added to the Crockett celebrity bandwagon. James Hackett, star of *The Lion of the West*, returned to the United States in 1835, after a production run in England, and revived his Crockett-like character. Furthermore, a race horse in Charleston's Macon's Central Course was named after him, and a schooner, the *Col. Crockett*, made journeys from the Bahamas to New York City and Boston.

Crockett's name was everywhere; however, his good name was subject to not only political ridicule from the Jacksonians but from others. French writer Alexis de Tocqueville dismissed the famous Tennessean as a worthy representative of the people in *Democracy in the United States*, which was published in 1835. "Two years ago, the inhabitants of the district in which Memphis is the capital, sent to the House of Representatives of Congress an individual named David Crockett, who has no education, can read with difficulty, has no property, no fixed residence, but passes his life hunting, selling his game to live, and dwelling continuously in the woods," noted Tocqueville, who also expressed his distaste for the "great number of vulgar men who occupy public offices."[61] Crockett was not as crude and illiterate as the Frenchman described; in fact, the frontier representative had learned the dynamics of Capitol Hill and the multiplicity of interests which seemed to underlie nearly every piece of proposed legislation. Like a political chameleon, Crockett could be a backwoods bumpkin among his canebrake constituents or a well-versed foe of Jacksonian policies while speaking in the halls of congress.

Once again, the Democrats waited for Crockett to begin his campaign run. They felt that the Tennessean was vulnerable because the Whigs were not enthusiastically behind him due to his independent stands on all issues. Since the pro-Jackson forces were successful against him in 1831, they believed they could repeat with another victory in the 1835 race. Adam Huntsman, who had written some anti-Crockett monographs during the previous campaign, ran against him. Huntsman was an aggressive candidate who used to stomp his wooden leg to underscore points of importance when he spoke to the voters of Tennessee's Twelfth District. According to the Democrats, Crockett was easy to exploit since his legislative resume contained no bills that had become law, and his anti-Jackson rants were getting tiresome. Furthermore, he lacked the funds to wage a successful campaign.

In the election, Huntsman topped Crockett 4,652 to 4,400. Crockett was devastated and angry. "You may all go to hell and I will go to Texas," he repeated a number of times to groups of constituents. When he returned home, his daughter, Matilda, remembered what he said to his wife. "Well, Bet, I am beat, and I'm off for Texas," recalled Matilda.[62]

Placing the burden, once again, of raising his family and maintaining the household on Elizabeth, Crockett sought Texas as a place of opportunity. However, Texas, then a part of Mexico, was experiencing a revolution. A decade earlier, Mexico had achieved its independence from Spain, and the new republic sought to expand its economy by offering Americans generous land grants to settle there. Emigrants from the United States poured into Texas, and soon the Anglo population outnumbered the native population. Mexico issued a decree in 1830, which forbade future settlement from the United States, but protests soon developed. The Mexican government, under the dictatorship of Gen. Antonio Lopez de Santa Anna, attempted to suppress the developing rebellion.

The Texas Revolution began on October 2, 1835, when a Mexican cavalry unit arrived at Gonzales with orders to confiscate an artillery piece. Under a banner that featured a cannon barrel and the words "Come And Take It," a small group of armed Texians fired upon the mounted troops. The Mexicans promptly retreated. The Texians later defeated a large Mexican force at the Battle of Bexar in December. Soon, Santa Anna organized an immense Army of Operations and led the troops back to Texas to punish the Texian pirates.

Crockett, at age forty-nine, headed west with his nephew, William Patton, and two neighbors, Abner Burgin and Lindsay Tinkle. The group departed Weakley County on November 1, 1835. Crockett's initial interest in Texas was personal; he was searching, once again, for another parcel of land that would benefit his family. Before he departed Tennessee, he undoubtedly heard about the events in Texas. Seemingly fascinated by the opportunities for adventure and the allure of joining another campaign with comrades in arms, Crockett went ahead. As he rode, he attracted others, and soon headed a mounted force "of thirty men well armed and equipped."[63] His last stop in Tennessee was Memphis, where he arrived on November 7. During his stay at the Union Hotel, he was celebrated and toasted by the locals, and repeated his "you may all go to hell and I will go to Texas" comment. James D. Davis recalled that "Crockett wore that same veritable coon-skin cap and hunting shirt, bearing upon his shoulder his ever faithful rifle."[64]

Many who had joined Crockett's ride through Tennessee did not continue beyond the Mississippi. Crockett and his company, albeit smaller in number, were ferried across the great river. They arrived in Little Rock on November 12, and later continued their travels across the Territory of Arkansas. Crockett's journey did not go unnoticed. Five days later, the *Arkansas Gazette* reported: "Among the distinguished characters who have honored our City with their presence, within the last week, was no less a personage than Col. David Crockett—better known as Davy Crockett, the real critter himself—who arrived on Thursday evening last, with some six or eight followers, from the Western District of Tennessee, on their way to Texas, to join the patriots of that country in freeing it from the shackles of the Mexican government. The news of his arrival rapidly spread, and we believe we speak within bounds, when we say, that hundreds flocked to see the wonderful man, who, it is said, can whip his weight in wild-cats, or grin the largest panther out of the highest tree."

Crockett entered Texas with great expectations, and found it immediately rewarding when he went on a buffalo hunt. Clearly, Texas was different, and it appealed to him. In a letter written to his daughter Margaret and her husband in early January 1836, Crockett stated: "Texas is the garden spot of the world. The best land and the best prospects for health I ever saw, and I do believe it is a fortune to any man to come here."[65] Texas was also perceived by some as a haven for those overburdened with debt. Some had carved "GTT," for "Gone To Texas," on their front doors and left their homes. But home still held an attraction for Burgin and Tinkle, who left Crockett and returned to Tennessee. Young Patton remained but later left his uncle to join Sam Houston's developing army.

As he traveled in Texas, Crockett would stop in a settlement and engage its residents on why he was there. "I was for some years a member of Congress," stated Crockett in an article published in Augusta, Maine's *The Age*. "In my last canvass, I told the people of my district, that if they would re-elect me, I would serve them as faithfully as I had done, but if not, they might go to hell and I would go to Texas. I was beaten, gentlemen, and here I am."[66]

During his journey to Texas, he parted with some personal items. He traded a gold watch to Isaac Jones "in exchange for Jones' less-expensive timepiece plus thirty dollars of sorely needed cash," and gave his copy of Benjamin Franklin's autobiography to W. H. Fullerton.[67]

In the letter to his daughter, Crockett added that he had "taken the oath of government and have enrolled my name as a volunteer." But Crockett was cautious about the oath's declaration that those who signed it would "bear true allegiance to the Provisional Government of Texas or any future government that may be hereafter declared." Concerned that a future government would reject democratic principles, Crockett added the word "republican" after the word "future." Considering his background as a Creek War veteran, two-term member of the Tennessee General Assembly, three-term member of the United States House of Representatives, and author, he viewed an independent Texas as a place where his political career could be revived. He shared his optimism with Margaret and her husband: "I am in hopes of making a fortune yet for myself and family, bad as my prospects have been."

On January 12, 1836, Crockett joined Capt. William B. Harrison's company in the Volunteer Auxiliary Corps of Texas at Nacogdoches. Still desperate for money, Crockett sold two rifles to Thomas Rusk for $60; however, the buyer only had $2.50. Crockett accepted a promissory note for the remainder.[68] Eleven days later, he arrived at Washington-on-the-Brazos where he was provisioned for his travel to San Antonio de Bexar. Crockett and his companions camped at several locations before arriving at an area where the El Camino Real meets the San Marcos River, the group's final camp site away from any settlement. On February 8, Crockett arrived in San Antonio where Col. James Bowie and Lt. Col. William Barret Travis held a joint-command. Despite his status as a militia colonel, Crockett expressed a desire to serve only as "a high private."

Like Crockett, nearly all of the men who served under Bowie and Travis had previously resided in other states (over thirty hailed from Tennessee) and countries. A contingent of Tejanos, native-born Mexicans like Juan Seguín and Gregorio Esparza, also aligned themselves against the dictatorship of Santa Anna.

On February 23, advance units of Santa Anna's army reached the outskirts of San Antonio. Approximately 150 armed Texians and about two dozen non-combatants entered the nearby Alamo mission-fortress for protection. The siege of the Alamo had begun.

Crockett's Arrival on the Outskirts of Bexar. Illustration by Gary S. Zaboly.

Travis, who assumed command of the Alamo garrison after Bowie became ill, sent out couriers with pleas for help from neighboring settlements. In one letter, written on February 24, Travis stated that he would "never surrender or retreat." On the next day, he wrote that Crockett was "seen at all points, animating the men to do their duty."[69] Years later, Alamo non-combatant Enrique Esparza, remembered Crockett during the siege. "Señor Crockett seemed everywhere," said Esparza, whose father, Gregorio, was an Alamo defender. "He would shoot from the wall or through the portholes. Then he would run back and say something funny."[70]

A small reinforcement of thirty-two volunteers from Gonzales arrived at the Alamo on March 1, and a message dated the same day from Maj. R. M. Williamson pledged more than six hundred armed Texians were on their way. "For God's sake, hold out until we can assist you," wrote Williamson. Another force of over four hundred, under the command of Col. James Fannin, was located at Fort Defiance at Goliad, less than ninety miles away.

A day later, at Washington-on-the-Brazos, delegates declared Texas an independent republic, but the Alamo defenders never found out. Instead, the men inside the besieged mission-fortress waited for reinforcements to arrive. The days passed.

In the predawn darkness of March 6, 1836, Santa Anna's soldiers attacked the Alamo. Cannons roared from the mission's walls and adversaries battled in bloody hand-to-hand combat while non-combatants huddled together inside the Alamo church. In about an hour or so, the Battle of the Alamo was over. When Susanna Dickinson, the wife of an Alamo officer, left the church she "recognized Colonel Crockett lying dead and mutilated between the church and the two story barrack building and even remember seeing his peculiar cap by his side."[71] According to Joe, Travis' slave, "Crockett and a few of his friends were found together with twenty-four of the enemy dead around them."[72] However, Mexican officer José Enrique de la Peña said that Crockett was one of some "seven men who had survived the general carnage" and were brought before Santa Anna. The Mexican commander immediately ordered their execution. "Though tortured before they were killed, these unfortunates died without complaining and without humiliating themselves before their torturers," said de la Peña.[73]

The question of how Crockett was killed and where he died remained an unanswered question. However, American newspapers provided explanations anyway. On March 28, the *Louisiana Advertiser* reported that "Col. Crockett is among the slain.... [He] fell like a tiger." On April 5, New York's *Monroe Democrat* proclaimed: "We are happy to state, on the authority of a letter from Tennessee, that the reports of the death of the eccentric Davy Crockett is not true."

Nevertheless, Crockett was dead. His body and the other Alamo defenders (except Gregorio Esparza, who was buried), were burned in funeral pyres. In the summer of 1836, a Captain Kimball of the ship *Mexico*, arrived in New York harbor bringing with him "a rifle, powder horn, bullet pouch," and other items allegedly belonging to Crockett.[74] Apparently, Kimball received the items from Col. Juan Bradburn, an American ex-patriot who served in Santa Anna's army. The next year, Col. Juan Seguín, who had fought under Gen. Sam Houston's command at the Battle of San Jacinto on April 21, 1836, returned to San Antonio where the remaining ashes of the Alamo defenders were gathered and interred in a ceremony at the San Fernando church. In a speech, Seguín acknowledged the sacrifices made by "our departed bretheren, Travis, Bowie, Crockett."

The legend of Davy Crockett had begun.

Section One Notes

1. Frederick Jackson Turner, *The Frontier in American History* (Mineola, NY: Dover Publications, Inc., 1996), 107. The author included a passage which summed up pioneers such as Crockett: "This then is the heritage of pioneer experience—a passionate belief that a democracy was possible which should leave the individual a part to play in free society and not make him a cog in a machine operated from above; which trusted in the common man, in his tolerance, his ability to adjust differences with good humor, and to work out an American type from the contributions of all nations—a type for which he would fight against those who challenged in arms, and for which in time of war he would make sacrifices, even the temporary sacrifice of individual freedom and his life lest that freedom be lost forever."

2. David Crockett, *A Narrative of the Life of David Crockett of the State of Tennessee* (Philadelphia: E. L. Carey & A. Hart, 1834), 37. Crockett's grandparents were Ulster-Scots who settled in North Carolina prior to the Revolutionary War.

3. Ibid., 21.

4. The original structure was located some twelve miles north of Dandridge, Tennessee. According to Sally Baker, Manager and Curator of the Crockett Tavern Museum in Morristown, Tennessee, the land which housed the original cabin and the recreated one was owned by the Canady family. Tim McCurry, who worked at the historic site said that the original building was deliberately burned to the ground in 1875, in order to curb the spread of smallpox. An historical marker outside the tavern states: "Here stood the Crockett Tavern, established and operated by John and Rebecca Crockett. It was the boyhood home of David Crockett (1786-1836), pioneer, political leader in Tennessee, and a victim of the Alamo Massacre at San Antonio, Texas." See William R. Chemerka, *The Davy Crockett Almanac and Book of Lists* (Austin: Eakin Press, 2000), 74.

5. Crockett, *Narrative*, 24.

6. Ibid., 26.

7. Ibid., 31.

8. Ibid., 36.

9. In his *Narrative*, Crockett said he traveled to "Montgomery court-house."

There was no community named Montgomery at that time, only a county with that name, which honored Revolutionary War Gen. Richard Montgomery, who died in the December 31, 1775 attack on Quebec. The busy town of Christiansburg had a court house, and that was the place that Crockett probably described.

10. Crockett, *Narrative*, 40.
11. Ibid., 43.
12. Joseph Swann, *The Early Life and Times of David Crockett in East Tennessee, 1786-1812*. Unpublished manuscript. Swann suggests that the "frontier exerted far less social pressure on its inhabitants than they had experienced in Europe and longer settled areas of America. They did not live as close together as earlier generations and the constraints of an established legal system and strong church were much less evident along the frontier areas." The author also pointed out that "the kindness and tolerance of John Canaday and the Quaker community gave David a different perspective. He was still an Ulster-Scot but a changed one."
13. Crockett, *Narrative*, 48.
14. Ibid., 49.
15. Ibid., 50.
16. In January 2006, Margaret Vance Smith of Tampa, Florida appeared on TV's *Antiques Roadshow* and displayed the framed license. However, a dispute arose as to who actually owned the document: Smith or Jefferson County, Tennessee. For many years, the document was displayed on the wall of the Jefferson County Courthouse in Dandridge, Tennessee. On the TV program, appraiser Frances Walhgreen of Christi's Auction House in New York suggested that the "irreplaceable" item should carry an insurance value of between $45,000 and $50,000. Lu Hinchley, the Director of the Jefferson County Archives told *The Crockett Chronicle* (February 2006) that the license "may have been missing for as many as seventy years." Smith claimed to have retrieved the document after the courthouse had been "clean[ed] out." In November 2009, Judge Allen Wallace of Humphreys County (Tennessee) Circuit Court ordered Smith to immediately return the document. In the January 2, 2010 edition of the *St. Petersburg Times*, Smith stated: "Well, they are not going to get it." Threatened with a $500-a-day fine if she did not return the document, Smith complied. Upon its return, the document was

placed in the protective custody of Lu Hinchley and the Jefferson County Archives.

17. Crockett, *Narrative*, 53-54.
18. Ibid., 69; Gert Petersen, *David Crockett, The Volunteer Rifleman: An Account of his Life, while a Resident of Franklin County, 1812-1817* (Winchester, TN: Franklin County Historical Society, 2007), 10. The name "Glaspie" appears on a September 11, 1779 land survey. However, the name and another variation of it, "Gillaspie," are actually misspellings of Gillespie. A modern highway marker identifies the rented land parcel: "Kentuck. The homestead which David Crockett named and occupied in 1812 is now marked by a well standing in a field 3½ miles south and to the east of this road."
19. Ibid., 189. Crockett's confrontation with the bear took place in early 1826.
20. President James Madison's War Message to Congress, Miller Center, University of Virginia. https://millercenter.org/the-presidency/presidential-speeches/june-1-1812-special-message-congress-foreign-policy-crisis-war
21. Crockett, *Narrative*, 72. Twenty enlisted men from Tennessee with the last name of Crockett, including three other men with the first name of David, served in the War of 1812. See Byron and Samuel Sistler, *Tennesseans in the War of 1812* (Nashville: Byron Sistler and Associates, 1992), 148.
22. Ibid., 74.
23. Ibid., 74-75.
24. John J. Jacobs, November 22, 1884 recollection in William R. Chemerka, *The Davy Crockett Almanac and Book of Lists* (Austin: Eakin Press, 2000), 202.
25. Crockett, *Narrative*, 82.
26. Ibid., 88.
27. Ibid., 90.
28. Ibid., 93.
29. The treaty included several provisions, including one which reflected the concern over the ongoing war with Great Britain and her allies: "The United States demand, that the Creek nation abandon all communication, and cease to hold any intercourse with any British or Spanish post, garrison, or town; and that they shall not admit among them, any agent or trader, who shall

not derive authority to hold commercial, or other intercourse with them, by license from the President or authorized agent of the United States." Interestingly, prior to the Civil War, the expression "United States demand" reflected the importance of state sovereignty over national sovereignty. After the war, similar expressions would have been changed to "United States demands."

30. Crockett, *Narrative*, 106.
31. The violence among the tribes was a violation of the Treaty of Fort Jackson, which stated: "A permanent peace shall ensue from the date of these presents forever, between the Creek nation and the United States, and between the Creek nation and the Cherokee, Chickasaw, and Choctaw nations."
32. Crockett, *Narrative*, 116.
33. Ibid., 124.
34. A. S. Colyar, "Nashville," *The New England Magazine* (October 1889), vol. 7, no. 2, 137-138, cited in Gary Zaboly, "More Crockett Bits," *The Alamo Journal*, no. 122 (September 2001), 17.
35. Crockett, *Narrative*, 125. There is no defintive date of Polly's death. She probably died in early 1815.
36. Ibid., 126. According to "Notes and Reminiscence from Uncle William Floyd given to Charles E. Gowen in the summer of 1904 when in his 84th year," a genealogical document now held in the University of Virginia Library, Elizabeth Patton "had about $800 in cash" in her possession at the time of her marriage to Crockett.
37. Ibid., 128.
38. Ibid., 132.
39. Ibid., 134.
40. Many years later, Crockett's second homestead in Lawrence County was commemorated with a Tennessee Historical Commission marker placed near Lawrenceburg's town square. The plaque states: "David Crockett's Home. Here David Crockett lived from 1819 to 1822. He was one of the commissioners who laid out the county and selected the site of Lawrenceburg, a colonel in the militia, justice of the peace, member of the legislature and operator of several industries here."
41. Crockett, *Narrative*, 143.

42. Ibid.
43. Ibid., 155.
44. Ibid., 171.
45. Ibid., 173.
46. Joseph S. Williams, *Old Times in West Tennessee*, Memphis 1873, 174-176, cited in Gary Zaboly, "More Crockett Bits," *The Alamo Journal*, no. 122 (September 2001), 17.
47. Crockett, *Narrative*, 206.
48. Ibid. Besides his opposition to Jackson's Indian policy, Crockett later championed the rights of Cherokees whose land had been taken by white claim jumpers. Crockett's reputation among the Cherokees remains strong. John Currahee's online reference blog, Chenoceta's Weblog [https://chenocetah.wordpress.com/tag/davy-crockett/], states in "The Cherokee Removal from Georgia, 1838-1839," that "Davy Crockett of Tennessee was a strong friend of the Cherokee, but he had left politics in disgust a few years before after losing an election, mostly because of his support of the Cherokee, had moved to Texas, and had died in the defense of the Alamo in March, 1836."
49. *David Crockett's Circular*, February 28, 1831, Rare Books Division, Library of Congress, cited in James R. Boylston and Allen J. Wiener, *David Crockett in Congress: The Rise and Fall of the Poor Man's Friend* (Houston: Bright Sky Press, 2009), 307. The authors assembled all of Crockett's known letters, selected speeches, and circulars in their comprehensive volume.
50. Before it opened at the Theatre Royal Covent Garden in England in 1833 as *The Kentuckian, or a Trip to New York*, the play was revised by William Bayle Bernard, a British dramatist, and then sent to the Lord Chamberlain's office for approval. Producers altered and toned down the Frances Trollope character to Mrs. Luminary. However, upon Hackett's return to the United States in 1835, Luminary was out and Trollope was back in. See Melvin Rosser Mason, "'The Lion of the West': Satire on Davy Crockett and Frances Trollope," *The South Central Bulletin, Studies by Members of SCMLA* [*South Central Modern Language Association*], vol, 29, no. 4, (1969), 143. Another popular fictional work was William Alexander Caruthers' *The Kentuckian in New-York; or, The Adventures of Three Southerns, by a Virginian*, which was published in 1834. The author's title character shared many of Nimrod

Wildfire's traits: "Our Kentuckian was no quiet man; but, like most of his race, bold, talkative, and exceedingly democratic in all his notions."

51. Crockett to Jones, August 22, 1831, University of Tennessee, Special Collections, Knoxville, Tennessee, cited in Gert Petersen, "On Tour to the Crockett Sites in Tennessee," *The Crockett Chronicle*, no. 8 (August 2004), 6.

52. *Urbana Record*, January 31, 1835. The March 10, 1834 issue of the *New-York Spectator* reported that the Mississippi delegation's invitation was sent on January 12, 1834, with Crockett's response coming later.

53. *American Advocate*, May 14, 1834. In another part of the newspaper, an article mentioned that Crockett had participated in a muzzleloading demonstration in New York where he "fired at a 25-cent piece, and sent the ball through the center at 40 paces!"

54. Bill Chemerka, "David Crockett and the Washington Cameo Pin," *The Alamo Journal*, no. 114 (September 1999), 6.

55. Jim Boylston, "Crockett, Boone, and the Chester Harding Matrix," *The Crockett Chronicle*, no. 1, (August 2003), 3. The author pointed out that Harding was "the only artist to have painted both Daniel Boone and David Crockett from life."

56. Crockett to Osgood, April 29, 1834, quoted in Boylston and Wiener, *David Crockett in Congress*, 246. When Robert Patton Crockett moved from Tennessee to Texas in 1854, he brought the Osgood painting with him. According to Ashley Wilson Crockett, Crockett's grandson, the original painting was larger and featured the frontier congressman seated at a table and holding a quill pen, but that lower portion of the canvas was not duplicated when a lithograph was made of the image. Robert Patton Crockett donated the original work to the Texas State Capitol where it was later destroyed in a fire on November 9, 1881.

57. Peter Stines, "Pretty Betsey: Davy Crockett's Fancy Rifle," *The Alamo Journal*, no. 60 (February 1988), 13.

58. "Col. Crockett's Speech, *Piqua Gazette*, August 2, 1834, quoted in Robert L. Durham, "David Crockett's Speech in Cincinnati, *The Crockett Chronicle* no. 7 (February 2005), 3; David Crockett [and William Clark], *An Account of Col. Crockett's Tour to the North and Down East* (Philadelphia: E. L. Carey and A. Hart, 1835), 151. Crockett's book identifies the speech having been delivered on July 14.

59. Joe Rainone, "The Davy Crockett Almanacs: Their Influence in American Popular Culture," *The Crockett Chronicle*, no. 24 (May 2009), 8. The author noted: "Over the years the content of the Crockett and other comic almanacs grew to mimic the themes seen on the stage. The first true minstrel shows started in 1843. Soon afterwards, many shows introduced blatantly racist and derogatory humor, reflecting the end of the post-Revolutionary War mentality and the beginning of the antebellum period when the issue of slavery was more contentious and polarizing. Minstrel show character songs continued to influence humor as well, though often presenting a negative interpretation of race, ethnicity, and politics in order to get a laugh and sell tickets. Obviously, not all stage shows were of the minstrel genre and not all minstrel shows were in bad taste; many, like the Christy Minstrels, were family oriented." The cover of the 1835 almanac featured an illustration from the preface of Sir Thomas Hood's 1833 *Comic Annual*.

60. See Michael A. Lofaro "Riproarious Shemales: Legendary Women in the Tall Tale World of the Davy Crockett Almanacs" in *Crockett at Two Hundred: New Perspectives on the Man and the Myth*, ed., Michael A. Lofaro and Joe Cummings (Knoxville: The University of Tennessee Press, 1989); Lofaro, *Davy Crockett's Riproarious Shemales and Sentimental Sisters: Women's Tall Tales from the Crockett Almanacs, 1835-1856* (Mechanicsburg, PA: Stackpole Books, 2001); and Richard M. Dorson, *Davy Crockett: American Comic Legend* (New York: Spiral Press, 1939).

61. George Wilson Pierson, *Tocqueville in America* (Gloucester, MA: Peter Smith, 1969), 385-386. The Frenchman's notes about Crockett were written on December 20, 1831. Crockett's reputation was outrageously avenged in "Crockett Paying Off Two Frenchmen for Insulting His Sweetheart," an article with an accompanying illustration, in the 1845 Crockett almanac. "I walked up, knocked the head o' one agin t'other, till they run off with the lockjaw," boasted the fictionalized frontiersman about his altercation with the men.

62. William Groneman III, *David Crockett: Hero of the Common Man* (New York: Tom Doherty Associates Book, 2005), 132.

63. Manley F. Cobia, *Journey into the Land of Trials: The Story of Davy Crockett's Expedition to the Alamo* (Franklin, TN: Hillsboro Press, 2003), 28.

64. James D. Davis, *History of the City of Memphis* (Memphis, 1873), 140.

65. Crockett to Wiley and Margaret Flowers, January 9, 1836. Copy in Alamo Library, San Antonio, TX.

66. Augusta, Maine, *The Age*, April 27, 1836.

67. James C. Kelly and Frederick S. Voss, *Davy Crockett: Gentleman From The Cane—An Exhibit Commemorating Crockett's Life and Legend on the 200th Anniversary of his Birth* (Washington, D.C.: National Portrait Gallery, 1986), 38. On the front of Franklin's autobiography, Crockett wrote: "I'll leave this truth for others when I am dead. Just be sure you're right and then go ahead." According to Kelly and Voss, Jones returned the watch to Elizabeth Patton Crockett, and "in 1896 Fullerton returned the copy of Franklin's memoir to Crockett's son, John Wesley Crockett." However, John Wesley Crockett died in 1852, and none of the other Crockett children were alive after 1890. The watch and Franklin's autobiography remain in a private collection.

68. Crockett may have acquired another rifle while in Texas when he traded one of his to an Andy Thomas. The weapon Thomas acquired is now owned by the Robert Darwin family and is currently on display at the Alamo; however, its provenance has never been firmly established. John L. Hinnant explained the rifle's history in "The Crockett Rifles (part 2): The David Crockett/Andy Thomas Rifle" in *The Alamo Dispatch,* no. 184 (Summer 2018): "According to Darwin family history, Andy met Colonel Crockett on the way to Texas in 1835, entering the Red River Province at Jefferson, Texas. The group made camp in a grove which had a large number of honey trees. That site was located just a few miles west of the present town of Honey Grove, Texas in Fannin County. It was at this site that Andy traded his lighter weight rifle for Colonel Crockett's heavy Tennessee rifle." In issue no. 185 (Winter 2018) of *The Alamo Dispatch,* Hinnant concluded: "The rifle displayed in the Alamo church was probably *not* presented to David Crockett in Nashville, Tennessee, as certain sources have claimed; the rifle could not have been converted from a flintlock; and the rifle *might* or *might not* have been owned by David Crockett. That question will remained unresolved for now."

69. Travis to Maj. Gen. Sam Houston, February 25, 1836.

70. Howard R. Driggs and Sarah S. King, *Rise of the Lone Star: A Story of Texas Told by its Pioneers* (New York: Frederick A. Stokes Co., 1936), 223.

71. James A. Morphis, *History of Texas from its Discovery and Settlement, with a Description of its Principal Cities and Counties, and the Agricultural, Mineral,*

and *Material Resources of the State* (New York: United States Publishing Co., 1874), 177.

72. *Commonwealth* (Frankfort, Kentucky), May 25, 1836.

73. Carmen Perry, ed. and trans., *With Santa Anna in Texas: A Personal Narrative of the Revolution, by José Enrique de la Peña* (College Station: Texas A & M Press, 1975), 43-56.

74. *Niles' Weekly Register*, July 30, 1836, 365; *New York Commercial Advertiser*, July 26, 1836. One item missing from Crockett's alleged possessions was his copy of Benjamin Franklin's autobiography. A few researchers and writers, such as Joseph Arpad ("David Crockett, An Original Legendary Eccentricity and Early American Character," Ph.D. dissertation, Duke University, Durham, NC, 1970), have suggested that he may have carried a copy of the autobiography with him to Texas. However, if he did, Crockett parted with the book prior to his entrance in the Alamo. The possibility that the book survived the destruction of March 6, 1836, and eventually ended up somewhere in the United States is highly unlikely. As note number 66 states, the book exists in a private collection.

SECTION TWO

The Davy Crockett of Popular Culture

> *You see, there's nothin' so absotutely unresistible as an old fashioned, good natured grin—like this! I started out on coons. I got so good at it one day an old coon throwed up his hands the minute he'd seen my teeth. "You got me, Davy," he hollered, and skinned down that tree and plopped himself in my sack before I knowed what was up.*
> — Fess Parker as *Davy Crockett*
> "Davy Crockett, Indian Fighter," 1954

Prior to his death at the Alamo, Crockett had been celebrated in staged productions, books, almanacs, newspaper articles, and music. Within a span of five years, from April 1831 to March 1836, the legend of Davy Crockett had been firmly established.

In 1831, playwright James Kirke Paulding had created a Crockett-like character named Nimrod Wildfire in *The Lion of the West*. Two years later, the first Crockett biography, *The Life and Adventures of Colonel David Crockett of West Tennessee*, ghostwritten by James Strange French, was published. The initial print run was so successful that a second edition, re-titled *Sketches and Eccentricities of Col. David Crockett of West Tennessee*, was published. Crockett's autobiography in 1834, *A Narrative of the Life of David Crockett of the State of Tennessee*, added to his growing celebrity.

In 1835, *An Account of Colonel Crockett's Tour of the North and Down East*, written by Crockett and William Clark; the first of the Crockett almanacs; and the publication of "'Go Ahead'—A March Dedicated to Colonel Crockett," elevated the canebrake congressman's popularity. His superhuman persona was magnified thanks to the 1836 almanac, which featured a cover image of him wading the Mississippi River on stilts and crutches. That same year, Carey and Hart published Richard Penn Smith's *Colonel Crockett's Exploits in Texas*, a work which incorporated newspaper stories and assorted books about Texas history. The book, "fiction marketed and consumed as fact, sold ten-thousand copies in the first year."[1] Despite its imaginative prose, *Exploits in Texas* would influence Crockett biographers for the next two centuries.

Yet, another ghostwritten Crockett book was in the works. An undated post-1836 newspaper advertisement stated: "Colonel Crockett's Life of Andrew Jackson...will stand alone—the only impartial history of the Hero of New Orleans."[2] However, the book was never published.

No longer alive to manipulate his own characterization, Crockett's image would constantly be reshaped, revised, and exaggerated by others. Even the Crockett almanacs became more animated and preposterous. The 1837 *Crockett Almanack*, which featured Edward Clay's cover lithograph illustration of *The Lion of the West's* Nimrod Wildfire, described the Tennesean's death at the Alamo in unbelievable heroic terms: "It was calculated that during the siege, he killed no less than 85 men, and wounded 120 besides, as he was one of the best shooters in the west, and he had four rifles, with two men to load constantly, and he fired as fast as they could load, nearly always hitting his man."

Death of Crockett in the 1837 *Crockett Almanack.*

Other almanacs such as *Crockett's Old Oldmanick* in 1837, and the *Crockett Awl-Man Axe for 1839,* were comedic publications offered by various New York publishers. These annuals used Crockett's name as a promotional device and rarely included content about the legendary Tennessean. No matter, the Crockett name sold.

On February 1, 1837, W. B. Porter, a character actor, starred in *Davy Crockett*, a Sterling Comedy Company production that was presented at Felt & Himes Hall in Brockwayville, Pennsylvania. Porter, like such fellow contemporary stage performers as James Hackett and John C. Mossie, helped enhance the Crockett legend by bringing the backwoods hero to "life" before appreciative audiences.

Crockett's last stand at the Alamo was acknowledged in Europe when *The London Musical Cyclopedia*, "a collection of about 400 of the most approved English, Scottish, and Irish songs," included "The Texian Lament on the death of Col. Fanning (sic) and David Crockett."

Among the election results for the Twenty-fifth Congress, which convened in 1837, was John Wesley Crockett's win over Adam Huntsman in the race for Tennessee's Twelfth Congressional District. It was a bittersweet victory for the twenty-nine-year-old Whig who succeeded the man who had defeated his father two years earlier. Young Crockett went on to win reelection in the Twenty-sixth Congress and was able to get a land bill passed that was somewhat similar to one his father had proposed years earlier. He was later elected attorney general by the Tennessee General Assembly, and served in that position from 1841-1843.

In the spring of 1837, Philip Thompson, William Craig, and Prewitt Sinclair built Fort Davy Crockett on the left bank of the Green River in Brown's Hole, in what is now Colorado. It was the first time that a fortification or a structure was named after the Alamo hero. During the next winter, Kit Carson, the famous hunter-trapper-guide, spent the first of four winters at Fort Davy Crockett.

Robert T. Conrad's song, "The Alamo or the Death of Crockett," which dates to 1837 and was sung to the melody of "The Star Spangled Banner," appeared in *Crockett's Free-and-Easy Songbook: A New Collection of the Most Popular Stage Songs, as Given by the Best Vocalists of the Present Day: and also of Favorite Dinner and Parlour Songs*. Conrad's composition began with, "To the memory of Crockett fill up to the brim!/The hunter, the hero, the bold Yankee yeoman." In a subsequent edition of *Crockett's Free-and-Easy Songbook*, a tune called "Go Ahead" featured the lyrics, "Hard fighting to the last, brave Crockett/Cried 'Go Ahead.'" Also in 1837, William Alexander Caruthers, an accomplished American novelist who had written the Nimrod Wildfire-like *The Kentuckian in New-York* three years earlier, wrote an initial draft of *David Crockett; or, The Nimrod of the West*, the first poem about the memorable hunter-hero.

The 1838 Crockett almanac reinforced the lively antics that were featured in earlier editions with such entries as "A Narrow Escape of a Woman from a Panther in Texas," "Mike Fink, the Ohio Boatman," and "Crockett and Santa Anna," but other than a basic day-by-day calendar, which included fundamental astrological information, the almanac and its successors concentrated on entertaining tall tales. No one seemed to mind.

The *David Crockett*, a keel boat that operated on the Colorado River in Texas, began its run in 1838. The next year, "Colonel Crockett: A Virginia Reel," a fiddle tune written by George P. Knauff, was published. Crockett was also mentioned in "Zip Coon" and "Pompey Smash," a pair of minstrel tunes which were popular in the 1830s and 1840s; in fact, the tunes continued to be favorites into the early 20th century.

Amidst Crockett's growing legend, a newspaper report revived a rumor that had been circulating for a few years. "Austin Gazette contains a letter from a person, William C. White, stating that in one of the mines in Mexico, which he visited, he met an American prisoner representing himself as Col. David Crockett," noted the *Vermont Chronicle* on April 29, 1840. The paper added that Crockett's eldest son, John Wesley, "has received information that leads him to believe his father is in a Mexican mine [and] steps will be taken to determine the truth and liberate him." John Wesley Crockett made inquiries through the "minister to Mexico" but nothing could be found to substantiate the claim. It was later determined that the letter and its author were fakes. White was none other than David L. Wood, who had arrived in Texas three years after the Battle of the Alamo. Wood's reason for inventing the story has never been determined.³

In the 1840s, the *Rough and Ready Songster*, a collection of songs, included "Yankees Light the Fires Bright," which features the lyric "Remember gallant Crockett's bones," a rallying cry to those who supported war against Mexico. The Crockett almanacs continued to include more wild tales, especially those in which the frontier hero was described encountering various animals, both real and mythological, in the backwoods.

On January 3, 1844, the New Orleans *Times-Picayune* stated: "They are playing a new drama at the theatre in Mobile called 'Col. David Crockett.'" Indeed, the production would have been new, but it probably was a retitled version of Paulding's well known *The Lion of the West*. Interestingly, a few years earlier, Paulding completed a three-year term as United States Secretary of the Navy under President Martin Van Buren, one of Crockett's political enemies.

The January 11, 1844 edition of the *Boston Evening Transcript* alerted "Antiquarians" that a bullet pouch supposedly to have belonged to Crockett was going to be exhibited at the city's Apollo Saloon. It was a way for those who had seen Crockett a decade earlier—and for those who had never seen him—to make a connection with the famous Alamo hero. Also on display at the saloon was a sword that purportedly had been used by Capt. Myles Standish of Plymouth Colony fame.

Besides the flatboats, steamboats, and schooners that were named after him, the sloop *David Crockett* sailed out of Philadelphia in 1842; the canal boat *David Crockett* operated at Harper's Ferry, Virginia in 1844; the whale boat packet *David Crockett* sailed out of Provincetown, Massachusetts in 1845; and the pilot boat *David Crockett* worked the waters between Alexandria, Virginia and the mouth of the Potomac River in 1851. Two years later, one of the most magnificent sailing crafts ever made would also bear his name.

In 1846, a new edition of *Crockett's Free-and-Easy Songbook* was published with the comprehensive title of *Crockett's Free-and-Easy Songbook: Comic, Sentimental, Amatory, Sporting, African, Scotch, Irish, Western and Texian National, Military, Naval and Anacreonic: A New Collection of the Most Popular State Songs, together with Glees, Duets, Recitations, and Medleys.* That year, the Mexican War began, and music fueled America's patriotic zeal. A number of the songs featured derogatory comments about Santa Anna, whose troops had killed Crockett a decade earlier at the Alamo. One song, "Wave, Wave, the Banner High," included lyrics which saluted the Alamo's most famous defender: "Each plain and wood/Stained by the blood/Of freedom's pilgrim sons, boys/There Houston led/And Crockett bled/And brav'd the tyrants guns, boys." The war ended in 1848, and the Treaty of Guadalupe Hidalgo gave ownership of the entire southwest to the United States.

The 1848 Crockett almanac reinforced the racial animosity the United States held for its southwestern neighbor when it included a woodcut titled "Death of Crockett." The image depicted Crockett with a sword and a knife plunged in his chest, but the apparent fatal thrust was made by a Mexican *soldado* who bayoneted him from behind, suggesting that the only way the famous Tennessean could be killed was to "stab him in the back."

In the 1850s, Crockett's name was commercialized on a number of products. "Davy Crockett" tobacco became one of the most popular brands offered by such distributors and warehouses as the

Virginia Tobacco Agency in New Orleans and Titus and Company in Memphis. "Davy Crockett" was sold throughout the United States, but would be unavailable to most northern states after the Civil War erupted a decade later. An "extra superfine" grade of flour called "Davy Crockett" was also a popular product, especially in Nashville markets. Of course, a century later, over 5,000 commercial items would be marketed with his name.

Throughout the 1850s, newspapers printed hundreds of stories and anecdotes about Crockett, ranging from his exploits in congress and his service at the Alamo to almanac-inspired tall tales. Also, Crockett's motto was frequently integrated into other advertisements and newspaper stories. For example, in the December 25, 1851 edition of Concord, New Hampshire's *Independent Gazette,* an ad described L. D. Brown, a hardware store owner, who pledged to "Go Ahead" after he had lost much of his merchandise in a recent fire. On June 15, 1863, the *Indiana State Sentinel* reported that Illinois Senator Lyman Trumbull said, "we have not adhered to David Crockett's motto, 'Be sure you are right and then go ahead,'" during a speech about loyalty and the restoration of the Union. On December 26, 1862, the *Sacramento Daily Union* proclaimed: "There was never a better motto than the homely one of David Crockett, 'Be sure you're right, then go ahead.'"

In 1851, poet T. F. Smith wrote "On The Death Of Colonel Crockett," which honored Crockett's service at the Alamo fifteen years earlier: "Tyrants shall tremble at thy honoured name/And blush to read the record of thy fame/While millions at their annual jubile/Shall toast—a Crockett lost—a nation free!"

The death of John Wesley Crockett, Crockett's first child, on November 24, 1852, in Memphis, was reported by newspapers across the country. In the stories, the former two-term congressman, was frequently referred to as the son of the "celebrated Davy Crockett." He had recently moved back to Tennessee after residing in New Orleans for nearly a decade where he served as an agent of produce sellers and editor of the *National* and the *New Orleans Daily Crescent*.

In 1852, Philadelphia's T. B. Peterson and Brothers publishing house promoted its *Pictorial Life and Adventures of Davy Crockett* as "the only complete and unabridged edition of the life of Davy Crockett ever published in the United States." In a review of the book in Philadelphia's *Dollar Newspaper* on December 1, 1852, the publication focused more on its unflattering opinion of Crockett than the biography itself. The newspaper noted his "rude and ridiculous" conduct in congress, and called him a "strange man" who "told many hard stories of himself, and told them so often, that... before he died, he really believed a part of them to be true."

During the decade, more race horses were named after the famous Tennessean. On April 1, 1854, Nashville's *Daily Union and American* described "Davy Crockett" as a fine animal whose offspring had also gained some notoriety.

On October 18, 1853, the majestic clipper ship *David Crockett* was launched. The 220-foot, 1,679 ton ship, which featured a carved wooden figurehead of Crockett made by Anderson of New York, sailed from New York to Liverpool, England, and New York to San Francisco. The *David Crockett* was later mentioned in a popular song, "The Leaving of Liverpool." The key lyrical passage of the song read: "I have signed on a Yankee clipper ship/Davy Crockett is her name/And Burgess is the captain of her/And they say she's a floating hell." The Burgess in the song refers to John A. Burgess, who served as captain from 1860 to 1874. Information about the *David Crockett's* arrival dates, cargo inventories, and departure dates were reported thousands of times in American newspapers during the ship's years of service.

In 1856, the last of the Crockett almanacs provided readers with more memorable tales from the seemingly indestructible frontier character. The final edition, *"I leave this rule for others, when I'm dead; Be always sure you're right, then go-ahead! Crockett 1856 Almanac*, featured thirteen animated woodcuts created by Philadelphia painter Joseph B. Howell and included "Crockett on Santa-Anna's Worldly effects," a satirical piece which mocked the victor of the Battle of the Alamo.

Twenty years after Crockett's death at the Alamo, newspapers reported that the Texas Legislature awarded "one league of land" to Elizabeth Patton Crockett, the "widow of the hero and martyr of Texas independence—Davy Crockett." She had earlier received her first parcel of Texas land a few years after the Texas Revolution as a result of her husband "having served faithfully and honorably."

The most macabre Crockett item appeared in the 1858 *Catalogue of the Surgical and Pathological Museum of Valentine Mott, M.D., LL. D.* The entry for item number 358 read: "Skull of the celebrated Davy Crockett, from an undoubted source," wrote Mott, a professor of surgery at the University of the City of New York, who had met Jim Bowie's brother, Rezin, in 1833. "Sent me by a professional friend, from Alamo, Texas." Mott never identified the "undoubted source."

Crockett's name was seemingly everywhere. Tennessee's Memphis Fire Department named one of its new hose carriages "Davy Crockett," and Maturin Murray Ballou's *The Arkansas Ranger; Or, Dingle the Backwoodsman, a Story of East and West*, a serialized novelette in Boston's *Flag of our Union*, included a reference to Crockett in its August 22, 1857 issue: "'These Eye-talians are a mighty curious set,' said our western hero to himself; 'They seem never to 'a heerd of David Crockett's notion – 'Be sure you're right then go ahead.'" Honolulu Hawaii's *Pacific Commercial Advertiser* printed an anecdote about him in its May 26, 1859 issue.

Crockett had become so synonymous with Paulding's *The Lion of the West* that on some occasions during the 1850s the play was simply promoted as *Davy Crockett*. The *Boston Herald* noted the title change when it provided information about a performance scheduled at the National Theatre on April 9, 1858.

Crockett's skull. Illustration by Gary S. Zaboly.

Ruben Potter wrote *The Fall of the Alamo: A Reminiscence of the Revolution in Texas,* the first published history of the famous siege and battle, in 1860. The booklet included a heroic explanation of Crockett's final moments during the conflict. "Crockett had taken refuge in a room of the low barrack near the gate," wrote Potter. "He either garrisoned it alone, or was left alone by the fall of his companions, when he sallied to meet his fate in the face of the foe, and was shot down."

Col. David Crockett, the Celebrated Hunter, Wit and Patriot was featured in a Beadles Dime Biographical Library edition in 1861, the same year the Civil War erupted. On February 13, 1861, Mississippi's *Oxford Intelligencer* printed a front page story titled "Death of Crockett." The article described his final moments at the Alamo and also included passages which underscored Mississippi's secession a month early. "In a voice of thunder, Crockett answered 'Surrender! No! I am an American,'" noted the newspaper, which concluded with, "So long as freedom has an abiding place in America, will their heroic deeds and proud names be held sacred."

East Tennessee, where Crockett was born and raised, was opposed to secession, but central and west Tennessee supported leaving the Union. Earlier, John Bell, who had served alongside Crockett in Congress, ran for President in 1860 as the standard bearer of the Constitutional Union Party, which attempted to find a conciliatory resolution to the impeding secession crisis. However, a June 8, 1861 referendum in Tennessee endorsed secession, and the state became the eleventh and final state to join the Confederate States of America.

Although names like Abraham Lincoln, Jefferson Davis, Ulysses S. Grant, Robert E. Lee, William T. Sherman, Thomas "Stonewall" Jackson, and other prominent political and military figures dominated newspaper and periodical stories for the next four years, stories about Crockett remained popular on both sides of the Mason-Dixon Line. Less than two weeks after the fall of

Fort Sumter, Massachusetts' *Salem Observer* printed an anecdote in which Crockett mocked a judge by comparing him to a baboon at a Washington menagerie. On October 31, 1861, the *White Cloud Kansas Chief* urged voters to cast their ballots for the fictional character Benjamin Harding in the race for Register of Deeds because he was "the friend and companion of Davy Crockett."

One of Crockett's grandchildren participated in the War Between the States. On May 30, 1861, the Baltimore *South* reported that "one of the rifle companies from Arkansas, now in Virginia, is commanded by Capt. Crockett, a grandson of the famous Davy Crockett. The company carries a banner upon which appears the inscription: 'Be sure you're right, then go ahead.'" Years later, a highway marker in Crockett's Bluff, Arkansas included the following: "The Crockett Rifles (Company H, 1st Arkansas Infantry), first Confederate company raised in Arkansas County and one of the first in the state, was recruited in this vicinity by Captain Robert H. Crockett in 1861."

Over a thousand miles away from where Union and Confederate troops were fighting at Fort Donelson in Tennessee, Paulding's *The Lion of the West,* once again retitled as *Davy Crockett,* was performed in Denver on February 12, 1862.

During the war, the clipper ship *David Crockett* made numerous Atlantic and Pacific runs without interference from the Confederate Navy, but its southern namesake did not do as well. On October 13, 1862, the USS *America* captured the Confederate schooner *David Crockett* as it attempted to run the Union naval blockade off Charleston, South Carolina.

On August 11, 1863, the *Charleston Courier* reprinted a northern newspaper's account of Confederate Gen. John Hunt Morgan's capture in Ohio on July 26, 1863. The daily stated that the cavalry commander surrendered "as gracefully as the coon did to Davy Crockett." Morgan escaped from a Union prison, returned to the battlefield, and was killed on September 4, 1864, in Greeneville, Tennessee, about a dozen miles from Crockett's birthplace.

In 1864, *Life and Adventures of Colonel David Crockett* was published as a Beadles Dime Biographical Library title, but it was actually a retitled offering of *Col. David Crockett, the Celebrated Hunter, Wit and Patriot* from three years earlier.

The most popular Crockett biography of the 19th century (and early 20th century) was *Life of David Crockett: The Original Humorist and Irrepressible Backwoodsman*, which combined Crockett's autobiography with Richard Penn Smith's ghost-written 1836 volume *Col. Crockett's Exploits and Adventures in Texas*. The book (complete title: *David Crockett: The Original Humorist and Irrepressible Backwoodsman comprising His Early History; His Bear Hunting And Other Adventures; His Services in the Creek War; His Electioneering Speeches And Career in Congress; With His Triumphal Tour Through the Northern States, And Services In The Texas War to which is added An Account of His Glorious Death at The Alamo While Fighting In Defence Of Texas Independence*), which included a few paragraphs written by Charles T. Beale, was edited by Alex J. Dumas for Philadelphia's J. E. Potter and Company in 1865. Over the years, several other publishers printed the book, including Chicago's W. B. Conkey Company, which featured a dapper-looking Napoleonic couple on the cover. The most interesting aspect of the book is its fictitious account of Crockett's final manuscript entry, dated March 5, 1836, the day before the fall of the Alamo: "Pop, pop, pop! Bom, bom, bom! Throughout the day. No time for memorandums now. Go Ahead! Liberty and independence forever!"

During the nation's Reconstruction Era, the April 1867 edition of Harper's *New Monthly Magazine* featured a six-page story titled "Davy Crockett's Electioneering Tour."

In 1871, Crockett County was created in the central part of west Tennessee from portions of four other counties. Coincidentally, the county seat is located in the town of Alamo, and the community's weekly newspaper was called *The Crockett Times* (originally *The Crockett Sentinel*). Crockett was also acknowledged in Gretna, Louisiana when the community's thirty-three-year-old fire company was renamed as the "David Crockett Steam Fire Company No. 1," in 1874. The volunteer unit's motto was "Be Sure You're Right, Then Go Ahead."[4] The next year, Crockett County was created in Texas.

Also in 1871, Edward S. Ellis, under the pen name Charles E. Lasalle, wrote *The Texas Trailer, or Davy Crockett's Last Bear Hunt*, a "dime novel" published by Beadles and Adams. Five years later, Harry Hazard (the pen name of Joseph Edward Badger) wrote *The Bear Hunter; or Davy Crockett as a Spy*, another Beadles offering.

Throughout the remainder of the 19th century, American newspapers continued to print Crockett stories, tall tales, and nostalgic remembrances. New books about Crockett were also published. In 1874, John S. C. Abbott wrote *David Crockett: His Life and Adventures*. In his introduction, the author assessed the significance of Crockett. "But there is probably not an adult American, in all these widespread States, who has not heard of David Crockett," noted Abbott. "His life is a veritable romance, with the additional charm of unquestionable truth. [This book] opens to the reader scenes in the lives of the lowly, and a state of semi-civilization, of which but few of them can have the faintest idea." Abbott later wrote *The Terror of the Indians; or, The Adventures of D. Crockett with*

Illustrations and *David Crockett*. In 1875, George Cary Eggleston added his *David Crockett* biography to the growing roster of books about the frontier hero, and a year later Wild Bill's "Young Davy Crockett; or, The Hero of Silver Gulch" first appeared as a story in *The Boys of New York* series.

Frank Mayo.

One of the most important cultural tributes to Crockett was the debut of Frank Murdock's play *Davy Crockett; Or, Be Sure You're Right, Then Go Ahead* in 1872. More serious than Paulding's *The Lion of the West,* this new production, which starred Frank Mayo, who helped rewrite the play for the next season, featured a noble and skillful backwoodsman who wins the heart of his grownup childhood love while fending off a suitor and a pack of wolves. The frontier play in five acts (1: "Saddle Mending;" 2: "Wolves at the Door;" 3: "A Living Barrier;" 4: "Lochinvar's Ride;" 5: "Quickest Marriage on Record") was considered "a highlight of the genre" and "almost the best American play ever written."[5]

Besides acting in the play, Mayo supervised the production. For example, in his prompt book entry for October 1, 1872, he included detailed notes about "moss covered" rocks, "stumps of trees," and painted props. One note declared: "Don't ring curtain bell until after chorus!"

The touring production ran for decades; in fact, by the spring of 1877, Mayo had performed the role 1,000 times. However, playing Crockett was dangerous work. A *New York Mirror* story of June 19, 1880, reported that Mayo fell through a center stage trap door which had been covered with leaves by the set decorator. Mayo landed eighteen feet below but sustained no serious injuries. Years later, he contemplated leaving the role, and on June 11, 1886, Lancaster Pennsylvania's *New Era* reported that Mayo wanted to be "a tragedian" instead of the frontier hero, "unless compelled by poverty to do so." Producers, theater managers, audiences, and some critics balked at the idea of him appearing in other staged shows. One newspaper wrote, "it was a long time before he realized the terrible fact that he was doomed to play Davy Crockett for life. Year after year, the local managers marketing for attractions in New York clamored for Frank Mayo. He in return offered them a season of Shakespeare with a picked company of forty actors. In vain he offered other elaborate productions, and which, by the by, has done the admirable actor infinite credit. But the local managers protested—'our patrons want Davy Crockett.'"[6] Mayo continued to portray Crockett on stage until he retired in 1891. He supposedly appeared in as many as 3,000 performances over a span of twenty years. He briefly returned to the stage in *Pudd'n-head Wilson* in the spring of 1895, but died the next year of a heart ailment while traveling on a train from Denver to Omaha. His son and grandson followed in similar thespian footsteps.

One of the most amusing publications about Crockett was Charles Dudley Warren's 1882 *Killb'ar, the Guide; or, Davy Crockett's Crooked Trail*, a Beadles and Adams publication, which told the tale of the famous frontiersman's adventures in Georgia. The publication was reissued six years later as *Rocky Rover Kit, or Davy Crockett's Crooked Trail*.

Ruben Potter, who wrote *The Fall of the Alamo* in 1860, responded to an article in the Woodbridge, New Jersey newspaper *The Independent Hour*, which suggested that Crockett surrendered to General Santa Anna's forces at the Battle of the Alamo. "David Crockett never surrendered to bear, tiger, Indian, or Mexican," stated Potter.

In 1883, the *Magazine of American History* featured an article on Crockett, and a year later the prolific author Edward S. Ellis wrote *The Life of Colonel Crockett*. A passage from the book concerning a congressional expenditure that was designated "for the benefit of a widow of a distinguished naval officer" was criticized by Crockett, who stated that "Congress has not the power to appropriate this money as an act of charity." Ellis, though, created the false scenario surrounding Crockett's stand which would be used a century later by fiscal conservatives who argued against similar spending.[7]

In February 1885, Wild Bill Hickok was identified as the author of "Young Davy Crockett; or, The Hero of Silver Gulch," which was first released without a full author credit in Frank Tousey's *Wide Awake Library* publication nine years earlier.

The popular Crockett name was placed on additional modes transportation in the final decades of the 19th century. In 1884, Henry Putnam's sloop, *David Crockett*, participated in the Dorchester, Massachusetts Yacht Club's annual regatta, and in 1888, a railroad Pullman palace car named "Davy Crockett" became part of the Pennsylvania Rail Road.

Also in 1888, Crockett was elevated to the highest echelon of frontier stardom when William F. Cody wrote *Story of the Wild West and Camp-Fire Chats, by Buffalo Bill (Hon. William F. Cody): A Full and Complete History of the Renowned Pioneer Quartette, Boone, Crockett, Carson and Buffalo Bill*. That same year, *The Young Men of America*, a "dime novel," included a story titled "Davy Crockett, Jr. or, Be Sure You're Right Then go Ahead."

In 1889, artist William Henry Huddle debuted his full-length portrait of Crockett, which depicted the frontiersman standing in the woods, wearing buckskin clothing, and holding a rifle in one hand and a coonskin cap in the other. The large canvas is currently displayed in the Texas State Capitol in Austin.

On August 17, 1889, the Davy Crockett Historical Society was formed. The organization celebrated the 103rd anniversary of Crockett's birth at his place of birth in Limestone, Tennessee on property that had been purchased and developed by Benjamin Rush Strong, a real estate entrepreneur and builder. A. E. Gillespie, the chairman of the event's executive committee and his associates proclaimed on printed invitations that "preparations are being made to have the grandest demonstration ever held in East Tennessee" at the Strong's Spring location. And grand it was. Music, parades, speeches, and an appearance by the Alamo hero's fifty-one-year-old grandchild, Robert Hamilton Crockett, (the son of John Wesley Crockett and his wife Martha), who exhibited "Pretty Betsey," made the day memorable for the thousands who attended. Among other items on display at Strong's hotel, the Strong Springs Inn, which had opened nine years earlier, were an ax that Crockett had brought back from the Creek War, a portrait painted by Rembrandt Peale, and a pocket watch.[8] A stone marker, supposedly from John Crockett's cabin, which read, "On This Spot Davy Crockett Was Born Aug. 17, 1786," was also displayed. Newspaper coverage of the event included tributes to Crockett, and the *Knoxville Journal's* August 19 edition was the most flattering: "He was of that honest, staunch, sturdy stock of pioneers that formed the basis of our broad, national character, and the celebration was a fitting recognition of his true worth and greatness."

The following year, on August 15, the society hosted a "Laying of the Cornerstone Monument" event for a proposed Crockett memorial which was budgeted at $5,000. Sadly, the monument was never built. However, nearly a century later, a memorial was constructed on grounds that became the David Crockett Birthplace State Park.

The August 17, 1892 Crockett birthday celebration picnic at Strong's Springs included "old time music [and] baseball," but visitors were warned: "No drinking or swearing allowed." Unfortunately, one man was shot to death in one of several drunken brawls. On the same day, another celebration took place in Rutherford where Crockett descendants took part in an elaborate program, which featured a dinner, music, and speeches, including a recitation of a speech originally delivered by Crockett against Martin Van Buren.

Crockett's name also translated into profitable commercial enterprises. The Davy Crockett Cabin at Strong's Spring welcomed visitors ($1.50 a day, $7.00 a week, and $25.00 a month), and retailers offered Davy Crockett Cigars for sale.

The legend of Davy Crockett became more nostalgic in the 1890s because the nation's frontier had finally closed, and stories about the rustic heroes of the past linked modern America to a unique part of its history. On July 12, 1893, historian Frederick Jackson Turner read his "The Significance of the Frontier in American History" paper at a meeting of the American Historical Association in Chicago. Turner argued that the ever-changing frontier had helped to create and maintain the country's democratic and egalitarian character. He pointed out the importance of the "moving mass" of settlers into the Piedmont region which included "the ancestors of John C. Calhoun, Abraham Lincoln, Jefferson Davis, Stonewall Jackson, James K. Polk, Sam Houston, and Davy Crockett," among others.[9]

On September 5, 1894, descendants of Crockett met for the first time at a large-scale reunion in Humboldt, Tennessee. Several photographs were taken of the event, including a group shot staged in front of a large banner that featured Crockett's motto. The December 1896 issue of *The Texas Magazine* included a pen sketch of Crockett created by William P. Ford on the cover, and the next year, Elbridge Gerry Littlejohn added to the Crockett legacy with *Texas History Stories; Houston, Austin, Crockett, La Salle.*

The 1890s was a particularly active decade for horse racing in the United States. Hundreds of tracks were open, and select venues from New Jersey to St. Louis featured races that included horses named "David Crockett."

However, the decade wasn't kind to the former clipper ship *David Crockett,* which had its masts removed during its transition to a coal barge in 1890. "Many an old-time clipper ship may be seen in New York harbor doing duty as a coal or oil barge and robbed of all semblance to her former glory," reported Massachusetts' *Springfield Republican.* "Among the most interesting relics of the kind is the David Crockett, at one time a famous Cape Horn clipper, with many fast voyages to her credit." Steam power was replacing sail power, and the former tall ships quickly became relics of the past. Adding insult to injury, bad luck seemed to follow the *David Crockett* wherever it was towed. In 1891, while being towed by the tugboat *Rattler* to Norfolk, the barge rammed and damaged a steamship off the Long Island, New York coast. Three years later, the barge sprung a leak off Cape Henry, Virginia, but was rescued by the ocean tugboat *Argus.* In 1897, the *Argus* broke her shaft as she was towing the *David Crockett* and another barge from Newport News to Boston. The following November, the barge was damaged in a storm. Shortly thereafter, what remained of the once majestic *David Crockett* was abandoned and left to rot, either on the Romer Shoal just north of Sandy Hook, New Jersey or nearby along the East River in Manhattan. But not all was lost. During the ship's early days, the attractive figurehead was moved from its bow to the deck where it was subject to less wear from the seas. The figurehead was eventually removed and stored on land. Years later, on July 1, 1924, the *San Francisco Chronicle* reported: "The figurehead from the old clipper ship Davy Crockett, which was recently presented to the marine department of the [San Francisco] Chamber of Commerce by the late A. B. Spreckles, now adorns a conspicuous place on the wall over the drinking fountain on the floor of the Merchants' Exchange. The figurehead was placed yesterday and within the next few days will be repainted and touched up." The figurehead is currently on display at the National Maritime Museum in San Francisco.

In 1898, the United States established itself as an imperialist world power as a result of its victory in the Spanish-American War. The nation celebrated Theodore Roosevelt, Commodore George Dewey, and other war heroes, but public demand for theatrical productions and printed material about the Old West, or what was perceived as the Old West, remained strong. The popular Buffalo Bill's Wild West shows and published stories about legendary frontier heroes and cowboys helped satisfy the public's nostalgic appetite. On a more sophisticated note, the David Crockett Literary Society in Texas was established in 1899.

Original works in the new millennium kept the life and legend of Davy Crockett alive. Throughout most of the 20th century, books that were marketed as non-fiction avoided the legendary exploits which had been featured in the almanacs and other published tall tales. Nevertheless, books portrayed Crockett in heroic terms, especially titles targeted for young readers.

In 1900, Frances M. Perry teamed with Katherine Beebe on *Four American Pioneers: Daniel Boone, George Rogers Clark, David Crockett, Kit Carson; a Book for Young Americans*. (Perry later released the Crockett chapter as *The Story of Davy Crockett For Young Readers*, a title in the Baldwin's Biographical Booklet series.) The authors wrote that Crockett was one of six defenders captured at the end of the battle. "The dauntless Crockett gave the spring of a tiger toward the dark leader, Santa Anna," they stated. "But before he could reach him he had been cut down by a dozen swords." Two years later, New York's Perkins Book Company published *The Life of David Crockett*, a combined reprint of his autobiography and his ghostwritten Texas exploits.

Artists also added to the Crockett legend. In 1903, Robert Jenkins Onderdonk's *Fall of the Alamo* depicted Crockett as the Alamo's central defender, and two years later Henry Arthur McCardle's *Dawn at the Alamo* included a determined Crockett positioned among scores of other combatants.[10] Both paintings showed Crockett fighting to the end.

In 1903, the Davy Crockett School was built in Dallas, and in the years that followed other schools in Texas and Tennessee were named after the canebrake congressman. Of course, it was somewhat ironic to have educational institutions named after someone who attended school for only six months.

Like the troublesome history of the *David Crockett* coal barge, the *Davy Crockett* locomotive, which operated on the San Antonio and Aransas Pass Railway, had its share of misfortunes. The *San Antonio Express* reported that locomotive killed two people who were crossing the tracks in San Antonio on August 9, 1903. It was deliberately derailed on September 16, 1905, and was damaged when a bridge collapsed on it near Yokum, Texas, on October 31, 1910.

The first decade of the 20th century was a fertile time for theatrical productions about Crockett, and the Murdock-Mayo play remained popular; in fact, the *Tacoma News* called it "one of the best known plays of the day." The play was produced on scores of stages by different production companies across the United States. For example, on January 7, 1900, The Baldwin-Melville Stock Company staged *Davy Crockett* at New Orleans' Grand Opera House, and the next month the play was performed by another troupe in Butte, Montana, with Harry Sedley in the title role. On October 19, 1900, the play was performed at Harrisburg, Pennsylvania's Grand Opera house, with Frank Cleaves in the lead. In 1901, R. E. French starred in Seattle's Third Avenue Theater's production, and James G. Morton handled the lead role at Biloxi's Dukate's Theatre. In 1903, the Huntley-Moore Stock Company staged the play at the Owens Academy of Music in Charleston, and Lester Lonergan was Crockett in Kansas City. The next year, Walter McCullough starred in another production at Biloxi's Dukate's Theatre. Playwright Augustus Thomas expressed interest in writing a new play about Crockett that was designed for Lionel Barrymore, but it was never completed.

However, all the *Davy Crockett* productions were about to be upstaged when a non-actor decided to follow in the footsteps of another non-actor in the ring of drama. In this corner: James J. Corbett, better known in boxing circles as "Gentleman Jim Corbett." Corbett, born thirty years after Crockett's death at the Alamo, became heavyweight champion of the world on September 7, 1892, when he defeated John L. Sullivan in a grueling 21-round match. Corbett, who was wonderfully portrayed by Errol Flynn in the Warner Bros. classic *Gentleman Jim* (1942), eventually lost his title and was unsuccessful in an attempt to regain it when he fought James J. Jeffries, his former training partner, in 1900. In a rematch on August 14, 1903, Jeffries defeated Corbett again.

Corbett's boxing career was over but his acting career was just getting started. In the autumn of 1904, Corbett was starring throughout New Jersey in a play called *Pals*. Jeffries got wind of it, and the competition between the two boxers was renewed when Jeffries also decided to act, even though he was still an active boxer. The champ selected the Murdock-Mayo play *Davy Crockett* as his heavyweight stage debut. An unfavorable dress-rehearsal review in the *Seattle Daily Times* stated that Jeffries was "knocked out in a bout with the drama." Nevertheless, he went on tour and opened in Carson City, Nevada in 1904. He continued in Colorado Springs before moving to other western cities. In between performances, Jeffries managed to retain his heavyweight title on August 24, 1904. The theater critics generally gave him a pass on his stage efforts. "Jeff does not lay claim to great Thespian abilities and so there is no complaint to make," noted the *Omaha World-Herald*. The *Baltimore American* provided an amusing Crockett-like take on his performance: "Be sure of your right and then get in an uppercut." He retired his Crockett characterization in 1905, and claimed that he had earned $33,000 playing the role; however, he said that he would not return to the ring.[11] The play, however, would continue to be staged regularly throughout the United States for another two decades.

In 1905, *Davy Crockett, Jr., or "Be Sure You're Right, Then Go Ahead"* was published as a "dime novel" in the Pluck and Luck series, and Harriet G. Reiter penned David *Crockett*, a 31-page booklet in the Instructor Literature series. Reiter's Crockett "stood alone like a lion at bay" in his final stand at the Alamo. She wrote that as one of six defenders who were captured at the end of the battle, Crockett tried to kill General Santa Anna: "But before [Crockett] reached [Santa Anna], a dozen bullets found their way into his heart." Also in 1905, Kirk Munroe authored the children's book, *With Bowie and Crockett, or Fighting for the Lone-Star Flag*.

In 1906, the Pluck and Luck series produced *Dead Game, or, Davy Crockett's Double,* and "Davy Crockett," a revised Pompey Smash-like tune, was published. The song's relevant lyrics consisted of: "Don't you want to hear about Davy Crockett, half horse, half man, and half sky rocket?/He went out one night when the folks were all asleep, the stars were lying on the ground about knee-deep."

President Theodore Roosevelt arrived in Memphis on October 5, 1907, and addressed a crowd that was interested in the federal government's plan to improve the channels of the Mississippi River in Tennessee. "Like Davy Crockett, the great Tennessean, I favor his motto, 'Be sure you are right, then go ahead,' and this deep water river problem is almost up to the 'go ahead' stage, but we want to be sure about it," said Roosevelt, who had co-founded the Boone and Crockett Club, the conservation-hunting organization in 1887.

In 1908, Edward Willett wrote *Davy Crockett's Boy Hunter,* a pulp publication in the popular Beadles Frontier Series. "A powerful bear hunter, and he has been to Congress," said the author. "He is a man all over, he is." Everett McNeil wrote *In Texas With Davy Crockett; A Story of the Texas War for Independence,* and provided a detailed description of Crockett's final moments: "He was bleeding from a gash across his forehead, his clothing was torn and cut by a hundred bayonet thrusts and knife-stabs; but still unconquered." McNeil added that Crockett, the last Alamo defender, was asked to surrender, but he shouted, "never!" According to the author, Crockett continued to fight but fell after he was bayoneted in the chest and subsequently stabbed with "a hundred knives and bayonets."

Bayonets were replaced by Cupid's arrows when in 1909 Crockett appeared for the first time on film in the silent production *Davy Crockett—In Hearts United.* The Bison Motion Pictures film, which ran approximately ten minutes, starred Charles K. French, who also co-wrote the romantic screenplay in which Crockett rescues a young woman named Anna from a loveless betrothal with a man named Blake. A promotional piece, on eye-catching pink-colored paper, in the May 8, 1909 issue of *Moving Picture World* proclaimed: "Anna is about to be married on the lawn of her Father's house to Blake, whom she now hates, when Davy rides in, grabs Anna, pulls her on the horse and rides away to a Country parson's house, marries Anna, [and] takes her home to his own Cabin."

The following year, the Selig Polyscope Company's *Davy Crockett*, another silent short, made its debut with Hobart Bosworth in the lead and Betty Harte as his romantic interest. The twenty-minute film was loosely based on the Murdock-Mayo play. The April 16, 1910 issue of *The Film Index* proclaimed: "No film presented in years will achieve the success from a historical and dramatic standpoint that this great subject will." Newspapers agreed. "The new picture last night [at the Bijou] was *Davy Crockett*, and it is well worth your time to see it," noted North Carolina's *Greensboro Record* on the front page of its June 21, 1910 issue. "The love making and the romantic experiences in the early life of Davy Crockett (historical), a great treat for the children," stated Little Rock's *Arkansas Gazette*. Interestingly, a year later, Bosworth played Daniel Boone in *The Chief's Daughter*, making him the first screen actor to portray the two famous frontiersmen, an achievement accomplished by Fess Parker fifty-four years later.

In 1909, the Crockett Hotel was built in San Antonio, on the edge of the original Alamo battlefield. The facility's six stories were augmented by a seven-story wing in 1927. A large reproduction portrait of *David Crockett 1812*, painted by John Nava in 1993, currently hangs in the lobby.

Several short, black and white silent films that included a Crockett character were released in the new century's second decade. The 1911, Georges Méliès' *The Immortal Alamo* included Crockett, and four years later in the Fine Arts Film Company's *The Martyrs of the Alamo*, A. D. Sears portrayed the legendary Tennessean.

A. D. Sears in *Martyrs of the Alamo* (1915).

Also in 1911, Charles Fletcher Allen wrote *David Crockett, Scout, Small Boy, Pilgrim, Mountaineer, Soldier, Bear-Hunter, and Congressman, Defender of the Alamo*. Besides its biographical content and Frank McKernan's illustrations, the author frequently added comments about Abraham Lincoln, Civil War battles, and accidental guns deaths in Chicago in 1910. Allen wrote that at the Alamo, Crockett "died in his tracks." Painter Frederick Coffay Yohn created *Battle of the Alamo*, which placed Crockett and a handful of defenders fighting oncoming Mexican soldiers in front of the Alamo church.

In 1911, Crockett's image was reproduced in the Royal Bengals Little Cigars "Men of History" card set. The front of card T-68, titled "Hon. David Crockett" and "Davy Crockett," depicted a somber-looking Tennessean wearing the clothes of a gentleman; the back of the card provided a biographical sketch which included the following: "At the battle of the Alamo he was one of the six survivors who fought to the end. When taken prisoner there was a ring of twenty dead Mexicans around him. Next day, March 6, 1836, he was treacherously executed by the order of General Santa Anna." The description is interesting because it suggests that the battle took place on March 5. Royal Bengals offered a five-cent Crockett cigar and promoted it with an image of the backwoodsman as an innocent cherub-like hunter, smoking a cigar, of course. Frank Mayo, who portrayed Crockett on stage for many years, was depicted on his own cigar box, which was produced by Philadelphia's H. B. Grauley company.

In 1914, Ray Myers portrayed Crockett in *Fall of the Alamo* (also titled *The Siege and Fall of the Alamo*), "a picture financed and produced by the State of Texas" and the Santa Monica, California-based New York Motion Picture Company, according to the 1914 edition of *Who's Who in the Film World*. The silent short is another lost film of the era.

The movement to grant women the right to vote in the United States received a Crockett-like acknowledgment from Arkansas' *Jonesboro Evening Sun* on October 8, 1915, when the newspaper noted that the suffragists "have been grinning for the President for a long time." Five years later, when the 19th Amendment was ratified (Tennessee was the important 36th state to ratify it), two of Crockett's granddaughters, Dorcas Matilda Crockett and Olivia Elvira Crockett, daughters of Robert Patton Crockett and his wife, Matilda, became eligible to vote in national elections.

In 1915, W. E. Browning starred in the Superba Company silent film *Davy Crockett Up to Date*. According to *The New Historical Dictionary of the American Film Industry*, Superba specialized in one-reel comedies, and true to the company's track record, the film was based more upon James Hackett's exaggerated characterization of Crockett than Frank Mayo's more recent interpretation of the famous backwoodsman. Unfortunately, like many of the early silents, *Davy Crockett Up to Date* remains a lost film. Also in 1915, William C. Sprague added to the Crockett biography roster with *Davy Crockett*.

On July 16, 1916, *Davy Crockett* debuted with Dustin Farnum, who had been called "the idol of the screen," in the title role. The silent film, produced by Pallas Pictures, was based on the famous Murdock-Mayo play; in fact, Mayo's grandson wrote the screenplay—a romance between the frontier character and Eleanor Vaughn (sometimes spelled Vaughan), played by Winifred Kingston. The film had been promoted months earlier by several industry publications, including *Moving Picture World*, which featured a full-page photograph of Farnum in its May issue. At the time, the film played was exploited as anti-Mexican sentiment because of Pancho Villa's raid on Columbus, New Mexico on March 9, 1916, which resulted in the deaths of eight American soldiers and over a dozen civilians. "Davy Crockett is a picture of particularly timely interest in view of the Mexican trouble," noted Cleveland's *Plain Dealer* on July 16, 1916.

The United States entered World War I in 1917, and the legacy of Crockett played a role in the nation's effort to promote the war. The rifle and silver tomahawk which were presented to him in Philadelphia in 1834 were placed on display along with other artifacts previously used by national heroes at the Smithsonian Institution in Washington D.C. In an article about German U-boats, Kentucky's *Lexington Herald* stated: "'Don't shoot,' said the coon. 'If you're Davy Crockett I come down.' 'Don't bomb me,' says the German submarine commander. 'If you have my range, I come up.'"

A year later, another Tennessean, who had also been born in a log cabin, gained fame as a Medal of Honor recipient for his incredible bravery against German forces in France on October 8, 1918: Sgt. Alvin York. The highly decorated soldier and Crockett became Tennessee's greatest heroes, and the two were frequently mentioned together in various media reports. York, who resided alongside the Wolf River, a tributary Crockett crossed when he left Tennessee in 1835, died in 1964. *The New York Times* acknowledged "the latter-day descendant of the American frontier, a plain-talking, no-nonsense sharpshooter" in York's obituary. "Later, when he was surrounded but not taken by fame, he extended the legend beyond the limits set by such as Davy Crockett."[12]

Dustin Farnum in *Davy Crockett* (1916).

Crockett's popularity continued in the 1920s. Books, songs, commercial promotions, and another motion picture celebrated him. Adrian, Michigan's *Daily Telegram* reported that Frank Mayo, the grandson of the famous 19th century actor, was scheduled to begin work on a film version of *Davy Crockett* for Universal. However, the film was not made. Young Mayo, though, went on to appear in over 350 motion pictures.

In 1920, Crockett appeared in a featured article published in *The Mentor: Pioneers of the Great West*. The next year, Yale University Press published *The Chronicles of America Series*, which included author Nathaniel W. Stephenson's Homeric-like passages about Crockett in Volume 24, *Texas and the Mexican War*: "David Crockett, who had come from his native Tennessee to throw in his lot with the Texans, sold his life amid the last massacre as grimly as a Norse Viking in an Icelandic saga." In 1922, Jane Corby wrote the children's book, *The Story of Davy Crockett*, and that same year, John T. McIntyre wrote *In Texas with Davy Crockett*, a fictional account which described the Alamo defender's final moments as "gallant." The life of Crockett was broadcast on radio for the first time when, on July 19, 1922, WJZ in Newark, New Jersey presented "Davy Crockett," a production by Capt. Frank Winch.

On September 14, 1922, a large statue of Crockett, built by Columbia, Tennessee's W. M. Dean Marble Company on the town square in Lawrenceburg, Tennessee, was dedicated in a formal ceremony. The statue's pose, similar to Crockett's appearance in John Gadsby Chapman's painting, suggests a greeting gesture to those who visit the Lawrence County community. One side of its base reads: "Erected by gift of the people and the legislature of Tennessee, to the memory of Col. David Crockett, born in East

Tennessee, August 17, 1786. And gave his life for Texas liberty amid the shooting walls of the 'Alamo' Sunday morning March 6, 1836." Coincidentally, when the statue was erected and publicly dedicated, two of Crockett's grandchildren were still alive: Ashley Wilson Crockett and Olivia Elvira Crockett. Both were the children of Robert Patton Crockett and his wife, Matilda.

In 1923, Hamlin Garland, who as a young man, saw the elder Frank Mayo portray Crockett on stage, made a satisfactory attempt in the introduction to the *Autobiography of David Crockett* (part of Scribner's "Modern Student's Library" series) to acknowledge the difference between the legendary Crockett and the actual man. "As set forth in his own books he is a long way from being a poet, although he loved the wilderness as profoundly as he hated Jackson and Van Buren," wrote Garland. "Somewhere between the coarse, bragging, stump-speaking politician and the Davy Crockett of the Murdock-Mayo play lies the real backwoodsman, whose fame is united with that of Daniel Boone as our typical pioneer." *Davy Crockett* continued to be staged in the 1920s, including performances that featured Frank Mayo's grandson in the title role.

The question of how Crockett died was addressed in S. E. Scates' *A School History of Tennessee*, which was published by the World Book Company in 1925. Scates, a professor of history and government at the West Tennessee State Normal School (now the University of Memphis), described the famous backwoodsman's last moments at the Alamo: "At last only Davy Crockett and five others remained alive. This immortal six surrendered, only to be massacred by the Mexicans." The "surrender" scenario was a distinctly different from James Phelan's earlier work, *School History of Tennessee*, which only said that "Crockett was among those who were taken prisoners and were killed by the Mexicans in cold blood."[13] However, no dispute arose among those who took sides in the different school book scenarios about Crockett's demise.

Actor J. Warren Kerrigan, who had the title role in *Captain Blood* (1924), said, "I shall surely do a motion picture of Davy Crockett before my film career ends." However, he never acted in films again. Another film with Crockett was soon on the way. In 1926, Sunset Productions released the silent film *Davy Crockett at the Fall of the Alamo*, starring Cullen Landis in the title role. Unlike the previous Crockett motion pictures, this six-reeler had a more dramatic and action-packed story line. Landis' death scene, in which he smiles first at his adversaries, is memorable, since it reflected a passage in the 1837 Crockett almanac which mentioned that "a smile of scorn played on his features" before he died.

Vernon Louis Parrington's *Main Currents of American Thought* (1927), which won the Pulitzer Prize for History the following year, focused more on Crockett's superficial reputation than his principled stands on behalf of Tennessee squatters and the displaced Eastern tribes. "Davy was a good deal of wag, and the best joke he ever played upon posterity [was] that he has swallowed up the myth whole and persists in setting a romantic halo on his coonskin cap," wrote Parrington, who also called Crockett one of the "Smart Alecks of the canebrakes."

Also in 1927, "The Ballad of Davy Crockett," a thirteen-verse tune based upon the Pompey Smash compositions, was released as sheet music. But even the legendary Davy Crockett—and just about everyone else—had to take a back seat in the 1920s while the nation celebrated Charles Lindbergh's trans-Atlantic flight, Red Grange's gridiron exploits, Gertrude Ederle's amazing English

Channel swim, Jack Dempsey and Gene Tunney's heavyweight boxing championships, and Babe Ruth's memorable sixty-home-run season.

In the 1920s, a number of businesses exploited Crockett's name and history to promote various products and services. The Southern Pacific Railroad used Crockett's image (firing a rifle atop the Alamo church) on its advertisements, and in 1928 the John Hancock Insurance Company produced a promotional sixteen-page booklet titled *David Crockett: Backwoodsman and Congressman*. The company wisely noted: "We do not know exactly how Davy Crockett died." Carefully reminding its customers about mortality and the need to secure proper insurance coverage, the company publication stated: "It is more probable that the brave woodsman died with his face to the foe, undaunted and resolute—on his lips, the words—'Go Ahead!'" The May 1929 issue of *Frontier Times*, a publication "devoted to frontier history, border tragedy, and pioneer achievements," featured a cover story on Crockett.

The Crockett legend evolved in the 1930s, thanks to more books, periodicals, songs, films, and radio programs. On October 15, 1931, vocalist Chubby Parker recorded "Davey Crockett," a 78-rpm disc on New York's Conqueror Records, which was released the following year. The rhythmic, upbeat single was the first commercial release of a Crockett recording, and like other approachable dance tunes of the time, provided listeners with a brief element of rhythmic escapism from the effects of the Great Depression.

The Murdock-Mayo play *Davy Crockett* and other stories about the famous frontier hero were popular on various radio stations. Hank Simmons' *Showboat* program on CBS radio presented *Davy Crockett* on May 3, 1930; the Corse Payton stock company's presentation of *Davy Crockett* aired on WOR radio in New York City on March 25, 1932; and DeWolfe Hopper starred as "Davy Crockett" in a dramatic presentation on Midwest radio on October 16, 1933.

For youngsters, Philadelphia's Gum company produced its Wild West Series Picture Puzzle Bubble Gum set, a 49-card assortment, in 1933. Although the set primarily featured cowboys, the first card in the series was titled "Davy Crockett Defending the Alamo." That same year, the Goudy Indian Gum card set included Crockett in a John Gadsby Chapman-like pose in its roster of 216 Native American chiefs, frontiersmen, military leaders, and assorted Western characters.

Half-Horse, Half-Alligator, a comedy about Crockett, written by Tennessee's John Philip Milhouse, was announced in the *Charlotte Observer* on March 22, 1933.

In 1934, Constance Rourke published *Davy Crockett*, a lively biography of the frontiersman. "Even in the most soaring of the many tales about Crockett there was truth," wrote Rourke, who was quite specific when it came to the location of Crockett's death at the Alamo: "Crockett fell in the thickest of the swift and desperate clash [at the] wall on the south side towards the barracks." The author included an epilogue-bibliography ("Sunrise in His Pocket" and "Behind This Book") which included a descriptive roster of the *Crockett* almanacs.

John W. Thomason, a decorated United States Marine, illustrated *The Adventures of Davy Crockett—Told Mostly by Himself*. The book's most memorable image was titled "Crockett led before Santa Anna," which depicted the battered and shirtless Alamo defender being escorted by two Mexican soldiers moments before his final fate. Two years later, the illustration was re-titled *Crockett Taken*

Before Santa Anna and displayed at the Forth Worth Woman's Club art gallery.

In 1935, C. R. Schaare penned *The Life of Davy Crockett in Picture and Story*, a book for young readers. The author, who also wrote biographies of Daniel Boone, Buffalo Bill, and Kit Carson, vividly stated that the Alamo hero's death was caused by a "dozen swords plunged into his body." That same year, Bud Geary, in an uncredited minor role, appeared as Crockett in the Mascot Pictures serial *The Miracle Rider*.

In 1936, the sesquicentennial of Crockett's birth was celebrated in Greeneville, Tennessee, and President Franklin D. Roosevelt proclaimed the Davy Crockett National Forest in Texas' Houston and Trinity Counties. The 150th anniversary was noted in numerous newspaper and magazine articles, like Zella Armstrong's "Davy Crockett, Boy and Man" in the *Chattanooga Sunday Times*. British author Hugh Poindexter produced *Go Ahead Davie*, a book about Crockett in his pre-Alamo days, and Columbia University's Morningside Players of Columbia gave a performance of "The Ballad of Davy Crockett," written by H. R. Hays. "His seven scenes he calls 'stanzas,' and preceding each stanza two verses telling of the high spots in Davy's career were sung," noted one newspaper. "Then upon the stage these episodes were enacted. Final scene: 'At the Alamo.'"[14]

The Battle of the Alamo's centennial was also commemorated in 1936, and many Texas newspapers remembered Crockett's participation in the historic event. The manner of his death became a hot topic once again, and the description of his final moments varied from publication to publication. On March 6, Brownsville's *El Heraldo de Brownsville* said that Crockett "was captured and put to death by Santa Anna." That same day, Clarence Wharton's "One

Hundred Years Ago In Texas," an article which appeared in *The Houston Chronicle* and *The Dallas Morning News,* suggested that a story of Crockett being the last man alive in the Alamo, before being shot to death, was a "rumor." The *Fort Worth Star-Telegram* stated that Crockett, "commanding the battery on the west wall, turned his guns on the Mexicans into the main area and inflicted heavy loss until he and his men were shot down."

In 1937, the Doughnut Corporation of America issued "Thrilling Moments in the Lives of Famous Americans," a 72-card set which appeared on the company's doughnut boxes. Eighteen card panels were included on each carton, and card number thirteen in the alphabetical roster was Davy Crockett, who was identified with the description, "Noted Scout and Alamo Hero." Among those on Crockett's panel were Babe Ruth, Paul Revere, Theodore Roosevelt, Abraham Lincoln, and Gertrude Ederle.

On September 24, 1937 Crockett was on the big screen again, this time in *Heroes of the Alamo.* The Sunset Productions' release starred Lane Chandler as Crockett, the film's second billed actor to Earl Hodgins' Stephen Austin. However, the focus of the film was on the Dickinson family, and Chandler's character receives limited screen time. At the end of the battle, Santa Anna, played by Julian Rivero, sees an unarmed wounded Crockett crawling near a ladder and orders: "Kill that!" The Tennessean manages to reach the second rung of the ladder (just where was he going, anyway?) before a *soldado* promptly clubs him in the head with the power of a Joe DiMaggio home run swing (By the way, the Yankee Clipper led the majors in 1937 with 46 homers). Crockett mumbles something like, "I'll be danged to ya," grabs his stomach with his left hand, and dies. Later that year, Sterling Waters portrayed the frontier hero in

The Alamo: "Shrine of Texas Liberty," a low budget, narrated educational film produced by the Kier Film Company.

Crockett's image on the Alamo Cenotaph. Illustration by Gary S. Zaboly.

The January 1938 issue of *Frontier Times* featured J. Marvin Hunter's cover story, "Crockett's Colorful Career Ended in Texas," which included the following statement: "Colonel David Crockett was one of the most remarkable men of the times in which he lived."

On December 31, 1938, a monument to Crockett was dedicated in Ozana, Texas. The large granite structure depicts a hatless Crockett, and the base features a revised version of his motto: "Be Sure You Are Right Then Go Ahead."

In 1939, a life-sized sculpted figure of Crockett was included along with other prominent Alamo defenders on the *Spirit of Sacrifice,* a large sixty-foot shaft of Georgia gray marble, created by Pompeo Coppini, that was erected on Alamo Plaza in San Antonio, Texas. One side of the impressive monument, which is commonly known as the Cenotaph, features Crockett and Alamo commander William Barret Travis, who are identified by name. Other nameless defenders stand with them, although the names of all who fought at the Alamo are inscribed on the Cenotaph's Texas granite base.

Also in 1939, Richard M. Dorson edited selections from various Crockett almanacs and published them as *Davy Crockett: American Comic Legend.* Dorson explained that the annuals represented "America's most authentic folk literature" and that "the Davy Crockett myth is closest of our scanty legend literatures to the national epics." Robert Barrat played Crockett in *Man of Conquest,* a Republic Pictures biography about Sam Houston, but it was not a major role. However, that was about to change.

On December 13, 1939, syndicated columnist Sheila Graham announced: "Joel McCrea or Walter Huston will get the role of Davy Crockett in Paramount's *Sunrise in my Pocket,* by Edwin Justus Mayer. The play, which centers round the Alamo, was all set for Broadway production when Paramount stepped in and offered Mayer $40,000 for the movie rights, plus $20,000 to write the scenario, on condition that it be made into a movie first. Production is scheduled for January."[15] Huston had made an earlier impression to Paramount when he portrayed Crockett on the *Kate Smith Hour* radio show on May 21, 1940. Unfortunately, the studio never advanced the project to the pre-production stage in 1940. *Sunrise in my Pocket* would remain in limbo until the spring of 1941, when Graham announced that the project was being sold to MGM as a Spencer Tracy vehicle. However, she mentioned in a subsequent column that McCrae was still being considered for Crockett. Once again a major studio placed the project on a back burner. In the meantime, Mayer completed his dramatic play, *Sunrise in my Pocket; or, The Last Days of Davy Crockett, an American Saga*.

Another year passed and more stories circulated about the film and its potential cast. In 1942, Raymond Massey was considered for a role in the stage version, scheduled to be produced by Cheryl Crawford. Massey had delivered a charming, folksy characterization of Abraham Lincoln in *Abe Lincoln in Illinois* (1940), and the veteran forty-six-year-old actor seemed to be an ideal choice to play Crockett, especially if the production focused on Crockett's later years. However, according to columnist Louella O. Parsons, Dennis Morgan was going to get the part, not Massey. There was talk of the play opening at a new theater being built in Maplewood, New Jersey, but the production, like the film, never materialized.

On the eve of World War II, stories about the legend of Davy Crockett continued in print, on the stage, and on the big screen. In 1940, San Mateo, California's Hillbarn Summer Theatre staged a production of *Davy Crockett,* the Murdock-Mayo original, and Frank Beals' *Davy Crockett* was published in 1941 as part of the Chicago-based Wheeler Publishing Company's "American Adventure Series." Beals' Crockett followed in the broad literary tradition which suggested that Crockett died fighting at the Alamo: "Davy stood there alone, Old Betsy in hand. 'Liberty and Texas!

Go ahead, America!' Then slowly he slumped over bodies of dead Mexicans." That same year, Crockett appeared in the first issue of *World Famous Heroes Magazine*, a comic book.

On July 15, 1941, Wild Bill Elliott debuted as Dave Crockett in Columbia Pictures' *The Son of Davy Crockett*, a classic Western six-gun shoot 'em up. The studio's press department noted: "The son of Davy Crockett, hero of the Alamo, hits the crime-fighting trail in a bullet blaze of glory to smash a renegade band and build the nation for which his father died." In the film, a bad guy named King Canfield is behind all the nefarious deeds, but Dave Crockett foils him in the end and wins the day. The film had a relatively strong run, playing in theaters around the country until early 1943.

Newspaper articles and magazine stories about World War II dominated the public's attention, but that didn't stop writers and publishers from delivering stories about Crockett. In fact, the Alamo hero became symbolic of the nation's fighting spirit, especially during the early years of the international conflict. On April 19, 1942, the S. S. *Davy Crockett*, a cargo-carrying Liberty ship, was launched by the Houston Shipbuilding Corporation at Irish Bend Island ship yard. According to the *Fort Worth Star-Telegram*, five Crockett descendants were on hand to witness the launch. Two years later, the attack transport USS *Crockett* (APA-148) was launched and served in the Pacific during difficult and challenging operations at the Philippines, Okinawa, and Guam.

In 1942, Dee Brown wrote *Wave High the Banner: A Novel Based on the Life of Davy Crockett*, and the April 1943 issue of *Esquire* magazine featured an eleven-page article titled "Davy Crockett: The Siege of the Alamo," which recalled the American defense of Wake Island in the Pacific sixteen months earlier.

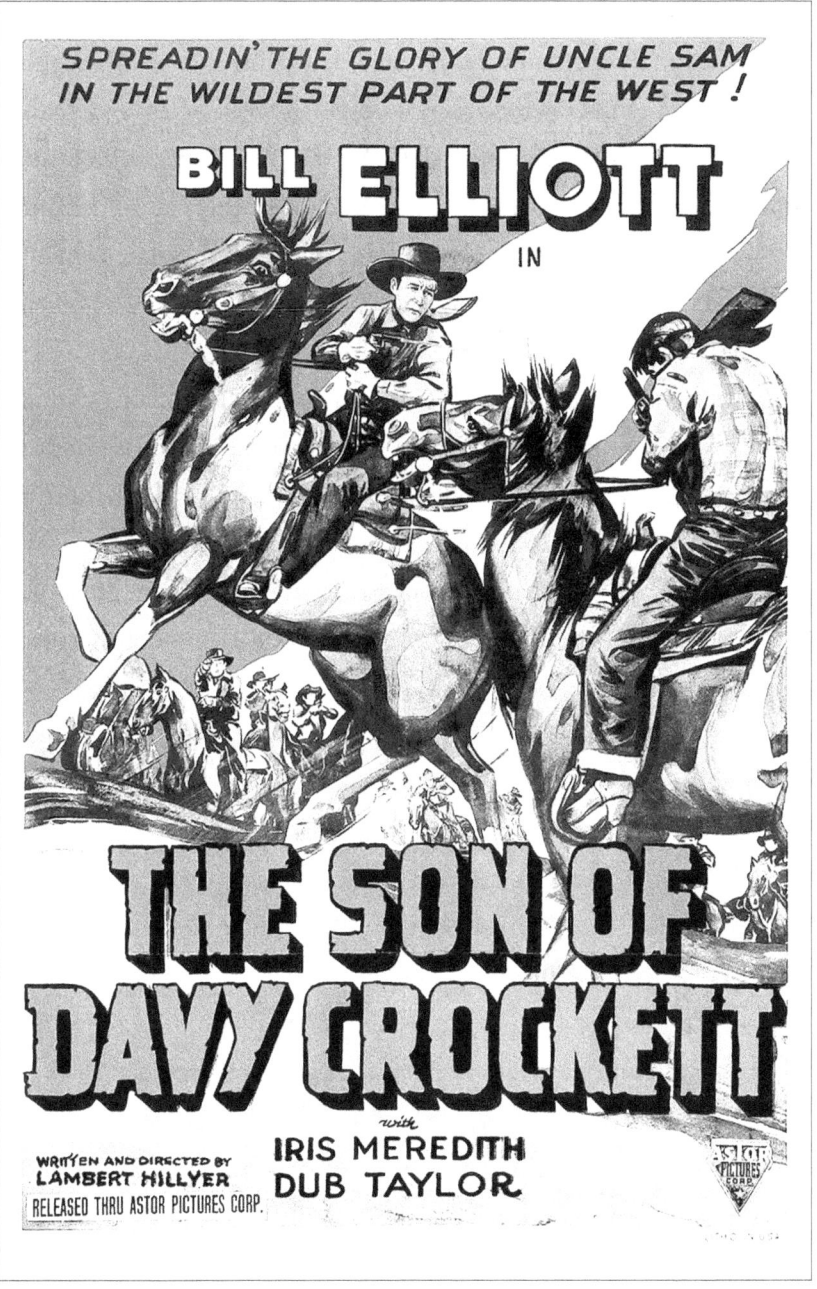

The Son of Davy Crockett (1941).

In 1944, Irwin Shapiro wrote *Yankee Thunder: The Legendary Life of Davy Crockett*, a lively fictional work aimed at young readers, and Arthur Tolliver wrote *The Wild Adventures of Davy Crockett: Based Mainly on the Writings of the Hero of the Alamo*, which questioned the "tradition that Crockett and five others were overpowered, and led as prisoners before Santa Anna [who] ordered them all killed." Tolliver concluded: "It was a good finish for a fighting man, and that's what Davy Crockett was."

Crockett was also the topic of radio programs during the war. Some stations around the country broadcast melodramas about his tall-tale legendary life, like KLRA-CBS in Little Rock on June 27, 1943, while others focused on his real life, like New Orleans WWL, which aired a show about Crockett at the Alamo on November 9, 1944. During the final year of World War II, Belden Kittredge wrote the children's book, *The Truth About Casey Jones and other Fabulous American heroes*, including Johnny Appleseed, Davy Crockett, Roy Bean, and Mike Fink.

Following the war, in 1946, Walt Disney asked artist Thomas Hart Benton to create a cartoon operetta based on Crockett's life. The well known Regionalist painter and muralist declined the offer because "he found it impossible to create anything satisfying within the constraints the studio imposed." Disney would wait another eight years before he attempted another Crockett project.

Cleveland's Barn Theatre staged its own version of the Murdock-Mayo play, directed by Miriam Kramer, in 1946, and plans about the pre-war Crockett film and another play were revived the following year. It was reported that Raymond Massey, then fifty-one-years-old, was once again scheduled to play Crockett in a 1947 Broadway production, this time directed by Margo Jones and produced by Haila Stoddard. Unfortunately, the play never received enough financial backing to open.

On February 13, 1947, Hollywood reporter Jimmie Fidler announced that "Paramount has scheduled a picture based on the life of Davy Crockett, hero of the Alamo." It was later reported that Alan Le May, who had written several recent Westerns including *Along Came Jones* (1945), *San Antonio* (1947), *Cheyenne* (1947), and *Gunfighters* (1947), was signed to write the screenplay. Film columnists continued to speculate about the casting. On August 19, 1947, Sheila Graham wrote that "Ray Milland, I hear, gets the top role of Davy Crockett in Paramount's *Sunrise in my Pocket*—and he'll do it when he finishes his current *Sealed Verdict*, in Europe." Milland finished the Nazi trial film but never played Crockett. John Wayne also expressed interest in a Crockett film. "Secret ambition of John Wayne, he confessed on the set of Argosy's technicolor production for RKO Radio, *She Wore a Yellow Ribbon*, is to play Davy Crockett in a picture based on the siege of the Alamo," reported the *Arkansas Gazette* on September 25, 1949. "I'd like to make him a well rounded human being, though," said Wayne, "not just a hero kids read about, but a real guy." Another actor's name was mentioned as a potential Crockett. On August 9, 1950, Hollywood columnist Hedda Hopper reported that Johnny Weissmuller, filmdom's *Tarzan*, was going to play Crockett in *The Alamo*, a motion picture that would be filmed in San Antonio and Mexico City, starring John Wayne in another role. The Weissmuller-Wayne project didn't happen. Wayne would wait nearly a decade to bring Crockett and the story of the Alamo to the big screen.

Sanford Tousey's children's book, *Hero of the Alamo*, was published in 1948, and that year Crockett appeared in the first issue of *Dead-Eye Western Comics.* Crockett also became a popular answer in newspaper crossword puzzles and question-and-answer columns. Many newspapers answered readers' questions about where he was born, his congressional service, and where he died, but one addressed the question about "how he died." In the December 31, 1948 issue of Illinois' *Evansville Press,* the newspaper's "Ask The Press" column responded to the following question: "Did Davy Crockett die defending the fort at [the] Alamo?" The daily replied: "Davy Crockett was one of six survivors who surrendered [at the] Alamo after [a] long siege, [and] all of them were then shot down by Santa An[n]a's order, say some historians. Texas history students staunchly maintain that all Alamo defenders died fighting." There were no critical responses to the newspaper's reply, although someone should have raised a question about its grammar.

Crockett's trademark coonskin cap became part of a national political fight in 1948, when Estes Kefauver ran for a United States Senate seat from Tennessee. He was challenged by the state's Democratic boss E. H. Crump, who supported incumbent Tom Stewart. The campaign became rather nasty when Crump accused Kefauver of working for the Communist Party "with the stealth of a raccoon." Like Crockett embracing the "gentleman from the cane" moniker and using it as an advantage, Kefauver donned a coonskin cap and stated: "I may be a pet coon, but I'm not Boss Crump's coon."[16] Kefauver successfully used the coonskin cap as a campaign symbol and won the primary and the Senate election. It was an amusing political victory for the Kefauver family since an ancestor, Joel Estes, "ran for Congress unsuccessfully against David Crockett In [1829]."[17]

In January 1949, "Davy Crockett's Last Fight" was featured

in the twentieth issue of Commended Comics' *Tex Granger*, and that same year Aileen Wells Parks authored *Davy Crockett, Young Rifleman*, a fanciful novel for young readers.

In 1950, interest in *Sunrise In My Pocket* received yet another lease on life when actor Paul Douglas said that he was going to play Crockett, but once again, Edwin Justus Mayer's play failed to be staged—at least as a dramatic piece. Interestingly, Mayer's play was set to be redesigned as a musical, with Rouben Mamoulian as director, bandleader-clarinetist Artie Shaw as arranger, and Frank Loesser as composer. Once again, the sun never rose on *Sunrise In My Pocket*. It would take decades, but the play was eventually produced.

During the early years of the 1950s, the story of the famous frontiersman was once again featured in print and on motion picture screens. *Davy Crockett—Indian Scout*, starring George Montgomery as the nephew of his famous namesake, was released in 1950. Directed by Lew Landers, the film, set in the post-1848 Southwest, featured Montgomery (wearing buckskins and a cowboy hat, and carrying a six shooter), Noah Berry Jr. as Tex McGee (wearing a fox-tail cap, which was more in tune with the original Crockett), and Robert Barrat, a former Crockett (*Man of Conquest*), who played James Lone Eagle, a mixed-race Native American chief. The film wasn't well received. "Someday someone is going to do a film about Davy Crockett with all the merit the character deserves," noted Massachusetts' *Springfield Union* on February 16, 1950.

On October 13, 1950, a David Crockett monument in Trenton, Tennessee was dedicated in a ceremony. The stone structure featured a stately bust and descriptive text which identified Crockett as a pioneer, statesman, and hero.

Davy Crockett—Indian Scout (1950).

Capitalizing on the Crockett name, Bob Schoenke wrote and illustrated *Laredo Crockett,* a Western comic strip, which ran from June 12, 1950 until January 27, 1968. *Laredo Crockett* was described as an "action-packed character of old-time Texas," but the stories were set in the decades following Crockett's death at the Alamo. On May 31, 1953, a Sunday comic strip, *Dick's Adventures in Dreamland,* created by Neil O'Keefe and Max Trell, featured a sleep-inspired sequence in which the title character goes back to the Alamo with "Davy Crockett, Jim Travis and a small group of friends and neighbors." Besides incorrectly identifying Alamo commander William Barret Travis (or was it Jim Bowie?), the strip mentioned that the famous siege lasted twelve days instead of thirteen. Crockett made several appearances in Norman Marsh's self-syndicated comic strip, *Dan'l Hale,* the coonskin cap-wearing pioneer who debuted as *Danny Hale* a year earlier.

Also in 1950, the song "Aha, San Antone," with its lyrical reference to Crockett ("When I was a kid I had a locket/And inside was a picture o' Davy Crockett"), was featured in a scene from Republic Pictures' *Rio Grande,* a classic John Ford-directed Western which starred John Wayne. That same year, the Crockett Theatre, a 1,265-seat venue, opened in Lawrenceburg, Tennessee, and *Coronet* magazine included a story on "Davy Crockett at the Battle of the Alamo" in its September 1950 issue.

The next year, Crockett appeared in several different published works. Meridel Le Sueur's *Chanticleer of the Wilderness Road: The Story of Davy Crockett,* a book for young readers, celebrated Crockett's adventurous life and death in rather sophisticated prose: "There came the moment when all that was Davy Crockett, made from the earth, from the flesh of others, his tall spired brain, his panther heart of imagination, fell down, and all at the Alamo were lost in that final and lonely place." Avon Periodicals published its first issue of *Frontier Fighter Davy Crockett,* Hillman Publishing included a story about Crockett in its second issue of *Dead-Eye Western* comics, and the Youthful company featured "Davy Crockett in Death Stalks the Alamo" in issue six of *Indian Fighter*. In 1952, Grosset and Dunlap published Enid Lamonte Meadowcraft's *The Story of Davy Crockett,* a children's book, which was wonderfully illustrated by Charles B. Falls.

On March 6, 1952, the 116th anniversary of Crockett's death at the Alamo, the *Beaumont Journal* featured an advertisement for *Return of the Texan,* which starred Dale Robertson as Sam Crockett, "heir to the fabulous name of Crockett—Davy Crockett, Indian fighter." Sam is a widower with two sons: Steve and Yo-Yo. That's right, Yo-Yo. The Twentieth Century Fox film, though, was set in modern-day Texas, and featured Crockett's favorite form of modern transportation—a jeep.

The Presidential election of 1952 had a touch of Davy Crockett when Tennessee Senator Estes Kefauver, wearing his trademark coonskin cap, defeated President Harry S. Truman in the New Hampshire primary. The March 24, 1952 *Time* magazine cover featured Kefauver wearing a coonskin cap. Kefauver, though, failed to win the nomination and was unsuccessful in securing the vice president position on Adlai Stevenson's Democratic ticket, which lost in November to Republican Dwight D. Eisenhower and his running mate Richard M. Nixon. Ironically, since Kefauver lost his bid to be the nation's VP, it was the new vice president, Nixon, who would get the opportunity to meet Fess Parker, Walt Disney's *Davy Crockett,* in Disneyland in August 1955. Eisenhower, though, became part of Crockett lore when in the autumn of 1955, while recuperating from a heart attack, he received a Davy Crockett necktie from members of the media. Kefauver became Adlai Stevenson's vice-presidential running mate in the next presidential election but the pair lost to Eisenhower and Nixon.

In "Alamo!," a story in the July-August 1952 issue (no. 28) of the comic book *Two-Fisted Tales,* Crockett is "trapped in the court yard" as Mexican soldiers advance.

On January 4, 1953, the CBS radio network broadcast "Wave High the Banner," starring Macdonald Carey as Crockett. The *Hallmark Playhouse* drama was based upon Dee Brown's 1942 book, *Wave High the Banner: A Novel Based on the Life of Davy Crockett.* Later that year, Trevor Bardette had a minor role as Crockett in Universal International's *The Man From the Alamo,* a film set in 1836 that quickly transforms into a conventional Western once star Glenn Ford leaves the famous mission-fortress. A year later, Frank Lee Beals penned *Real Adventures with Great American Pathfinders: Lewis and Clark, Davy Crockett, Daniel Boone;* Marion Michael Nunn wrote *The Forgotten Pioneer: The Life of Davy Crockett;* and the prolific author Elizabeth Jane Coatsworth penned the children's book *Old Whirlwind: A Story of Davy Crockett.* Coatsworth's book was promoted with the following description: "What happens when Davy Crockett is hired out to a cruel drover gives an inkling of the rugged backwoods childhood of this American frontiersman." At first, these books weren't particularly successful, but a year later, like other previously written Crockett titles, they started flying off book store shelves.

Then 1954 arrived, and Crockett was about to be elevated to popular heights that no one anticipated or imagined. On October 27, 1954, during the debut episode of *Disneyland* on ABC-TV, host Walt Disney described his forthcoming Frontierland production about "real people who became legends, like Davy Crockett, the first coonskin congressman. Davy's life was so fantastic it was hard to tell where fact left off and fancy began."[18] Next, Norman Foster, the production's director, introduced Fess Parker, a handsome, thirty-year-old native-born Texan who was contracted play the featured character in the forthcoming three-part miniseries, TV's first. In the segment, Parker, dressed in buckskins and accompanied by three backwoods-looking vocalists-musicians, sang a few verses of "The Ballad of Davy Crockett," a tune written by Tom Blackburn and George Bruns for the show. Blackburn also wrote the lively teleplay, which was based in part on Crockett's *Narrative* and Edward S. Ellis' 1884 book, *The Life of Colonel David Crockett*.

Not much was mentioned in the media about the first *Davy Crockett* episode until six weeks later; as a matter of fact, the only piece of advance national publicity for the production was a December 5, 1954, cover article, "Davy Crockett Lives Again," in *Parade*, the national Sunday newspaper supplement.

The first action-packed episode, "Davy Crockett, Indian Fighter," aired on December 15, 1954, and Parker appeared as a natural in the role. With his buckskin clothing, flintlock rifle, and coonskin cap, Parker's Crockett looked quite different from the ten-gallon-hat-wearing and six-gun-toting TV and film cowboys like Hopalong Cassidy, Gene Autry, and Roy Rogers. He looked comfortable in his costuming, and he depicted a character who actually seemed to know the woods and the critters and people who resided in them. Disney elevated the authenticity of the production by providing the principals with original early 19th century flintlock rifles.

Parker's scripted actions as Crockett were even more memorable.

Using the deceptively innovative "Crockett's Charge," he successfully battled a Creek war party with only one other man, his sidekick, George Russel, played by Buddy Ebsen. He also skillfully rode a horse, interpreted moccasin tracks, killed a bear in an off-screen knife fight, accurately imitated the sounds of an owl and a Tennessee Thrush, fired a flintlock rifle with deadly accuracy, walked bravely alone into a Creek camp to save his captured sidekick, and fended off an attack from an alligator. Not bad for less than an hour's worth of television entertainment. Parker's character emerged from the first episode as a sure-shot man of action, honor, and integrity.

Blackburn's script also empowered Crockett with a sense of rebelliousness (his unauthorized departure from camp in "Davy Crockett, Indian Fighter") and a disobedient attitude which questioned authority (his door-slamming entrance into the House of Representatives in "Davy Crockett Goes to Congress"). These expressions would resurface among counter-culture Baby Boomers in the next decade.

Nothing that Parker did on screen seemed awkward or artificial, and most importantly he handled a flintlock rifle like an experienced marksman, a skill that not every film and TV Crockett mastered. Had Parker appeared or acted in any unconvincing way, kids everywhere would have dismissed him; instead, they embraced him with admiration and affection, a reaction that would reach unprecedented levels. With Davy Crockett in mind, some school kids temporarily forgot about duck-and-cover air raid drills, the threat of atomic warfare, and mushroom-like clouds forming on the horizon. A coonskin-capped hero became a temporary antidote to the potential horrors of the Cold War, which was made evident when the Soviet Union detonated a 40-kiloton atomic test weapon the previous September.

The response to the first episode was extraordinary from both viewers and retailers. Disney prepared no advance merchandising for the hour-long program, but manufacturers' representatives contacted his office in the days that followed the initial broadcast, looking to make something, anything, associated with Crockett. Although the first Davy Crockett items failed to meet the Christmas deadline, hundreds of items eventually reached the market place over the next months.

"Davy Crockett Goes to Congress" debuted on January 26, 1955. The episode's story line focused on Crockett's defense of Indian rights, from his confrontation against Big Foot Mason, who confiscated Native American Charlie Two Shirts' land, to his impassioned stand against Jackson's Indian removal policy. "Expansion ain't no excuse for persecutin' a whole part of our people because their skin is red and they're uneducated to our ways," says Parker's character during a speech in the House of Representatives. The scene was filmed only months after the historic United States Supreme Court *Brown v. The Board of Education of Topeka* decision which stated that "separate educational facilities are inherently unfair." For many Baby Boomers, Davy Crockett's sentiments about race were taken to heart. The dramatic "Davy Crockett at the Alamo" aired on February 23, which coincided with the 119th anniversary of the famous battle. The final episode showed Crockett fighting off every Mexican soldier who advanced against him. Before viewers can witness his ultimate fate, the camera shifts to a scene of the modern Texas flag, which ends the episode. It is one of the most memorable scenes in TV history, and it would later generate arguments about Crockett's actual death for decades to come.

Three days after the Alamo episode was broadcast, singer Bill Hayes' version of "The Ballad of Davy Crockett" entered *Billboard* magazine's "Best Sellers in Stores" chart at the number sixteen position. Hayes had recorded the song in one take on December 16, 1954, the day after "Davy Crockett, Indian Fighter" debuted. The song had twenty verses, but Hayes needed only six of them, and a memorable chorus ("Davy, Davy Crockett, king of the wild frontier!"), to reach the top of the charts on March 26. Hayes stayed at number one for an impressive five weeks.

"The Ballad of Davy Crockett" sung by Bill Hayes.

Fess Parker released a rendition of the song that eventually reached the number five spot on the "Best Sellers" chart, and Tennessee Ernie Ford's recording of the catchy tune reached number five on *Billboard's* "Most Played by [Disc] Jockeys" chart. Walter Schumann's chorus—The Voice of Walter Schumann—released a cover version which managed to reach the number fourteen position on the "Jockeys" roster. Mac Wiseman, the accomplished bluegrass musician, recorded a rendition which reached number ten on *Billboard's* Country chart. The tune was seemingly everywhere.

The song became a staple part of *Your Hit Parade*, a weekly TV program which showcased the nation's biggest hits. "The Ballad of Davy Crockett" was such a popular recording that one version of the song, Tennessee Ernie Ford's rendition, remained on *Billboard's* "Most Played in Juke Boxes" chart until July 23, 1955, two weeks after Bill Haley and his Comets reached the top of the charts with "Rock Around the Clock." Three versions of "The Ballad of Davy Crockett" were included on *Billboard's* Top 30 Songs of the Year (based on the publication's "Best Sellers in Stores" chart): Bill Hayes (no. 6), Fess Parker (no. 22), and Tennessee Ernie Ford (no. 24). Approximately ten million singles were sold, and eventually over one hundred artists released versions of the Blackburn-Bruns composition.[19]

Besides "The Ballad of Davy Crockett," Disney produced other Crockett recordings, including dramatic productions which featured scripted dialogue, sound effects, and music from each of the original episodes. The individual recordings were also combined on the album *Walt Disney's Davy Crockett King of the Wild Frontier*. Other Disney recordings included "Davy Crockett's Motto—Be Sure You're Right (Then Go Ahead)" b/w "Old Betsy (Davy Crockett's Rifle)," which was performed by Fess Parker and Buddy Ebsen. Disney also published sheet music for all of the Crockett tunes.

Davy Crockett guitar.

ABC-TV's ratings for the original three episodes were so successful that Disney broadcast them again on April 13, April 27, and May 11, 1955, respectively. By this time, Disney joined the merchandising bandwagon and produced over 200 items labeled with "Walt Disney's Davy Crockett King of the Wild Frontier starring Fess Parker." Among the authorized items were plastic rifles, rubber knives, clothing, powder horns, glassware, belts, gloves, mittens, paint sets, furniture, cups, plates, soap, towels, napkins, pencil boxes, schoolbook bags, suit cases, rings, toothbrushes, curtains, musical instruments, serving trays, comic books, pocket knives, a wonderful series of Davy Crockett at the Alamo playsets produced by Louis Marx and company, and, of course, coonskin caps.

During the early months of 1955, the price of raccoon fur went from around 25-cents a pound to several dollars a pound. The demand continued to increase and the price for fur tails climbed to almost eight dollars a pound. J. B. Simpson's Alaska-Arctic Furs in Seattle had its two million fur-pelt inventory depleted in a manner of months. The Associated Press (AP) reported that the "Davy Crockett craze has created a $2,000,000 boom in the fur industry." In the article, Louis Cohen, President of the American Fur Merchants Association explained that rabbit, raccoon, and opossum fur were "doing a land office business." The AP report noted that the "headpiece fad had also cleaned out the wolf tail market." In addition, a run was made on Australian rabbit, skunk, and imitation fur. It wasn't a particularly pleasant time for fur-bearing animals.

The Crockett Craze blossomed as the U.S. economy expanded and consumer optimism increased. The nation's Gross Domestic Product growth rate for 1955 was an outstanding 7.1%, a figure not topped until 1984's 7.2%.

Approximately 5,000 non-Disney Crockett items were produced, including lamps, chalk, record players, hat racks, bicycle mud flaps, waste paper baskets, grills, board games, note pads, lariats, party poppers, clothing, iron-on patches, sunglasses, rubber horse shoes, pin-back buttons, rugs, fabric, banks, wallets, decals, rings, water pistols, badges, flashlights, faux coonskin caps, band-aids, and pith helmets—yes, pith helmets! Besides toys, games, clothing and the like, manufacturers also produced ice cream, soda, canned oysters, honey, diaper bags, and many more items under Crockett's name.

A Popular Culture and Historical Calendar

Davy Crockett at the Alamo comic book. 1955. © Disney

Crockett also made cameo appearances in other comic books. In issue no. 39 of *Forbidden Worlds*, a science fiction comic, "The Davy Crockett Mystery" told the story of Crockett who drinks from a fountain of youth and gets to fight on every American battlefield up to and including World War II. The frontier hero also appeared in *It's Game Time, Mickey Mouse in Frontierland, Marmaduke Mouse,* and *Donald Duck Beach Party.*

Numerous Crockett comic books were produced. Dell Publishing produced the most popular ones in 1955: *Davy Crockett: Indian Fighter, Davy Crockett at the Alamo,* and a Giant issue, *Davy Crockett: King of the Wild Frontier,* which included a "Davy Crockett Goes to Washington" story. That same year, Classics Illustrated published its *Davy Crockett* title. Other publishing firms produced such series as *New Adventures of Davy Crockett: Frontier Fighter, Fighting Davy Crockett, Davy Crockett Western Tales,* and *Frontier Fighters featuring Davy Crockett.* Another offering for young readers was the Crockett-like *Billy Buckskin Western* comic book series, which featured the front cover phrase, "Tales of the Wild Frontier."

Commercial give-away booklets included American Motors' *Walt Disney's Davy Crockett in the Raid at Piney Creek,* Cities Service Petroleum's *Davy Crockett Safety Trails,* the Ben Franklin Stores' *Hunting With Davy Crockett,* Vital Publications' *Life of Davy Crockett For You to Color,* Sears' *Davy Crockett Christmas Book,* and several *Captain Fortune* promotional comics, which included such titles as "Young Davy Crockett," "Davy Crockett in Episodes of the Creek War," and "Davy Crockett in Congress," among others. In the field of folk literature, the Caxton Club published Franklin J. Meine's *The Crockett Almanacks: Nashville Series, 1835-1838.*

Capitalizing on the popularity of the Crockett series, Disney edited the three original episodes, which were filmed in 35mm color, and released them in theaters as *Davy Crockett, King of the Wild Frontier* on May 25, 1955. Using the motion picture as a promotional tool, retail stores across the country responded by placing thousands of Davy Crockett merchandise ads in newspapers. For example, the day before the film opened at the Bradley Theater in Columbus, Georgia, the June 8, 1955 edition of the *Columbus Daily Enquirer* featured ads from J. J. Newberry Company ("Your Davy Crockett headquarters!"), Woolworth's ("For the most complete assortment of Davy Crockett items!"), Shulte United ("Davy Crockett Trading Post!"), Hofflin and Greentree ("Davy Crockett's complete frontier shop!"), and Sears Roebuck and Company ("Your Davy Crockett headquarters!").

At the same time the motion picture was released, Fess Parker went on a national tour of forty-two American cities. The reception was unprecedented. Thousands of kids turned up wherever Parker was scheduled to appear: department stores, civic events, government buildings, movie theaters, schools, sports stadiums, historic sites, hospitals, and airports. Over 2,000 people welcomed him when he flew into Beaumont, Texas' small airport; 5,000 greeted him in Austin; and 10,000 awaited his arrival at the Birmingham, Alabama airport. Crowds also lined the streets to see him as his motorcade passed by. Later on the tour, Buddy Ebsen joined him.

In Philadelphia, members of the National Rifle Association presented Parker with an original 19th century flintlock rifle that was built by J. Bender, a Lancaster gunsmith. Medal of Honor recipient Merritt Austin Edson, a World War II Marine veteran, and Pennsylvania congressman William A. Barrett were among the dignitaries at the ceremony.

The *Davy Crockett* trilogy helped the *Disneyland* TV show win the 1956 Emmy Award for "Best Action or Adventure Series," but Fess Parker was edged out by George Gobel who won the award for "Most Outstanding New Personality."

The Crockett Craze also helped revive an interest in the real man and his birthplace. On June 12, 1955, *The Knoxville News-Sentinel* printed a photo of the cabin that Crockett was born in, and included the following caption: "It's now about 250 yards from the Davy's birthplace marker in Greene County. Greeneville and Limestone organizations plan to make a shrine of the old building. Roscoe Stonecypher, who owns the cabin, has been using it as a granary." In the 1880s, the Stonecypher family had dismantled the cabin and moved its parts to a different location on their property where they rebuilt the structure.

In August 1955, the Davy Crockett Birthplace Association, a non-profit organization, obtained a charter "to restore and maintain the cabin in which the frontiersman was born." The group purchased land from the Stonecypher family and helped create what would later be known as the Davy Crockett Birthplace State Park, a site by the Nolichucky River in Limestone, Tennessee. The park's recreated log cabin includes a door stone that the Stonecypher family claimed was from Crockett's 1786 home. The impact of decades of rain and the need to recreate a more accurate looking cabin led to the construction of a new cabin in the 1980s; however, that one was replaced by another in 2016. Over the last few years, additional out buildings and structures which were commonly built in eastern Tennessee in the late 18th century were added to the park.

Patty Williams, Miss Tennessee of 1955, wore a coonskin cap during a United Press International photo shoot in the nation's capital before arriving at the Miss America Pageant in Atlantic City,

New Jersey. Alas, Williams didn't win the crown on the nationally televised event on September 10, 1955; Sharon Ritchie of Colorado became the new Miss America.

Numerous books about Crockett were published in 1955 and 1956. The printed works ranged from serious biographies to tall tale accounts aimed at kids. The major problem for authors and publishers was selecting a title—more appropriately a sub-title—which would separate their book from the rest of the printed pack.

Walter Blair, a University of Chicago professor, provided an interesting examination of the Crockett legacy in *Davy Crockett—Frontier Hero: The Truth as He Told It—The Legend as His Friends Built It*. Ardis Edwards Burton wrote the authorized Disney children's book *Legends of Davy Crockett*; Russel B. Shaw penned *Davy Crockett: Fabulous Frontier Fighter—The Life Story of an Amazing American Hero*; Hazel Davis authored *Davy Crockett: Frontiersman and Scout*; and James Duncan Lawrence wrote *Davy Crockett and the Indian Secret*, a fictional tale about a treasure chest in a cave. Harriet Evatt wrote *Davy Crockett, Big Indian, and Little Bear*; Nat Wilson created *Davy Crockett: Danger From the Mountain*, a "Triple Nickle Book," which described the frontier hero's adventures with the Crow tribe; Stewart H. Holbrook penned *Davy Crockett: From the Backwoods of Tennessee to the Alamo*; and Janet Frank's children's book about Crockett was published as two different titles: *Davy Crockett and the Indians* and *Straight-shootin' Davy*.

Vincent Frank Taylor's 1955 children's book, *David Crockett: The Bravest of Them All Who Died at the Alamo*, featured an adult-like graphic ending: "But there were too many aiming muskets now, too many bayonets coming closer," wrote Taylor. "They shot him, and then they stabbed his lifeless body dozens of times." Bruce Grant's children's book, *Davy Crockett: American Hero,* featured a more delicate description of the frontier hero's death: "No one, not even Davy Crockett, came out of the battle of the Alamo alive." Felix Sutton's *The Picture Story of Davy Crockett,* another book for youngsters, featured splendid illustrations by H. B. Vestal. Irwin Shapiro's *Davy Crockett's Keelboat Race,* and the Little Golden Book, *Walt Disney's Davy Crockett, King of the Wild Frontier,* which featured the artwork of Mel Crawford, were best sellers among children's books. Another authorized Disney title for young readers was Elizabeth Beecher's *Walt Disney's Davy Crockett: King of the Wild Frontier.*

Albert Ross Hogue's *Davy Crockett and Others in Fentress County Who Have Given the County a Prominent Place in History,* a 32-pager, celebrated Crockett's life, although the author should have also placed the county's most famous citizen, Alvin York, in the title—but, after all, it was 1955, the main year of the Crockett Craze. The John Hancock Insurance Company dusted off its 1928 pamphlet about Crockett and updated it with six additional pages in 1955.

The July 16, 1955 issue of *Look* magazine promoted the next day's opening of Disneyland in Anaheim, California, where Fess Parker and Buddy Ebsen sang "Bang Goes Old Betsy." The tune, written by Gil George and George Bruns, provided the backdrop to a fun-filled choreographed hoe-down which featured dancers dressed in pioneer garb. The two actors had just returned from an on-location shoot in Ohio where two new Crockett episodes were being filmed.

Disneyland's Frontierland featured the Davy Crockett Arcade, which was filled with "King of the Wild Frontier" merchandise. Two life-sized mannequins of Parker and Ebsen were placed in an area where fans could have their photos taken with Crockett and Russel.

Although Crockett died at the Alamo, Disney resurrected the famous frontiersman by producing TV's first prequels: "Davy Crockett's Keelboat Race" and "Davy Crockett and the River Pirates," which initially aired on November 16, 1955, and December 14, 1955, respectively. *TV Guide* considered the prequels a major television event and announced them in a cover headline: "Davy Crockett Rides Again."

With Jeff York playing Mike Fink, the "king of the river," the two episodes reflected a bit of the Crockett almanac's absurdities. York's Fink delivers a classic boast when he meets Crockett for the first time. He also engages in feats of strength, displays a lusty appetite for brawling, and constantly reminds his keel boat crew who is in charge. Of course, it's Crockett who ultimately outwits Fink, and in Disney fashion the two join forces and successfully battle the river pirates. Disney repeated the two new episodes the following January and February.

The two keel boats featured in the episodes, the *Bertha Mae* and the *Gullywhumper,* were eventually brought to Disneyland where they became the Mike Fink Keel Boats attraction. The *Gullywhumper* went into operation on Christmas day 1955, and the *Bertha Mae* followed the next spring. "Davy Crockett and the River Pirates" was nominated for an Emmy Award in the "Best Single Program of the Year" category but lost to *Peter Pan*.

When the craze subsided the next year, over $300 million worth of Crockett merchandise had been sold, which adjusted for inflation, is nearly $3 billion in current dollars. One can only imagine what the retail sales figure would had been if Disney and other manufacturers had products ready for sale during the 1954 Christmas buying season.

Time magazine reported in its August 8, 1955 issue that the Boston Museum of Fine Arts was displaying "John Neagle's 1828" portrait of David Crockett, but in order not to confuse kids "Museum Director Perry Rathbone exhibited the portrait beside a full-scale Disney cutout of television's "King of the Wild Frontier." Years later, the 19th century painting was identified as an 1834 work created by Chester Harding.

Thousands of newspaper and magazine articles chronicled the craze and also help stimulate it; however, there were some adult critics who tried to undermine the popularity of Disney's character by associating him with unpleasant elements in Crockett's actual life (living in a tavern, running away from school, questionable campaign tactics, etc.), but the kids ignored the criticisms. Another exploitation of the Crockett Craze was Irving Stone's multi-part romantic story, "Four Loves of Davy Crockett," which appeared in the *American Weekly* and catered to adult readers.

There were also the zany media reports. Among the more off-beat articles was *Cockeyed* magazine's spoof on the next Presidential election. The magazine suggested a Democratic Party tandem to challenge President Dwight Eisenhower and Vice President Richard Nixon: Italian actress Gina Lolabrigida and Crockett. Of course, one part of the team wasn't an American citizen and the other had been dead since 1836. The Crockett Craze had finally gone crazy.

On November 24, 1955, Fess Parker, costumed as *Davy Crockett,* and Walt Disney rode horses on Disneyland's Main Street, U. S. A. as grand marshals in the opening parade of the Mickey Mouse Club Circus. The ringmaster was Jimmy Dodd of TV's *Mickey Mouse Club,* who had recorded two Crockett tunes, "Be Sure You're Right" and "Bang Goes Old Betsy."

Stories about Crockett were featured in several newspaper comic strips. "He's here...Davy Crockett. See today's comic page," stated newspapers from across the nation in 1955 when *Davy Crockett, Frontiersman* debuted. France Edward Herron wrote the stories and

Jim McCardle created the illustrations (with occasional contributions from Jack Kirby, and Jim Christiansen) for the Columbia Features daily strip, which ran regularly until 1957, although some of the strips appeared until 1959. In the lively illustrated panels, Crockett crossed paths with numerous characters, including Mountain Joe, the self-proclaimed "strongest man in the world."

The *Walt Disney's Treasury of Classic Tales: The Legends of Davy Crockett*, which was drawn by Jesse Marsh, was heralded with the following advance promotional statement: "Davy is captured by the Comanches in the Red River wilderness. The Indians admire Davy's courage, test him against their heroes. The final match is the trial by endurance—Davy against the chief's three giant sons. It looks hopeless for Davy, until...." The strip ran from July 17, 1955 to January 8, 1956.

Another newspaper comic strip was *In The Days of Davy Crockett*. Disney also came out with *Li'l Davy*, a much younger comic book version of the "King of the Wild Frontier," who appeared in *Frontierland* no.1 (May 1956); *Donald Duck Beach Party* no. 3 (July 1956), no. 4 (July 1957), and no. 5 (July 1958); and *Disneyland Birthday Party* no. 1 (November 1958).

Davy Crockett Says, was a part story, part moral comic strip which provided readers with examples of proper conduct and behavior. For example, one strip noted: "A man has to do right by his country [and] do right by his family." Another stated: "Don't be discouraged by hard knocks. Davy Crockett wasn't. They give you character, if you keep on working hard for what you want." Sadly, the lessons would be replaced a half century later by an "Everybody-is-a-Star" philosophy that endorsed participation trophies, non-competitive athletic games, and other kid gloves-like activities for young people.

Seemingly lost in the Crockett mania was the August 3, 1955, theatrical release of Republic Pictures' *The Last Command*, an Alamo film that featured Arthur Hunnicutt as a grizzled, coonskin cap-wearing Crockett. In the Frank Lloyd-directed film, which debuted three weeks after Disneyland opened, Crockett delivers a well received speech to his admirers ("Anyway, in Washington they told me either to go to Hell or go to Texas, so naturally not wantin' to be took for a coward, I chose Texas."), reassures a sick Jim Bowie ("They'll eat snakes before they get in here!"), and torches a gunpowder barrel, which blows up and kills him, along with a few Mexican soldiers.

Arthur Hunnicutt in *The Last Command* (1955).
Illustration by Gary S. Zaboly

That same week, *The Kentuckian*, a United Artists film which was directed by its star, Burt Lancaster, debuted. Ironically, the motion picture was promoted with an original Thomas Hart Benton painting that was commissioned by Lancaster's production company. Benton, who a decade earlier rejected Disney's offer to create a cartoon operetta about Crockett, was seemingly more comfortable painting a single canvas. Another 1955 release, *Bad Day at Black Rock,* had a minor Crockett touch. Ernest Borgnine's Coley Trimble character confronts Spencer Tracy's John J. Macreedy with a threatening Crockett-like boast: "I'm half horse, half alligator."

In 1956, following in the staged 19th century footsteps of James Kirke Paulding's *Lion of the West* and Murdock and Mayo's *Davy Crockett; or, Be Sure You're Right, Then Go Ahead,* Wilbur Braun (under the pen name of Alice Chadwicke) wrote *Davy Crockett: A Robust Comedy Drama in Three Acts Based Upon the Life of America's Heroic Young Backwoods.* Ernest T. Thompson's booklet *The Fabulous Davy Crockett: His Life and Times in Gibson County, Tenn. Including Tall Tales and Anecdotes of the Western Wilds* added to the famous frontiersman's legacy. That same year, Top Pictures Corporation released the low-budget *Frontier Woman: Daughter of Davy Crockett,* starring Cindy Carson in the title role as Polly Crockett. The screenplay, which was filmed in something called Vistarama, involved a lover's triangle, Indian attacks, and a happy ending for Polly. The most interesting thing about the film was that an uncredited extra, a child named Ron Howard, went on to co-produce *The Alamo* in 2004, a Disney film, which featured Billy Bob Thornton as Davy Crockett.

On December 17, 1956, a Woody Woodpecker cartoon, *Woody Meets Davy Crewcut,* debuted in theaters. A commercial recording, "Woody Woodpecker Meets Davy Crockett," featuring the voice of Mel Blanc, was also released in 1956.

Cindy Carson in *Frontier Woman: Daughter of Davy Crockett* (1956).

Although the Crockett craze was winding down in the United States in 1956, it was just getting started in Europe. Disney's *Davy Crockett, King of the Wild Frontier* was released in Great Britain on November 9, 1955. The motion picture was released in Italy on February 7, 1956; Denmark on March 23; France, Belgium, the Netherlands, and Sweden in April; and West Germany and Finland in August. It was also released in Yugoslavia, Greece, the Soviet Union, and several other nations.

"The Ballad of Davy Crockett" was particularly popular in Great Britain, and became a best seller on the British music charts. As in the United States, Bill Hayes generated the biggest hit. His version of the song entered the British charts on July 1, 1956, at number thirteen. Two weeks later, he was at the number two position; however,

Hayes never reached number one. He stayed at the number two slot for three weeks, held back by Tennessee Ernie Ford's "Sixteen Tons." Hayes remained on the UK vinyl roster for a total of nine weeks. Coincidentally, the recording fell off the charts during the week of the Alamo battle's 120th anniversary. Other successful versions of the song were recorded by Tennessee Ernie Ford, who reached number three, and Dick James (with Stephen James and his Chums), who reached number fourteen. Max Bygraves was the fourth British artist to score a UK hit with "The Ballad of Davy Crockett." The popular vocalist, who had received acclaim as a teenage soloist in the 1930s, scored a top twenty hit with the Blackburn-Bruns tune on February 18, 1956, but the song fell off the vinyl roster the next week.

Dejvi Krocket (Davy Crockett, King of the Wild Frontier). Yugoslavia poster (1956).

In 1956, the famous Tennessean was depicted in a Billy Smart Circus production titled "The Wild West Show Presenting Davy Crockett," a popular British entertainment which recalled the excitement of Buffalo Bill's Wild West show. The performance consisted of seven "displays" under the big top that included such imaginative scenes as "Indians and Cowboys led by Davy Crockett," "The Roundup presented by Davy Crockett," "On the Trail," "The Cherokee Indians Attack and Capture the White, Pale-Face Girl," "Chief Sitting-Bull's Encampment," "Davy Crockett to the Rescue and the Death of Chief Sitting-Bull," and the "Grand Finale." The show, which was later titled "Billy Smart's Circus and Davy Crockett Western Spectacle," was action packed, and no one seemed to care that Sitting Bull died fifty-four years after Crockett's death.

More Crockett creations originated in Europe. Annie Cordy, the popular Belgian-born actress and vocalist, reached the top of the French record charts with the "Ballade de Davy Crockett." Her version of the song stayed at number one for five weeks during the summer of 1956. That same year, the Dutch performer Serge Singer recorded a *Davy Crockett* EP, which included "Ballade Van Davy Crockett," "Betsy," "Davy Crockett's Woord," and "Vaarwel." Singer also recorded a French version of the EP. In Denmark, Preben Uglebjerg recorded the tune, and in Norway, Karen Brunes, using the pseudonym Tom Hill, wrote the first of her sixteen Crockett books for young readers. Several other Western European nations printed Crockett comic books, too.

The Crockett Craze wasn't completely over in the United States. In 1956, the Topps company, which specialized in baseball cards, printed two eighty-count sets of Disney's *Davy Crockett, King of the Wild Frontier* collector cards, which were sold in one-cent and five-cent packs. The one-cent pack contained a card and a flat piece of bubble gum; the five-cent pack contained several cards and gum. The handsome display boxes included 120 one-cent packs and 24 five-cent packs. The first set, which had an orange-colored background on the card's reverse side, featured such lively titles as "Bear Meat For Dinner," "Tomahawk Terror," "Face To Face With Death," and "Fists Against Gun." The second set, which had a green-colored background on the card's reverse side, were enhanced with such imaginative captions as "Blazing Bullets," "Jaws Of Death," "Rough And Tumble," and "5,000 Against 200." The popular cards remain among the most highly sought after Crockett collectibles.

Disney wasn't finished with Davy yet. On July 18, 1956, *Davy Crockett and the River Pirates* debuted in theaters nationwide. The 35mm color film was edited from the two TV episodes, "Davy Crockett's Keelboat Race" and "Davy Crockett and the River Pirates." Like *Davy Crockett, King of the Wild Frontier,* the motion picture also opened in Europe. It debuted in Great Britain on August 24, 1956, and made its initial appearances in France and Sweden later in the year. Over the next few years, it was released in other European, South American, and Asian countries.

A generic set of sixteen non-Disney Davey (sic) Crockett Exhibit Supply cards were also released in 1956. The sepia toned cards depicted such illustrated scenes as "Young Davey Crockett Shooting a Bear," "Davey Crockett Buffalo Hunter," and "Davey Crockett at the Alamo Awaiting the Attack." Ed-U-Cards produced the 36-card "Davy Crockett Adventure Card Game," which featured such assorted scenes as "Fighting a Bear," "Indian Encounter," and "Alamo in Sight."

The Louis Marx company issued another playset in 1956: Walt Disney's Official Davy Crockett at the Alamo, which included a wonderful assortment of 54mm plastic "Texan Frontiersmen" and "Mexican Infantry" figures, a tin Alamo church and walls, artillery pieces, and assorted accessories. Like the previous Marx playsets, it included "The Story of Davy Crockett and the Alamo," a four-page insert that was both informative and interesting. "He was not a statesman or a politician, but had a glib tongue and was a renowned yarn teller," noted the publication. As for Crockett's fate at the Alamo, the Marx booklet provided no details except the following: "Not one of the defenders of the Alamo was left alive."

Chicago's Genco Manufacturing and Sales Company produced a Davy Crockett Moving Target Rifle Gallery which featured a real .22-caliber rifle that was "designed especially for boys and girls from 6 to 16." Speaking of weapons, the United States Department of Defense joined the Crockett bandwagon in 1956 when it manufactured the Davy Crockett Weapon System (sometimes erroneously called the "Davy Crockett Nuclear Bazooka"), a tactical recoilless surface-to-surface gun that fired a nuclear missile. The Cold War continued and a decade later, many of the kids who had played with plastic flintlock rifles were carrying M-16s in the jungles of Vietnam.

Also in 1956, James Griffith portrayed Crockett, a supporting role, in Allied Artists' *The First Texan*, a bio-pic about Sam Houston's (Joel McCrea) participation in the creation of the Lone Star Republic.

Although the Crockett Craze was finally over, the phenomenology of the coonskin cap-flavored zaniness would continue to be analyzed by sociologists, psychologists, and pop-culture investigators. Academic types suggested everything from the socio-economic impact of the Baby Boom generation, the influence of the Cold War, the effects of television, and other factors as to why so many kids got hooked on TV's "king of the wild frontier." The answer, though, was fundamental: It was a great story told by a great story teller, Walt Disney, and flavored with a catchy pop song and a memorable, larger-than-life performance by Fess Parker. For kids, it was fun playing Davy Crockett, and their imaginations transferred suburban backyards, rural fields, and urban streets across the nation into Creek warrior camps, bear-filled forests, and the Alamo. The same cerebral analysts would be at it again a decade later when Beatlemania struck.

The most important book ever written about Crockett, up to that time, was the June 1956 publication of James Atkins Shackford's *David Crockett: The Man and the Legend*, a thorough examination of the historical Tennessean's life. The book was the first comprehensive attempt to segregate the real man from the legendary character of popular culture. Shackford, though, had suffered from a "progressive muscular atrophy" since the early 1950s, and his brother, John B. Shackford, helped organize the finished manuscript. "David Crockett symbolizes the essential man, that vital 'common stock,' that has played a most important part in this new land in the shaping of that philosophy of the new spiritual frontier," wrote James Shackford, who offered the best assessment of Crockett's death at the Alamo. "Too much has been made over the details of *how* David died at the Alamo," he wrote. "Such details are not important. What is important is that he died as he lived. His life was one of indomitable bravery, his death was a death of intrepid courage. His life was one of wholehearted dedication to his own concepts of liberty. He died staking his life against what he regarded as intolerable tyranny."

For young readers, William O. Steele wrote *Davy Crockett's Earthquake*, which described the frontiersman's various encounters with bears, and Stanley J. Folmsbee authored *The Early Career of David Crockett* in 1956, *David Crockett: Congressman* in 1957, and *David Crockett in Texas* in 1958.

On April 21, 1958, the Crockett Tavern Museum opened in Morristown, Tennessee. Groundbreaking for the recreated structure had taken place on August 17, 1955, after proceeds from Morristown's Centennial celebration in 1955 had been raised by the local Association for the Preservation of Tennessee Antiquities chapter in order to build a memorial to the Crockett family. The replica structure features a downstairs area that is filled with period tools, spinning wheels, quilts, manuscripts, and assorted collectibles. The main room depicts what the original Crockett home may have looked like.[20]

In the special 1958 Classics Illustrated issue (no. 144A), *Blazing Trails West,* Crockett appears armed with a rifle and a fiddle in the "Texas and the Alamo" story.

Walt Disney kept the legacy of his *Davy Crockett* production alive on September 12, 1958, when "Davy Crockett, Indian Fighter" was broadcast on ABC-TV's *Walt Disney Presents* (formerly *Disneyland*). "Davy Crockett Goes to Congress" and "Davy Crockett at the Alamo" aired over the next two weeks.

In 1959, David Crockett State Park in Lawrenceburg, Tennessee opened, and Fess Parker, costumed as Crockett, made an uncredited cameo appearance in the Bob Hope comedy *Alias Jesse James,* a United Artists production, which debuted on March 20, 1959. That same year, John Wayne directed *The Alamo,* a big screen epic in which he played Crockett. Several weeks before *The Alamo* premiered at San Antonio's Woodlawn Theatre on October 24, 1960, "Davy Crockett's Keelboat Race" and "Davy Crockett and the

River Pirates" were rebroadcast on ABC-TV's *Walt Disney Presents*. The airings were a reminder of sorts that Fess Parker was still *Davy Crockett, King of the Wild Frontier*.

The Crockett Tavern Museum. *Alamo Journal* illustration by Gary S. Zaboly.

In *The Alamo,* Wayne's Crockett was bold, confident, and appreciative of liberty, loyalty, and patriotism; in fact, the actor was essentially portraying himself on the big screen. "Republic, I like the sound of the word," says Wayne's character to Laurence Harvey's William Barret Travis. "Means people can live free, talk free, go or come, buy or sell, be drunk or sober, however they choose." Like Arthur Hunnicutt's Crockett in *The Last Command,* Wayne goes out with a bang when he torches the Alamo's entire gunpowder supply, an event which never happened in 1836. The film received seven Academy Award nominations, and won for Best Sound, but it wasn't initially successful at the box office. It would take over a quarter of a century for another Crockett to appear in a major role on television or in the movies.

Also in 1960, Virgil Baugh wrote *Rendezvous at the Alamo: Highlights in the Lives of Bowie, Crockett & Travis.* The author's pages on Crockett were primarily based on the 1834 *Narrative,* which Baugh had read as a young man. In 1961, Anne Ford's children's book, *Davy Crockett: A See and Read Biography* was published, and Edward S. Ellis' 1884 book, *The Life of Colonel David Crockett,* was reissued as *Sockdolager! A Tale of Davy Crockett in which the Old Tennessee Bear Hunter Meets up with the Constitution of the United States.* Walter Lord, author of *A Night to Remember* and *Day of Infamy,* included a "Did David Crockett Surrender?" section in his *A Time to Stand,* a splendid work about the Battle of the Alamo. Lord suggested that there was "a good chance that Crockett lived up to his legend." In 1962, British author Jeff Jeffries wrote *Remember the Alamo! The Story of Davy Crockett.*

The three original *Davy Crockett* episodes were broadcast in September 1963, on NBC-TV's *Walt Disney's Wonderful World of Color* (formerly *Walt Disney Presents*), and the next year "Davy Crockett's Keelboat Race" and "Davy Crockett and the River Pirates" were aired.

John Wayne in *The Alamo* (1960). Image created by Charles Martin Brazil.

Also in 1963, Gold Key published *Walt Disney's Davy Crockett: King of the Wild Frontier*, a twelve-cent comic book, which reissued the contents of the 1955 Dell *Davy Crockett at the Alamo* comic. The color cover, which featured a green background behind its title, utilized the same cover as Dell's *Davy Crockett: Indian Fighter* comic from 1955. Its inside cover proclaimed: "This is a story about one of those valiants whose fame shone brightly on the horizons of our early frontiers." In 1969, Gold Key printed another *Walt Disney's Davy Crockett: King of the Wild Frontier* title, which sold for fifteen cents. The issue featured a red background behind its title, and included the partial contents of the Dell Giant *Davy Crockett, King of the Wild Frontier* comic. Like its similarly titled 1963 version, it featured the cover of *Davy Crockett: Indian Fighter*. During the 1960s, Crockett comic books were published in a number of nations, including Australia, Yugoslavia, Great Britain, and Norway.

In 1967, after reaching the top of the *Billboard's* Hot 100 chart ten times, the Supremes recorded "The Ballad of Davy Crockett," but the Motown recording, in which Mary Wilson sang lead, wasn't released until it was included on the *Never Before Released Masters* LP twenty years later. The song was primarily the Blackburn-Bruns composition but some extra lyrics were included, for example, "At night he walked to the woods alone/Winding his beard/Way back home/A hero's curse, a man alone." Wilson enjoyed the recording. "It was fun to do, and I got a chance to sing lead," said Wilson during a 2018 interview. "I think we recorded that when we did our country and western album." However, the song was not included on *The Supremes Sing Country, Western and Pop*, which was released in 1965. The group's version may have been recorded in 1967 for the unreleased *Diana Ross & The Supremes Sing Disney Classics* album that was scheduled for release the next year.

Like the USS *Crockett* (APA-148), the attack transport which served in World War II, the "king of the wild frontier" went to sea again during the Vietnam War as the gunboat USS *Crockett* (PG-88). The ship was launched on June 4, 1966, and commissioned on June 24, 1967. The next year, Fess Parker made the first of several visits to Vietnam where he met young soldiers who grew up watching him as Disney's *Davy Crockett*. He surprised the wounded at Long Binh hospital when he entered the facility. "Wow, it's Davy Crockett," said Jerome "Jerry" Greenwood, who received three Purple Hearts. "I had only been in Vietnam for a few months, and seeing Fess Parker brought back memories of home. I think his visit was really an up day for everyone."[21]

On August 17, 1967, the 131st anniversary of Crockett's birth, the United States Post Office issued a first-class five cent Davy Crockett stamp. Created by Robert Bode, a New York-based artist, Crockett, wearing buckskins and a coonskin cap, is shown partly in shadow, carrying his rifle, in front of a tree line. The Post Office made an initial printing run of 120 million stamps. Numerous mailing envelopes depicting Crockett were also sold at the time.

On August 15, 1965, a memorial was erected at the David Crockett Birthplace State Park. The monument reads, in a vertical arrangement:

Davy Crockett

Pioneer

Patriot

Soldier

Trapper

Explorer

State Legislator

Congressman

Martyred at the Alamo

1786-1836

One side of the monument reads: "Monument replaced at Davy Crockett celebration August 15, 1965. By the Limestone Ruritan Club." Another side reads: "Original monument placed by Davy Crockett Historical Society Aug. 15, 1890." The structure is partially encircled by stonewall sections which designate the fifty states.

During the decade's final summer, Disney's three original *Davy Crockett* episodes aired once again on Walt Disney's *Wonderful World of Color*. At that time, Fess Parker, wearing another coonskin cap, was entering his sixth and final season as *Daniel Boone* on NBC-TV.

Crockett's life and legend received a thorough academic study in December 1969, when Joseph John Arpad delivered his doctoral dissertation, *David Crockett, An Original Eccentricity and Early American Character*. Three years later, Arpad edited *A Narrative of the Life of David Crockett of the State of Tennessee*, currently available as one of the titles in Rowman and Littlefield's Masterworks of Literature Series.

On March 16, 1971, Crockett became part of a *Beverly Hillbillies* episode titled "The Clampetts Meet Robert Audubon Getty Crockett." The episode was described in newspapers as "Bremerkamp [Mike Minor] makes Granny [Irene Ryan] believe he's related to Davy Crockett and tries to elope with Elly [Donna Douglas]." The episode's obvious Crockett connection was Buddy Ebsen, who starred as Jed Clampett on *The Beverly Hillbillies,* played George Russel in the five Disney *Davy Crockett* episodes from 1954-1955. The next week, the final episode of *The Beverly Hillbilies* aired.

On May 19, 1971, Davy Crockett's Explorer Canoes (known since July 4, 1956 as the Indian War Canoes) debuted at Disneyland. Each 35-foot-long canoe was guided by a Disneyland cast member, who was dressed in faux buckskins and a coonskin cap; paddle-wielding guests provided the power. The theme park's Crockett-canoe connection originated in Crockett's autobiography, which included several stories about canoes. Also, the opening scene from Walt Disney's "Davy Crockett at the Alamo" features Crockett and his sidekick, George Russel, paddling a canoe towards a riverboat.

Fred Gwynne in *You Are There* episode (1971).

In October, Fred Gwynne portrayed the famous backwoodsman in "Defense of the Alamo," a color episode on CBS-TV's *You Are*

There. Narrator Walter Cronkite exaggerated the casualties when he said that "Santa Anna lost almost eight thousand men," a figure nearly twice the size of the Mexican commander's entire Army of Operations.

On October 1, 1971, Walt Disney World opened in Lake Buena Vista, Florida, and the Magic Kingdom's Frontierland section included a number of Davy Crockett-related attractions. The Country Bear Jamboree featured a rollicking musical finale that included portions of "The Ballad of Davy Crockett," sung by Henry the bear and Sammy the raccoon, two audio-animatronic figures. Aboard the Mike Fink Keel Boats, a cast member operator told a lively story about Fink and Crockett. "Well, that cheater Davy Crockett, tried every trick in the book to beat me, and he even got to the dock before I did," noted the attraction's script. "But even he knew that that shortcut through the bayou made me the winner. You can't have a river race unless you stay on the river, ain't that right?" Frontierland also had the Davy Crockett Explorer Canoes, and the park also offered imitation coonskin caps, toy flintlock rifles, and rubber hunting knives for sale. "Davy Crockett's Keelboat Race" and "Davy Crockett and the River Pirates" were rebroadcast on NBC's *The Wonderful World of Disney* (formerly *Walt Disney's Wonderful World of Color*) in September 1972. Also that year, Wyatt Blassingame wrote the children's book *How Davy Crockett Got a Bearskin Coat*. On December 9, Vincent Van Patten voiced the Possessed Davy Crockett Mannequin character in "The Phantom of the Country Music Hall," an episode of the CBS-TV series *The Animated Scooby-Doo Movies*. The next year, the Davy Crockett Birthplace Association transferred its ownership of the land where Crockett was born to the David Crockett Birthplace State Park.

In the wake of the Vietnam War and Watergate, a revisionist sentiment began its pervasive expansion in academic and journalist circles. This post-modern orthodoxy dissected and reassessed American institutions and heroes in order to fulfill certain socio-political expectations. To be sure, Crockett came under scrutiny. His experience with poverty, his support for Tennessee squatters' land rights, and his noble stand against Jackson's Indian Removal legislation, made him exempt from severe revisionist criticism. And rightly so. But the unanswered question surrounding the manner of his death at the Alamo provided an opening for new wave iconoclasts, the publish-or-perish crowd, and others to try and tarnish "king of the wild frontier's" crown.

A few innocuous titles were published in the mid-1970s, such as a pair of young readers books: Matthew G. Grant's *Davy Crockett, Frontier Adventurer* and Barbara Hazan's *Davy Crockett: Indian Fighter,* which was based on Tom Blackburn's script for *Disneyland's* "Davy Crockett, Indian Fighter" episode. In 1974, New York's Arno Press reprinted *Sketches and Eccentricities of Col. David Crockett of West Tennessee,* and a year later Crockett's illustrated image was featured on the four of hearts card in U.S. Game Systems' "The American Historical Playing Card Deck." The entire hearts suit was titled the "Frontier Suit," and it included Daniel Boone, Kit Carson, and Sam Houston, among others.

In 1975, all hell broke loose when Texas A&M University Press published Carmen Perry's edited translation, *With Santa Anna in Texas: A Personal Narrative of the Revolution by José Enrique de la Peña,* which suggested that Crockett survived the final battle and was summarily executed. Some modern-day Crockett defenders were appalled that anyone would dare suggest that the Alamo hero died any other way except fighting. But the debate over how Crockett died was just heating up. On March 4, 1977, Dan Kilgore addressed the Texas State Historical Association and acknowledged the Mexican soldier's claim of Crockett's death. The next year, Kilgore's controversial book *How Did Davy Die?*, an amended version of his talk, reached a wider audience and generated criticism from those who believed Crockett fought to the death. Dean Lipton, writing "In Defense of Davy" in the May 14, 1978 issue of the *San Francisco Chronicle,* said that in "the old sport of debunking...Kilgore manages to out-debunk all previous debunkers." Among the imaginative newspaper headlines were "Did Davy Crockett Have Feet of Clay?" "Davy Crockett No Hero, Texas Historian Says," "Crockett Legend Assailed," "Author Disputes Legend," "Diaries Dim Crockett Luster," and the poorest written one, "Davey Crockett Didn't Die Hero?" The acrimonious debate about the Alamo defender's death would continue.

Earlier, NBC-TV's *The Wonderful World of Disney* rebroadcast "Davy Crockett's Keelboat Race" on September 12, 1976, and "Davy Crockett and the River Pirates" on September 19, 1976. On November 20, 1976, *Davy Crockett on the Mississippi,* an animated program produced by the successful William Hanna and Joseph Barbera partnership, aired on CBS-TV. The production told the story of Crockett (voiced by Ned Wilson); "Honeysuckle," his pet bear; Mike Fink; Matt Henry, an orphan; and some other historical and fictional characters. It was amusing and fun. In 1979, Naunerle C. Farr authored the children's dual biography, *Davy Crockett/Daniel Boone,* and the Hallmark company issued several seven-inch, historical dolls made of cloth, including one of Davy Crockett.

The 1980s marked a renaissance of sorts for all-things-Crockett. In 1981, HBO broadcast Disney's three original *Davy Crockett* episodes, and Frank A. Driskill wrote *Davy Crockett: The Untold*

Story, a book for young readers. Driskill provided one of the most vivid and dramatic descriptions of Crockett's death at the Alamo. "The last to go was Davy Crockett," wrote the author. "He had no powder left and used Betsy as a club. He stood there, one arm useless. He had a deep gash in his cheek where he had been cut by a saber. At his feet were the bodies of many Mexicans who had failed in an attempt to reach him in hand-to-hand combat. His Bowie knife, a gift from Jim Bowie, had served him well."

Anticipating the upcoming 100th anniversary of Crockett's birth, the Direct Descendants of David Crockett (later called the Direct Descendants and Kin of David Crockett) was formed in Tennessee in 1981, and a few years later the group held its first organization meeting in Greeneville, Tennessee. The descendants' purpose is to "preserve the heritage of the legendary David Crockett," and they share their research and Crockett-related news in *Go Ahead*, a periodic newsletter. The organization holds bi-annual reunions in Tennessee and Texas. At each gathering, special T-shirts, which usually feature Crockett's famous motto or his defiant "You may all go to hell and I will go to Texas" statement, are offered for sale.

The August 19, 1982 issue of *Disneyland Line,* a weekly publication of Disneyland's Cast Communications, featured a cover story, "Folk Hero and Fad: The Legend of Davy Crockett," which included eight black and white photos of Disney, Fess Parker, and Crockett-adoring youngsters. The issue sparked an interest among Disney Studios executives about a possibility of creating a new series about the "king of the wild frontier." It took a while, but that idea finally manifested itself as a new production series six years later.

Paul McCartney sang the lyrical line "at the time of Davy Crockett" from "Ballroom Dancing," a track on his 1982 album

Tug of War. The next year, an illustration of Crockett appeared on the cover of Dr. James A. Hanson's *The Long Hunter's Sketchbook,* which included instructions on how to make a real coonskin cap.

Greenwood Press published Richard Boyd Hauck's *Crockett: A Bio-Bibliography* in 1982, a careful examination of the man and the myth. The next year, Lee Bishop's steamy romantic paperback *Davy Crockett: Frontier Fighter* and Laurence Santrey's children's book, *Davy Crockett: Young Pioneer* were published. Santry's book mentions Crockett's adult life in one paragraph on the last page, and states that he was killed on March 5, 1836.

In 1984, Leo Lenvers' *Davy Crockett: Le Coureur Des Bois,* a French publication, entered the market. That same year, the Davy Crockett Long Hunters, a David Crockett State Park-based group of historical interpreters, was formed. According to the organization, its members are "dedicated to the preservation and advancement of the lifestyle, ideals, patriotism and freedoms of the American pioneer." The members of the private, non-profit organization participate in living history demonstrations and black powder shoots, promote muzzle loading gun safety, and celebrate the frontier legacy of Crockett at such events as the annual "Crockett Days" each August.

In 1985, Fess Parker's recording of "The Ballad of Davy Crockett" played on a jukebox during a scene in *Back to the Future,* and Caron Lee Cohen wrote the children's book, *Sally Ann Thunder Ann Whirlwind Crockett,* a fictional tall tale about Crockett's wife who behaved more like her husband of the 19th century almanacs.

Also in 1985, Michael A. Lofaro's *Davy Crockett: The Man, The Legend, The Legacy, 1786-1986,* was published. LoFaro's volume provided an entertaining and informative exploration of the many facets of the Crockett story, which included Richard Boyd Hauck's

"Making It All Up: Davy Crockett in the Theater" and Margaret J. King's "The Recycled Hero: Walt Disney's Davy Crockett," among other essays. Also reaching the public in 1985 were James Wakefield Burke's *David Crockett, The Man Behind the Myth* and Connecticut's Academic Industries' abbreviated biography, *Davy Crockett*. In the world of popular music, British rocker Paul Young kicked off his "The '9' Go Mad With Davy Crockett World Tour" in 1985, but fans of the "king of the wild frontier" were disappointed when the performer sang songs like "Every Time You Go Away" and "Come Back and Stay" instead of "The Ballad of Davy Crockett."

The bicentennial of Crockett's birth and the sesquicentennial of his death at the Alamo in 1986, were marked with commemorations, especially at events which were held in Tennessee, Texas, and Washington D.C. The Volunteer state appropriately acknowledged Crockett with celebratory activities at the David Crockett Birthplace State Park in Limestone, the David Crockett State Park in Lawrenceburg, and the Crockett Tavern Museum in Morristown. A newly-constructed log cabin, depicting the place of Crockett's birth, was erected at David Crockett Birthplace State Park.

The Witte Museum in San Antonio showcased an extensive display of Crockett memorabilia; displayed Eric Von Schmidt's massive painting, *The Storming of the Alamo,* which features Crockett; showed a 16mm color print of *Davy Crockett, King of the Wild Frontier;* and hosted a group of historical interpreters who portrayed Crockett and his fellow Alamo defenders.

Numerous stories about Crockett's 200th birthday were printed in newspapers and magazines, including a cover story in *Texas Monthly* titled "Davy Crockett: Hero or Hype?" The cover featured a skeptical question which was critical of both the Crockett of history and the Crockett of popular culture: "Should we all believe in a man who wasn't born on a mountaintop, hardly ever wore a coonskin cap, and surrendered at the Alamo?" Yet the article, written by Paul Andrew Hutton, a professor of history at the University of New Mexico, was titled "Davy Crockett, Still King of the Wild Frontier, and a Hell of Nice Guy Besides." The author, however, went beyond de la Peña's description of Crockett's capture at the Alamo, and stated: "It's true—he surrendered at the Alamo." Hutton, though, focused more on Crockett's "independence and honesty" rather than the debatable details of his death.

Other voices in 1986, like *USA Today* ("Coonskin Cap a Myth, Experts Say"), the Tennessee Municipal League's *Tennessee Town & City* ("David Crockett Not the Idol You Think, Debunkers Say"), the *Wall Street Journal* ("Davy Crockett Was No Great Shakes, The Debunkers Say") jumped on the anti-heroes bandwagon, but despite the critics' efforts to defrock the famous Tennessean's legacy, Crockett's legend survived and continued to "Go Ahead!"

The most impressive bicentennial event was the Smithsonian Institution's "Davy Crockett: Gentleman From The Cane—An Exhibit Commemorating Crockett's Life and Legend on the 200th Anniversary of his Birth." On display were such items as Crockett's marriage bond with Polly, his first rifle, images and portraits, "Pretty Betsey," Crockett almanacs, and assorted ephemera. Surprisingly, in the exhibit's catalog, co-author James C. Kelly, called Crockett "an authentic, if minor, American hero." The exhibit was later displayed in the Tennessee State Museum in Nashville. Several Crockett pop culture items were displayed at The Walt Disney Story attraction in Walt Disney World's Magic Kingdom, including the 1956 Emmy Award for the *Davy Crockett* trilogy and a coonskin cap that Fess

Parker wore in "Davy Crockett's Keelboat Race."

Another 1986 publication, Gary L. Foreman's *Crockett: The Gentleman from the Cane: A Comprehensive View of the Folkhero Americans Thought They Knew* traced Crockett's life and legend with scores of assorted images and vivid photos, many taken by the author. "He was an intelligent, witty man who possessed an unusual amount of physical strength, humor, and above all, independence," wrote Foreman, who later assisted the Direct Descendants and Kin of David Crockett with their bi-annual gatherings in Tennessee and Texas. Under the editorship of Jim Dumas, the organization published its first newsletter, *Go Ahead,* in June 1986.

Another Crockett bicentennial publication was Felicity Trotman and Shirley Greenway's *Davy Crockett,* a poetic-like book for young readers, which stated: "Davy was killed where he stood, one of the last defenders of the Alamo." The Tennessee Historical Commission published Herbert L. Harper's *Houston and Crockett: Heroes of Tennessee and Texas.*

On August 18, 1986, the Crockett Tavern opened at Fort Wilderness in Walt Disney World. The facility offered such items as "Davy's Lemonade" (according to the original menu, the original concoction was made of "Jack Daniels, triple sec, sour, and a touch of lime") and a "Crockett's BBQ Sandwich." The bar and dining area were eventually decorated with a few images of Crockett; a miniature wooden replica of the *Gullywhumper,* Mike Fink's keel boat; a taxidermied bear; and some anachronistic mountain man prints.

Crockett was back on the small screen in 1986, in *Houston: The Legend of Texas,* but viewers didn't see much of him until his corpse (portrayed by an uncredited Guy Arnold) was briefly shown in a post-Battle of the Alamo scene. In 1987, Brian Keith played a more prominently featured Crockett in the NBC-TV production *The Alamo: 13 Days to Glory*. His on-screen demise is one of the more awkward Crockett death scenes since he seems to pull a Mexican soldier's bayonet into his own chest. At the time of filming, Keith, at age sixty-five, became the oldest actor to portray Crockett until the next year when Merrill Connally appeared as the memorable backwoods hero in the IMAX film *Alamo...The Price of Freedom*. Connally, the brother of former Texas Governor John Connally, was sixty-six years old during filming, and had one of his two stunt doubles, David Kanawah, perform Crockett's death scene. Near the film's conclusion, Crockett battles oncoming *soldados* in front of the Alamo church, and then a Mexican officer strikes him in the head with a sword guard. Crockett falls and several *soldados* finish him off with their bayonets. *Alamo...The Price of Freedom* has been shown daily at the IMAX Rivercenter Theatre in San Antonio every day since its debut.

Tom Townsend's 1987 book for young readers, *Davy Crockett: An American Hero,* stated that Crockett survived the Battle of the Alamo and attempted to slay Gen. Santa Anna with a Bowie Knife, but was stopped when "a dozen muskets fired" at him. That same year, Robert Quackenbush wrote the children's book, *Quit Pulling My Leg: A Story of Davy Crockett,* and Harry Borden Roberts, a veteran teacher and Greene County, Tennessee historian, published *Davy Crockett—Explained and Defined,* which stated the following about his final moments: "He had been through too many personal experiences to recoil for the specter of death." Michael Lofaro provided an informative introduction to *The Tall Tales of Davy Crockett; The Second Nashville Series of Crockett Almanacs, 1839-1841,* which was published by the University of Tennessee Press in 1987.

In 1987, Fess Parker, star of Walt Disney's *Davy Crockett, King of the Wild Frontier*, was voted the "Best Crockett" in a poll of The Alamo Society's members. The results were published in the June 1987 issue of *The Alamo Journal*, the official publication of the organization. Parker narrowly edged out John Wayne (*The Alamo*) 37% to 34%. Arthur Hunnicutt (*The Last Command*) placed third with 24%. Parker was also interviewed by *The Alamo Journal*, and over the next several years he participated in a number of interviews in the quarterly.

In 1987, during a twelve-day visit to Canada, Great Britain's Duchess of York, affectionately known as Fergie, was photographed wearing a coonskin headband and tail, which prompted one British tabloid to proclaim: "Fergie Crockett: Queen of the Wild Frontier."

On September 20, 1987, singer-song writer Mac Davis became the newest TV Crockett when he starred in "Davy Crockett," an episode of the Showtime cable series *Shelly Duvall's Tall Tales & Legends*. According to a Showtime press release, a seventh grader uses a "special" book about Crockett to travel back in time where he meets the famous frontier hero. "The legend of Davy Crockett represents the backwoods spirit of the American frontier," stated the release. "A self-made man, Davy Crockett died a hero's death fighting for Texas' independence in 1836." Critics enjoyed the program, especially Davis' confident performance. "As Crockett, Davis has a part that suits him perfectly," wrote Daniel Ruth, the cable television critic of the *Chicago Sun-Times* on September 21, 1987.

The Disney Studios took advantage of the Alamo-Crockett anniversaries by issuing *Davy Crockett, King of the Wild Frontier* on videocassette. More importantly, Disney produced a new Davy Crockett series for NBC television. Starring Tim Dunigan in the title role, "Davy Crockett: Rainbow in the Thunder" debuted on November 20, 1988, with Johnny Cash appearing as an elder Crockett who reflects on his past. The subsequent episodes were "Davy Crockett: A Natural Man" (December 18, 1988), "Davy Crockett: Guardian Spirit" (January 13, 1989), "Davy Crockett: A Letter to Polly" (June 11, 1989), and "Davy Crockett: Warrior's Farewell" (June 18, 1989). As a promotional tie-in, a Disney cast member portrayed Crockett on his own float during the daily afternoon parade at Walt Disney's World's Magic Kingdom in 1989.

Dunigan was likable enough, and he even had a Buddy Ebsen-like loyal sidekick in Gary Grubbs' George Russell (as opposed to Ebsen's George Russel), but the charismatic ghost of Fess Parker's larger-than-life characterization and the production's inappropriate British Columbia, Canada filming locations contributed to the program's lack of success. Unfortunately, ratings were poor. "Davy Crockett: Rainbow in the Thunder" ranked forty-seven out of sixty-five prime time programs for the week, and "Davy Crockett: Guardian Spirit," ranked sixty-two out of eighty other small screen productions. The other episodes also did not do well in the ratings.

At the same time the new Crockett series aired, Fess Parker got into the wine making business. After purchasing land in Los Olivos, California, he consulted with wine experts and eventually planted 5½ acres of Johannisberg Riesling in 1989. Other plantings followed, but all the wines shared the same image on their respective labels and corks: a tiny coonskin cap.

For several years, the Crockett Tavern at Walt Disney World's Fort Wilderness Campground provided two different plastic mixed drink stirrers: one featured a coonskin cap and the other featured an Indian headdress similar to the one worn by Pat Hogan's Red

Stick character in "Davy Crockett, Indian Fighter." The tavern also distributed cocktail napkins that depicted Crockett holding Old Betsy, but once the inventory was exhausted, the three items were never reordered. Today, the items are among the rarest later-day Crockett collectibles.

The Alamo Society polled its members again about their favorite Alamo films and actors, and the results were published in the August 1989 issue of *The Alamo Journal*. Fess Parker (*Davy Crockett, King of the Wild Frontier*) was name the "Best Crockett," according to 44% of the membership. John Wayne (*The Alamo*) was supported by 31% of the membership; Arthur Hunnicutt (*The Last Command*) 25%; Merrill Connally (*Alamo... The Price of Freedom*) 7%.[22]

The decade's most informative book was *Crockett at Two Hundred: New Perspectives on the Man and the Myth,* which was edited by Michael A. Lofaro and Joe Cummings. The book contained an excellent assortment of essays, including "Why Davy Didn't Die" by Dan Kilgore, "Davy Crockett and the Tradition of the Westerner in American Cinema" by William Eric Jamborsky, and "Cats, Coons, Crocketts and other Furry Critters—or, Why Davy Wears an Animal for a Hat" by John Seelye, among others.

In 1989, Billy Joel mentioned the *Davy Crockett* of Walt Disney mini-series fame in "We Didn't Start the Fire," the singer-songwriter's ode to post-World War II American history. In the Chris Blum-directed video of the song, a small boy wears a cowboy outfit, a Richard Nixon mask, and a coonskin cap. The next year Crockett was acknowledged in the TV special *Texas and Tennessee: A Music Affair,* a production based on a previous 1982 incarnation. On December 22, 1990, the Hanna-Barbera animated TV series *Bill & Ted's Excellent Adventures* featured an episode titled "A Grim Story of an Overdue Book," in which the title characters meet Crockett and other historical figures.

Director-producer-writer David Zucker, a collector of original Crockett letters and pop culture memorabilia, hosted the first of several Davy Crockett Rifle Frolics at his Ojai, California home in 1989. Fess Parker was the special guest at his 1991 event, which featured live flintlock shooting contests and tomahawk-throwing demonstrations. Parker was two-for-two at the shooting range, which generated enthusiastic cheers from those in attendance, most of whom had seen the original Disney *Davy Crockett* episodes as children. Zucker hosted additional frolics in 1992, 1994, and 1999.

In the 1990s, Zucker planned to create a feature film based upon Crockett's life. "I still think that Crockett's life was—and is—a great story, because he was a great character," said Zucker, who worked with Paul Andrew Hutton and Robert LoCash on the scripts. "But his story is that of an American tragedy because he never got to achieve his goals. He never got his Tennessee land reform bill passed; he failed to stop Andrew Jackson's Indian Removal bill from passing; he tried to make money but failed; as a matter of fact, he was just about broke most of the time. He had success in promoting his own legend but it never generated any kind of materialistic or financial success for him or his family. He was always on his way to something but he never accomplished it. Still, he was basically a decent guy who wanted fairness for the settlers and the Indians."

Casting the film was crucial. "Early on, I extended invitations to most of the A-list actors at the time—Mel Gibson, Tom Hanks, Kevin Costner, Tom Cruise, Tim Robbins—to see what their interest would be in playing the role of Davy Crockett," said Zucker. "When I met Mel Gibson, he asked if he would have to wear a coonskin cap. It appeared that he didn't want to wear one. I said he would have to but only in certain winter scenes. Nobody wore a coonskin cap in the summer, I assured him; it wasn't practical. I said most of the hats he would wear would be the regular headgear that gentleman wore, what the politicians wore at the time. And, I pointed out that he would never wear a hat in the indoor scenes. Gibson felt a bit more comfortable after I explained the hat situation." Zucker's good friend, Robert Weil, an artist who ran a photography lab, created several images of Gibson in 1830s clothing and sporting a period hair style. The finished photos looked impressive. "But Gibson eventually declined," said Zucker.

Zucker recalled his discussion with Tom Hanks, who had just completed the highly regarded *Philadelphia* in 1993. "Tom Hanks loved the script," he said. "He told me he was surprised at how much he liked it. But he was reluctant to take on the role of Crockett because he wasn't sure how audiences would approve of his next release about another Southern character: *Forrest Gump*." Hanks passed.

Zucker continued the search but met Kevin Costner by chance. "Kevin Costner and I had a brief chat over lunch after I met him in the parking lot of Sony studios," said Zucker. "We didn't go much into detail about the Crockett script but he didn't rule it out completely." But Costner had another period piece on his schedule: *Wyatt Earp*, not Davy Crockett.

Tom Cruise, who had starred in *A Few Good Men* in 1992, and *The Firm* a year later, was also on Zucker's list. "I contacted Tom Cruise through his agent," said Zucker. "Tom and I had been on the same week-long journey along the Amazon River earlier in the nineties, so we knew each other. His agent seemed open to the Crockett story and I sent him a copy of the script. I don't know whether Tom actually read it or not but I eventually heard about a month later, through his agent, that his answer was 'no.'" The next year, Cruise filmed *Interview With the Vampire: The Vampire Chronicles*. For the actor, it was fangs instead of flintlocks.

Zucker moved on. "I met with Tim Robbins at his place in New York," said the director, "but things didn't work out." However, after numerous script revisions the project never reached the pre-production phase.[23] Despite a few silent films with Crockett's name in the title and Disney's *Davy Crockett, King of the Wild Frontier,* Zucker's film would have been the first major bio-pic about the famous frontier hero. In the years that followed, Zucker considered rewriting his Crockett project as a TV miniseries, since it would allow him to develop a more comprehensive story about his central character. Unfortunately, no progress was ever made on the small screen production.

More books were written about Crockett in the 1990s than any other decade, except the 1950s. In 1990, author Jeff Long set an iconoclastic standard in *Duel of Eagles: The Mexican and U. S. Fight for the Alamo* when he described Crockett's last moments at the Alamo: "David Crockett made a choice. The Go Ahead man quit. He did more than quit. He lied. He denied his role in the fighting."

In 1991, Elizabeth R. Moseley wrote the children's book, *Davy Crockett: Hero of the Wild Frontier*, and Eliot Dooley's hard-bound comic book, *Davy Crockett,* stated that the Alamo hero died after being "hit savagely on the back of the head." That same year, Margery Evernden's children's play, *Davy Crockett and His Coonskin Cap,* was performed in a limited run at the Casa Manana Playhouse in Fort Worth, Texas.

On a more innocuous note, the Kentucky Headhunters, a country rock quintet, released a hard hitting version of "The Ballad of Davy Crockett" in 1991. "We needed to come out with 'Davy Crockett,' make it fast, make it rock," explained Fred Young, the band's drummer, in a 1991 *Alamo Journal* interview. The group's accompanying video was a zany slapstick adventure which featured a determined bear and an enthusiastic coonskin cap-wearing audience. The tune, which was on the band's *Electric Barnyard* LP, peaked at number forty-seven on *Billboard's* Country singles chart.

A year later, actor Nicholas Cage narrated the children's audio cassette *Davy Crockett,* a Rabbit Ears Entertainment production, featuring the music of David Bromberg. "Young folks out to know their history, and how a person gets to be a legend," says Cage's tall tale-talking Crockett. "So these here are the naked, green skin facts of my life—and a lot of it is the truth, too." It was a fun filled effort, and Cage's wonderful portrayal was as good as anyone who ever attempted to recreate the legendary frontier hero.

With a band playing "The Ballad of Davy Crockett," Fess Parker received a Disney Legend award during ceremonies held at the Walt Disney Studios in Burbank, California on October 22, 1991. Disney CEO Michael Eisner hosted the event, and Roy E. Disney made the presentation. Parker was escorted during the event by Goofy, who wore faux buckskins and a coonskin cap.

If any proof was needed to confirm that Crockett's legacy was part of American culture in the late 20th century, all one had to do was view "Treehouse of Terror II," an episode on TV's *The Simpsons*, which aired on January 31, 1991. The half-hour program told the story of nuclear power plant entrepreneur C. Montgomery Burns and his creation of a Homer Simpson-like robot. Burns celebrates by dancing around with Homer Simpson's brain on his head and shouting, "Look at me, I'm Davy Crockett!" On April 23, 1992, another Crockett reference appeared on *The Simpsons* in "The Otto Show," an episode in which Selma Bouvier, Bart Simpson's aunt, sees Homer Simpson wearing an old fringed jacket at a rock concert. "There goes Davy Crockett and his baldskin cap!" remarks Bouvier. Furthermore, Simpson's hometown of Springfield was founded by Jebediah Springfield, a Crockett-like pioneer who wore buckskins and a fur cap. It may have taken over 150 years, but the Crockett almanacs were finally topped for ridiculous absurdity.

On June 28, 1991, *The Naked Gun 2½: The Smell of Fear* opened in theaters nationwide, and director David Zucker, costumed as Davy Crockett, made a cameo appearance in the Paramount Pictures production.

During the decade's early years, Disney Press released six new Crockett books for young readers: *Davy Crockett and the King of the River* (written by A. L. Singer), *Davy Crockett and the Creek Indians* (Justine Korman), *Davy Crockett and the Pirates at Cave-In Rock* (A. L. Singer), *Davy Crockett and the Highway Men* (Ron Fontes and Justine Korman), *Davy Crockett Meets Death Hug* (Ron Fontes and Justine Korman), and *Davy Crockett at the Alamo* (Justine Korman). The last title erroneously stated that "the enemy soldiers finally overran the Alamo, killing every man, woman, and child within its walls." Mary Dodson Wade used poetic-like phrases in her 1992 children's book, *David Crockett—Sure He Was Right*.

In 1993, an effort was made to have a statue of David Crockett funded, built, and placed in Washington D.C. Supporters of the proposal included film director David Zucker, members of The Alamo Society, and Crockett descendants. "His courageous efforts on behalf of the struggling pioneer settlers he represented, and his valiant defense of Native American rights, have become an enduring part of the

American story," explained Frances John, the President of the Direct Descendants and Kin of David Crockett. "Few Congressman have attained such a legendary status."[24] Unfortunately, the idea lacked support from Vice President Al Gore, who was from Tennessee, and was never sponsored by a member of Congress.

David Zucker, Director of *The Naked Gun 2½: The Smell of Fear.*

Mark Derr's 1993 biography, *The Frontiersman: The Real Life and the Many Legends of Davy Crockett* weaved the usual biographical tale; however, the book is not error free. Derr stated that "white men in greasepaint" portrayed the Creek warriors in "Davy Crockett, Indian Fighter," although all of them were Cherokees. The author also said that after Crockett was captured at the Alamo he explained to Santa Anna's soldiers why he was there. "Crockett told his captors that he had been exploring the country around Bexar when he heard of the Mexican advance and...had sought refuge with the Anglos in the Alamo," wrote Derr, who promptly described Crockett's execution. Walter Retan contributed to Crockett lore when he wrote *The Story of Davy Crockett, Frontier Hero*. Also in 1993, videographer Brian Huberman produced *Death of Davy Crockett*, which described the various artistic interpretations of the Battle of the Alamo and Crockett's subsequent legend.

A few Davy Crockett toy figures were produced since the glory days of the Crockett Craze, and the most imaginative one was created by the Mattel toy company in 1993. Authorized by Disney, the 11½-inch plastic figure of Davy Crockett came complete with faux buckskin clothing and a coonskin cap, footwear, a hunting bag, and assorted plastic weapons. The back of the sealed box featured a description which reflected more legend than history: "Tall and strong in his coonskin hat and fringed buckskin Davy Crockett suddenly appears from out of the woods. 'I'm hear for the big knife-throwin' match,' he shouts. He takes his bowie knife from his sheath, aims and flings it at the target. It hits with a whack that echoes off the green Tennessee mountains. 'Yahoo! Bulls eye!' Once again, Davy proves he's the King of the Wild Frontier."

On March 6, 1994, Fess Parker appeared at the annual Alamo Society Symposium in San Antonio, which was held at the Emily Morgan Hotel, a towering structure located across the street from the Alamo. The event was appropriately titled "Fess Parker:

Still King of the Wild Frontier." With opening music from *Davy Crockett, King of the Wild Frontier* playing through the room's sound system, Parker, dressed in buckskins and wearing a coonskin cap, entered the room. The mostly Baby Boomer crowd stood and cheered. Amusingly, Parker introduced himself as Davy Crockett, and quoted part of the introduction speech that he delivered in "Davy Crockett Goes to Congress," the second episode of Disney's TV trilogy. "I'm Davy Crockett," he said. "I'm half horse, half alligator and a little touched with snappin' turtle. I've got the fastest horse, the prettiest sister, the surest rifle and the ugliest dog in Tennessee!" Again, the crowd filled the room with applause. Parker spoke about the *Davy Crockett* series and the importance of the Alamo. He was later presented with a plaque "for inspiring a generation with his dignity, humility and compassion in helping us to remember the Alamo." Following his appearance, Parker walked to the Alamo and held an impromptu press conference in which he stated his support for efforts which would help an Alamo restoration effort based on recommendations suggested by the Alamo Foundation, a group organized by historian Gary Foreman.

In the 1990s, Walt Disney World offered a new assortment of Davy Crockett collectibles in Frontierland: a rubber knife in a sheath, two different sized plastic canteens, a bag of marbles, a small lariat, a bag of jacks, two different sized flashlights, and a mini six-gun. All the items were enclosed in light brown cowhide and featured a "Davy Crockett" tag. But the collectibles were only offered for a limited time. Years later, the Frontierland wooden toy rifles, which featured Crockett's name on them, were soon replaced by pink and blue-painted pirate rifles. After a while, all the toy firearms disappeared from Walt Disney World. However, the

Frontierland arcade, which features rifles that shoot beams of light at various moving and stationery targets, remains.

Bill Groneman's *Defense of a Legend: Crockett and the de la Peña Diary* in 1994 suggested that some of the papers attributed to the Mexican officer who claimed that Crockett was executed after the Battle of the Alamo were forgeries. The author didn't have the last say on the subject because a year later a ferocious debate erupted among Alamo and Crockett historians.

Cameron Judd's 1994 book *Crockett of Tennessee: A Novel Based on the Life and Times of David Crockett* was a fictionalized tale of lusty adventure, but the author praised the Alamo hero's final moments: "David, pierced again and again by bayonets, taking the assault without an outcry, claimed his destiny, going to his glory-time like the bravest of soldiers."

Davy Crockett was represented by several music acts during the 1990s. In 1992, the Headcoatees, a post-punk British group, released "Davey Crockett," an original tune that recalled the McCoys' "Hang on Sloopy" and the Premiers' "Farmer John." The Rolling Stones included a reference to Crockett in "Mean Disposition," a track from the band's 1994 *Voodoo Lounge* album. The song, written by Keith Richards and Mick Jagger, contained the lyrical lines, "I'm going have to stand my ground/Like Crockett at the Alamo." Guitarist Adrian Legg performed "Crockett Waltz," a folksy Celtic-flavored instrumental, on his *High Strung Tales* CD in 1994, and re-recordings of the Blackburn-Bruns "Ballad of Davy Crockett" appeared on several compilation CDs by various performers.

On April 16, 1995, Crockett returned to television in *James A. Michener's "Texas,"* a movie which featured John Schneider as the Alamo hero. The actor was only thirty-four years old during production, making him the youngest performer to portray the forty-nine-year-old Alamo defender in a film or TV movie. Also in 1995, Steven Kellogg wrote and illustrated the children's book, *Sally Ann Thunder Ann Whirlwind Crockett.*

In 1995, Disney artist Charles Boyer created *Fond Memories,* a wonderfully nostalgic painting about the Crockett Craze. Made into a limited edition of 600 lithographs and sold exclusively at Disneyland and Walt Disney World, *Fond Memories*' certificate of authenticity states that the illustration "depicts America's beloved hero Davy Crockett surrounded by autograph seeking children and Mickey, Minnie, and Donald." Boyer's Crockett is clearly Fess Parker, but the accompanying certificate made no mention of the actor.

Thomas F. Feely and Nancy E. Nagle published *Crockett's Last Stand: A Diorama,* a colorful booklet in 1995, which coincided with the debut of "Crockett's Last Stand," Feely's large 54-mm Alamo diorama at The Texas Adventure in San Antonio, Texas. The attraction featured a lively holographic image of Crockett portrayed by Noel Webb. Feely's diorama included the Alamo church, the front courtyard, the palisade, the horse and cattle corrals, the southern corner of the Long Barrack, hundreds of detailed figures, "exploding" artillery pieces, and a synchronized audio track which featured music by Michael Boldt. *Crockett's Last Stand* was displayed at The Texas Adventure until 1999 when the attraction closed.

At the 1995 annual meeting of the Texas State Historical Association in San Antonio, an Alamo Society panel featured Bill Groneman who explained to the audience the problems associated with the de la Peña papers' account of Crockett's capture and execution at the Alamo. During a question and answer period, Groneman's conclusions were challenged by James Crisp, a professor of history at North Carolina State University. Thus began a debate that recalled a bloodless version of the Gunfight at the O. K. Corral, except this war of words carried on for years. The two antagonists were different, and seemed to reflect the cultural classes that Crockett commented about in his autobiography. Groneman was a New York City firefighter who graduated from Manhattan College with a degree in history; Crisp earned his Ph.D. from Yale.

The two continued the debate in the Fall 1995 issue of *Military History of the West* via Groneman's "The Controversial Alleged Account of José Enrique de la Peña" and Crisp's "When Revision Becomes Obsession: Bill Groneman and the de la Peña Diary." Crisp followed up with "Truth, Confusion, and the de la Peña Controversy—A Final Reply" in the publication's Spring 1996 issue.

The Crockett death debate became more animated when Texas researcher Thomas Ricks Lindley wrote "Killing Crockett: It's All in the Execution" in the May 1995 issue of *The Alamo Journal*. Lindley cast doubts and raised questions about several contemporary sources which suggested that the Alamo hero survived the battle and was subsequently executed. Lindley followed up with "Killing Crockett (part 2): Theory Paraded as Fact" in the July 1995 issue of *The Alamo Journal*. Lindley's conclusions were criticized by James Crisp in "Davy in Freeze-Frame: Methodology Paraded as Fact" in the October 1995 issue of *The Alamo Journal*, which also contained Lindley's "Killing Crockett: Lindley's Opinion." In the December 1995 issue of *The Alamo Journal*, Crisp countered with "Trashing Dolson: The Perils of Tendentious Interpretation," which focused on Sgt. George M. Dolson's interview with a Mexican officer who had witnessed Crockett's execution. The issue also contained an article titled "Lindley-Crisp Debate Generates Membership Feedback," which described assessments of Lindley's and Crisp's arguments about the manner of Crockett's death. Crisp also wrote "Back to Basics: Conspiracies, Common Sense, and Occam's Razor" in the March 1996 issue of *The Alamo Journal.*

The debate over Crockett's death continued when Lindley wrote "The José Enrique de la Peña Petard" in December 1997 issue of *The Alamo Journal.* Alamo Society member Alan Wiener attempted to end the argument with "Who Cares How Davy Died" in the March 1999 issue of *The Alamo Journal,* but Lindley returned in the next issue with "The Prima Facie Evidence that De La Peña is a Forgery." The battle over the manner of Crockett's death didn't end; it merely evolved into a temporary cease fire.

On August 15-17, 1996, the Direct Descendants and Kin of David Crockett held their bi-annual gathering in East Tennessee, which was in the state's First Congressional District. When Crockett family members from others states arrived they noticed political campaign signs on roads and highways that read "Crockett For Congress." The Crockett on the signs was David Crockett, a district attorney from Washington County who was not related to the famous frontier hero but was running for Congress in the Republican primary. However, he and ten other candidates came up short; Bill Jenkins won the primary and the November election. Although the campaign and election were over, several "Crockett For Congress" signs remained on roadways, and Crockett descendants and various friends of the organization went after them as if they were on a scavenger hunt. The signs became the primary memento from the weekend's celebration.

In 1996, William R. Sanford and Carl R. Green wrote *Davy Crockett: Defender of the Alamo,* which concluded with, "Davy Crockett died a hero's death that day in 1836." David A. Adler wrote

A Picture Book of Davy Crockett, an excellent book for young readers, and Steve Warren's play, *The Confessions of Davy Crockett,* starring Ernie Taliaferro, had a run at the Hyde Park Theater in Austin, Texas, following performances at the David Crockett State Park in Lawrenceburg, Tennessee. "Warren's script coupled with Taliaferro's reenactment capture Crockett's pioneer persona and spirit, which, in a way, captures the image that made Americas choose to have about themselves, rugged and ready to fight to defend our liberty, without making us question why," reported the *Austin Chronicle* on October 18.

The film *High School High* opened on October 25, 1996, and once again David Zucker, who produced the motion picture, added some Crockett touches to the comedy. Most notable was a large reproduction portrait of Crockett, based on the original John Gadsby Chapman canvas, which was prominently placed in the school's interior.

Barzo Playsets offered a "Davy Crockett Wilderness Playset" for Baby Boomers who enjoyed the Marx "Davy Crockett at the Alamo" playsets from the 1950s. The new set, which carried a $139.95 price tag, contained a six-cabin refuge fort, forty plastic action characters, trees, bushes, and various accessories. For an additional $20, the Illinois-based company also offered a "giant set" which included fourteen more figures. Paul Anderson wrote *The Davy Crockett Craze: A Look at the 1950's Phenomenon and Davy Crockett Collectibles,* which included a "forward" (sic) by Bill Hayes.

Over a three year period, 1996-1998, David Thompson (real name David Robbins) churned out eight fictional novels about Crockett: *Homecoming, Sioux Slaughter, Blood Hunt, Mississippi Mayhem, Blood Rage, Commanche, Texican Terror,* and *Cannibal Country.* The following year, British artist Mark Churms painted *Crockett's Last Sunrise,* which featured the famous Alamo defender loading his rifle as he stood by the mission-fortress' palisade.

On March 1, 1997, a Thom Ross exhibition debuted at the Keene Gallery in San Antonio, Texas. Among the displayed acrylic-on-paper paintings were *Davy Crockett and His Fiddle* and *Davy at the Doorway.* That same year, Alex Shoumatoff created Crockett's unsubstantiated demise in *Legends of the American Desert: Sojourns in the Great Southwest.* "Davy Crockett...hid under a bed throughout the fighting [at the Alamo] and tried to surrender rather than fight to the death." claimed the author. Also in 1997, Paul Andrew Hutton contributed "Sunrise in His Pocket," an essay on "The Crockett Almanacs and the Birth of an American Legend" in *Frontier and Region: Essays in Honor of Martin Ridge.* According to Hutton, the Crockett of the almanacs "mirrored an emerging, still evolving, national character—celebrating its crudeness, its toughness, its daring, its egalitarianism, and, above all, its wit."

Michael Lind's *The Alamo: An Epic,* a modern-day blend of the classic heroic poem and the historical novel, treated Crockett stylishly. Lind described Crockett through Alamo commander William Barret Travis' eyes:

A well-dressed gentleman of fifty years,
    with graying hair beneath a round felt hat,
the kind that farmers wore, the wild frontier's
    most celebrated son was far from that
        cartoon in almanacs, the half bobcat,
half alligator brute who loved to fight.
The man was quiet, courtly and polite.[25]

In 1998, noted Civil War historian William C. Davis penned the comprehensive *Three Roads to the Alamo: The Lives and Fortunes of David Crockett, James Bowie, and William Barret Travis.* The author described Crockett not as a Jacksonian Era "common man" but as a "self made man" with a "spirit of adventure." Also that year, the popular G.I. Joe toy figure took a step back in time when he was costumed as a Crockett-like "Alamo Patrol" figure. Crockett's name was mentioned in "outer space," courtesy of the TV series *Star Trek: Deep Space Nine*, which featured a scale model Alamo fortress that served as a gathering site for historical debates aboard the space station.

In 1999, David Wright, a highly regarded painter who specialized in early American historical scenes and characters, painted *Crossroads of Destiny*, which depicted Crockett, Andrew Jackson, Sam Houston, and Dr. Charles McKinney in 1813, at Camp Blount during the Creek War. Rod Timanus created *On The Crockett Trail*, which traced Crockett's 1835-1836 journey from Tennessee to Texas in a series of informative maps and photographs. Bill Groneman concluded the decade's book roster with *Death of a Legend: The Myth and Mystery Surrounding the Death of Davy Crockett*, which examined all of the literature associated with the fatal events of March 6, 1836. Besides eight comprehensive chapters, the author included three appendixes which chronicled the Crockett death controversy in books, periodicals, newspapers, and films. Groneman remains skeptical about any theory which claims, with metaphysical certitude, *the* exact manner of Crockett's final moments at the Alamo.

Filmmaker Steven Spielberg acknowledged the importance of Crockett's "Be always sure you're right, then go ahead" motto in a March 15-22, 1999, issue of *People* magazine. "That was the Davy Crockett motto and I've lived by it all my life." Two years later, Spielberg served as the executive producer of HBO's *Band of*

Brothers, a series about American soldiers in World War II. When asked by *Entertainment Weekly* magazine if he played World War II soldier during his childhood, he replied: "No. I played Davy Crockett. When that Fess Parker movie came out, all my friends wanted to be King of the Wild Frontier."

On the eve of the new century, the hottest Crockett collectible on the market since the 1950s appeared when Disney contracted a Chinese manufacturer to produce a line of metallic "Countdown to the Millennium" pins, which were offered for sale at Disney Stores stores nationwide. The handsomely made colorful pins celebrated the studio's productions and characters, and pin no. 94 identified "Davy Crockett," which featured a coonskin cap resting on an old TV with its "rabbit ears" antennae and the date 1947. Nineteen forty-seven? A short time later, corrected pin no. 94-A was issued with the date 1954, which acknowledged the correct date of the "Davy Crockett, Indian Fighter" episode. Over the next several years, Disney Stores and its theme parks offered more Crockett pins for consumption, including "Davy Crockett at the Alamo," "Davy Crockett and the River Pirates," "Ballad of Davy Crockett," "Davy Crockett, King of the Wild Frontier," and "Davy Crockett's Journal," which was a tiny metallic book that actually opened. On other Disney pins, Crockett's coonskin cap was worn by such characters as Mickey Mouse, Chip and Dale, Goofy, and Tinker Bell. At about the same time, Donald Duck, wearing a faux buckskin jacket and a coonskin cap, was stationed in Walt Disney World's Frontierland where the costumed cast member signed autographs and posed for photographs.

The Davy Crockett Almanac and Book of Lists, by this author, ushered in the new millennium; Marianne Johnston wrote *Davy*

Crockett for young readers; Henry Godines painted *Davy's Last Stand;* and J. R. Edmondson penned *The Alamo Story: From Early History to Current Conflicts,* which provided the most common sense analysis of the never-ending debate over the manner of Crockett's death. "Although it is now in vogue to assume that David Crockett was executed, the evidence is hardly conclusive, wrote Edmondson, a talented historical interpreter. "In fact, more accounts exist supporting his death in combat."[26]

In 2000, Stephen Harrigan's *New York Times* best seller, *The Gates of the Alamo,* an excellent fictional novel, crafted Crockett in captivating prose. Above all, Harrigan's Crockett is a leader among leaders, a man other men gravitated to. Yet, he maintains a sense of sense of humor, seasoned with a touch of sarcasm, as the world seemingly begins to collapse around him. When Crockett suggests a joint command between Travis and Bowie as a way of curbing their mutual hostility towards each other, he adds that in case of disagreements "common sense will prevail." When an Alamo defender asks, "Who decides what's common sense?" Crockett responds, "I do, by virtue of my long experience of the matter in the United States House of Representatives." [27]

Rosalyn Schanzer updated a tall tale from the Crockett almanacs in her children's book, *Davy Crockett Saves the World,* in 2001. In a fun-filled way, Schanzer's book raised the question: "What will happen when the great Davy Crockett comes head to head with Halley's Comet?" Interestingly, the famous comet passed the earth in 1835, the year when Crockett left Congress and departed Tennessee for Texas.

The next year was a particularly active one for modern Crockett culture. "Sunrise in His Pocket: The Life, Legend and Legacy of

Davy Crockett," an excellent exhibit of history and popular culture at the Bob Bullock Texas State History Museum in Austin, Texas, had a pre-opening reception event on February 27, 2002, and Fess Parker was the featured guest. The exhibit, which opened to the general public on March 2 and ran until August 18, included wonderful artifacts and memorabilia. One of the most impressive displays was a recreated kid's bedroom from 1955 that was filed with hundreds of Crockett collectibles donated by Murray Weissmann. The exhibit also featured an edited version of the Gary Foreman-directed History Channel production *Boone & Crockett: The Hunter Heroes* on a video monitor. During the exhibit's run, the museum hosted book signings, presented a Davy Crockett symposium, and offered a new set of Crockett collectibles in its gift shop.

A minor controversy arose following the publication of the February/March 2002 issue of *True West* magazine in which a guest editor altered the original content provided by the writer of an "Alamo Myths" article. The published article stated that Crockett's "fighting like a tiger" death was a myth, and included information supporting the memoirs of Mexican officer José Enrique de la Peña who recalled that Crockett was captured and executed. The original article contained a more balanced assessment of Crockett's death: "Could Crockett have been one of the executed defenders? Certainly. But when it comes to an absolute certainly about the king of the wild frontier, the jury is still out on this one."[28]

In 2002, the skillful musician Dean Shostak released *Davy Crockett's Fiddle*, a CD collection of traditional tunes which featured "The Legend of Davy Crockett," a composite piece that included two different versions of "The Ballad of Davy Crockett." Shostak utilized a fiddle that allegedly belonged to Crockett, and is now on display at the Witte Museum in San Antonio.[29] That same year, new music written about Crockett appeared on K. R. Wood's *The Crockett Chronicles,* a Texanna Records CD collection of twenty-five spoken word and music tracks. The CD included the Michael J. Martin-penned song, "I Am With my Friends," which was based on Crockett's letter of January 9, 1836, to his daughter Margaret and her husband, Wiley Flowers. The letter concluded with, "Do not be uneasy about me. I am among friends," an expression which Wood and his band reinterpreted and delivered with poignancy on the track.

Also in 2002, Jack Jackson wrote and illustrated the magnificently detailed *The Alamo: An Epic Told From Both Sides.* "With Crockett, as with Bowie, I stick to the mass of evidence and make no apologies for doing so until someone can prove beyond a reasonable doubt that the capture/execution [of Crockett] took place," noted Jackson in his end-of-text essay. Kathy Feeney wrote *Davy Crockett: A Photo-Illustrated Biography* for young readers.

In the summer, *The Anarchist Cookbook,* a low-budget film about young anti-establishment types, featured a scene in which an actor playing Davy Crockett (Justin S. Simons) in a no-frills outdoor production about the Battle of the Alamo is confronted by Puck (Devon Gummersall) and Johnny Red (John Savage) during a question-and-answer sesssion. "Exactly what it was that Davy Crockett fought and died for?" asks Red. "It's a little thing we call freedom," replies the Crockett character. "Whose freedom?" replies Puck, who follows up with comments about slavery and Mexican rights in early Texas. Inspired by Puck's remarks, members of the audience charge the stage.

In 2002, Edwin Justis Mayer's *Sunrise In My Pocket* opened at the Paul Green Theater in Chapel Hill, North Carolina, starring Ken Strong as Crockett. Adapted and directed by Jeffrey Hayden, the Playmakers Repertory Company presentation received a so-so review from *Variety* writer Robert C. Page III. "Ken Strong, a versatile and experienced actor, is upbeat as Crockett, maybe too polished for a frustrated three-term congressman-turned-fighter and trailblazer," said Page. "Too corny for adults, play's best hopes in its present form rest with youthful audiences, who were moved from sympathy to laughter."[30]

That same year, Arkansas gunmaker Danny Caywood offered hand-crafted copies of Crockett's first rifle, which is now owned by Tennessee's Joe Swann, for $12,500. The beautifully reproduced shoulder arm features a forty-six inch, swamped octagon .48-caliber barrel, a four piece brass patchbox, a reverse Indian head finial, a full relief-carved maple stock, and a sterling silver thumb piece. Caywood presented President George W. Bush with rifle number one in 2002.

Later in the year, the three original Disney *Davy Crockett* episodes ("Davy Crockett, Indian Fighter," Davy Crockett Goes to Congress," and "Davy Crockett at the Alamo") and the two subsequent prequels ("Davy Crockett's Keelboat Race" and "Davy Crockett and the River Pirates") were superbly restored by veteran editor Tony Malanowski and reissued as *Davy Crockett: The Complete Television Series*, a two-disc DVD collection packaged in an attractive metallic tin. However, a number of mistakes were included in the supplemental material, a part of the DVD which Malanowski had nothing to do with.

In 2003, Thomas Ricks Lindley's *Alamo Traces: New Evidence and New Conclusions* suggested that Crockett left the Alamo during the siege in order to locate Col. James Fannin's command at Goliad. According to Lindley, Crockett's mission resulted in a second Alamo reinforcement of approximately fifty mounted Texians who arrived during the morning of March 4, 1836. If substantiated, such an alleged action by Crockett—riding through Santa Anna's lines twice and risking contact with Mexican cavalry patrols—would elevate the Alamo hero's status beyond its established legendary position.

Also in 2003, Elaine M. Alphin wrote *Davy Crockett*, a title in the ABDO Publishing's History Maker Bios series. The publisher's promo boldly stated that Crockett never wore a coonskin cap, despite 19th century evidence to the contrary. Also that year, the first issue of *The Crockett Chronicle*, a quarterly dedicated to the life and legend of David Crockett, was published. In the periodical, Fess Parker had his own column, "Talkin' With Fess," which was featured in every issue until his death seven years later.

An interesting description of Crockett's dead body at the Alamo was described in Ned Huthmacher's fictional 2003 work *One Domingo Morning: The Story of Alamo Joe*. "A look of pain contorted Crockett's once jesting lips, while blood soaked up his buckskin shirted torso," wrote the author. "An ugly saber cut had evidently laid open Davy's forehead, for great clots of crusty black scab matter splashed across his weathered features." For Huthmacher, Crockett died fighting.

The fiftieth anniversary of Walt Disney's *Davy Crockett* series was particularly memorable for its star, Fess Parker. On March 5, 2004, Parker donated the 19th century flintlock rifle that had been given to him during his 1955 *Davy Crockett, King of the Wild Frontier* promotional tour in Philadelphia to the Alamo. The Smithsonian Institution's Museum of American History hosted "Fess Parker—Celebrating an American Icon" in its Carmichael Auditorium on March 30, 2004. Prior to his appearance, the standing-room-only audience spontaneously broke out singing the chorus to "The Ballad of Davy Crockett." Despite Parker's high profile in 2004

(*USA Today* did a feature article, "Hats Off to 'Davy,' Fess Parker in its March 26, 2004 issue), *TV Guide* raised a question in its May 2-8 issue: "What Ever Happened to Fess Parker?"

Billy Bob Thornton in *The Alamo* (2004). Image created by Charles Martin Brazil.

Disney's *The Alamo* in 2004, starred Billy Bob Thornton as Crockett. The talented actor resembled 19th century images of Crockett but portrayed him as a reluctant warrior who played the violin and told his fellow Alamo defenders that he only "did a little scoutin,' but mostly...fetched venison for the cook fire" during the Creek War. In one reflective scene, carefully crafted by director John Lee Hancock, Thornton's character dramatically describes the horrors of war during the Battle of Tallusahatchee to a small group of men around the campfire. It's an effective scene, but the film said nothing about the other battles and skirmishes Crockett participated in. Of course, Crockett did much more than fight in one battle and hunt during the conflict.

An interesting line of dialogue in the film renewed a debate about Crockett's first name when Micajah Autry, played by Kevin Page, states: "He prefers David." Crockett signed his extant letters David and he identified himself as David in his autobiography, but he was called Davy by many, including Goliad defender John Sowers Brooks in 1836, journalists, and his son, Robert Patton Crockett.[31] It is difficult to believe that Crockett insisted his neighbors call him David when he met them at taverns and rifle frolics or when he was with them on hunting expeditions. Thornton's Crockett lost his credibility as an accomplished marksman when he repeatedly flinched when firing his flintlock rifle. The film bombed at the box office.

The most expensive Crockett figurine debuted for sale at the "2004 Blast to the Past" Walt Disney Art Classics convention held at Disneyland on May 14-16, 2004. The 8¾-inch porcelain, limited edition figure (only 500 were made) of Fess Parker as *Davy Crockett* was designed by Kent Melton, and carried a $199 price tag.

On December 15, 2004, the fiftieth anniversary of "Davy Crockett, Indian Fighter," was commemorated at Disneyland when Fess Parker was escorted to Frontierland by a cast member costumed as coonskin cap-wearing Mickey Mouse. "The nice folks at Disneyland dedicated a storefront window in my name and happily, included my old friend Buddy Ebsen in the renaming of the building's facade," said Parker about the "Crockett and Russel Hat Company" designation on the Pioneer Mercantile building.

Also in 2004, Riders in the Sky, a Western-Cowboy quartet, released *Davy Crockett, King of the Wild Frontier*, a CD collection which included all twenty verses of "The Ballad of Davy Crockett," "Be Sure You're Right, And Then Go Ahead," "Old Betsy," "Farewell," and five other selections. The Rounder Records production included a booklet which described Crockett's life and legend; however, the text stated that the Alamo hero died in 1835.

In 2005, several Crockett books reached the market. William Groneman wrote *David Crockett: Hero of the Common Man*, an insightful and interesting examination which confirmed the frontier congressman's status as an American champion. James E. Crisp's *Sleuthing the Alamo: Davy Crockett's Last Stand and Other Mysteries of the Texas Revolution* was an expanded personal essay about the historical process and an analysis of how Crockett died at the Alamo. Once again, the author concluded that Crockett was one of a handful of Alamo defenders who was captured at the end of the battle and executed. Randell Jones penned *In The Footsteps of Davy Crockett*, which provided readers with biographical and travel information, but for some reason the book did not mention New Jersey and Massachusetts, two states where Crockett traveled to in 1834. The book also contained a few errors, including Crockett's birth date. It also identified San Antonio and Béxar as two separate places. Furthermore, the author stated that "Crockett was always known as David, not Davy."

Also in 2005, Buddy Levy wrote *The Real Life Adventures of Davy Crockett*, and an amusement ride, "Davy Crockett's Tall Tales," opened on Alamo Plaza in San Antonio. Members of The Alamo Society held the organization's first "Fandango" at the Crockett Tavern in Walt Disney World's Fort Wilderness Campground on April 30, 2005, in honor of the 50th anniversary of *Davy Crockett, King of the Wild Frontier's* theatrical release. Fess Parker sent a personal greeting which was printed in the event's program.

On November 4, 2006, *Disney: The Music Behind the Magic*, a national traveling exhibit that featured an assortment of Davy Crockett items, opened at Seattle's Experience Music Project, a non-profit music museum. Among the Crockett collectibles on display were record sleeves, sheet music, a board game, a Frontierland pencil case, a doll, a toy guitar, and a coonskin cap from this author's collection. Two years later, the exhibit traveled to Vancouver, Canada's Science World in 2008, before finishing its run at Chicago's Museum of Science and Industry during the winter of 2008-2009.

Crockett's name was once again mentioned in Congress when Missouri representative Todd Akin debated Iraq War funding on April 23, 2007. "So to say that we're gonna support our troops but we're not going to send them any reinforcements is on the face of it contradictory," said the Republican from the state's Second District. "Could you picture Davy Crockett at the Alamo looking at his Blackberry getting a message from Congress? 'Davy Crockett, we support you. The only thing is we are not going to send any troops.' I'm sure that would really be impressive to Davy Crockett."

Also in 2008, K. R. Wood released *Davy Crockett's Fiddle Plays On: Live at the Alamo,* a seventeen tune collection (fourteen tracks were recorded inside the Alamo church on February 25, 2007) which included "Crockett Plays his Fiddle Tonight," "Ballad of the Alamo," and the title track. Like Dean Shostak on his *Davy Crockett's Fiddle* in 2002, musician W. B. Fowler played the Witte Museum's Crockett violin on Wood's CD.

Nearly every piece of music associated with the Crockett of history and popular culture was included in Allen J. Wiener and this author's *Music of the Alamo: From 19th Century Ballads to Big-Screen Soundtracks* in 2008. Music, as much any other art form, has promoted the Crockett legend for public consumption for nearly two centuries. The authors secured back-cover endorsements from Fess Parker and rock music icon Phil Collins, a collector of 19th century Crockett memorabilia. Also that year, Gert Petersen, an excellent Danish researcher, wrote the detailed *David Crockett: The Volunteer Rifleman*, which traced the famous backwoodsman's life from 1800 to 1817.

In 2009, Walt Disney's *Davy Crockett* series from the 1954-55 TV season took sixth-place honors in the Western Writers of America's "All-Time Greatest Western TV Series, Movies and Miniseries" category. *Lonesome Dove,* the 1989 CBS production, took top honors.

The most serious examination of Crockett's political career came in 2009 with James R. Boylston and Allen J. Wiener's *David Crockett in Congress: The Rise and Fall of the Poor Man's Friend*. The authors included every known letter and speech which Crockett created, several broadsides, and nine contemporary images of the frontier congressman. "Ultimately, despite his own best efforts to control the [legendary] image during his lifetime, Crockett's mythological persona eclipsed the plainspoken gentleman from the cane, and, while his sacrifice in defense of Texas liberty should never be forgotten, his tireless efforts on behalf of his poor and working-class constituents should also be honored," concluded the authors, who added that Fess Parker was the actor who best represented Crockett in film.[32]

Also in 2009, Mary Dodson Wade wrote *David Crockett: Hero and Legend,* a book for young readers; however, the Bright Sky Press publication is filled with such errors as the wrong date of Margaret Crockett's birth, the incorrect number of children born to Crockett and his second wife, and the wrong date of Crockett's tour of the northeast. Still, the author praised Crockett and stated that "he was more than a tragic hero." In the March 2009 issue of *Texas Monthly,* Crockett was listed first on an alphabetical list of the "30 Most Stylish Texans of All Time."

In 2009, an expanded display of Crockett images and items debuted at the Crockett Tavern at Walt Disney World's Fort Wilderness

Resort and Campground. The museum-like salute to Crockett includes a new wall-mounted showcase that holds the title page from the 19th century publication *Life of Colonel David Crockett*, a fringed hunting pouch, a powder horn, a small reproduction Crockett portrait painted by Chester Harding in 1834, Fess Parker's introductory speech from "Davy Crockett Goes to Congress," six printed lyrical lines from "The Ballad of Davy Crockett," rifle balls and flints, a postcard from Tennessee's Crockett Tavern Museum, and, of course, a coonskin cap, among other interesting items. A handsome, framed color portrait of Fess Parker as Crockett, painted by Jim Noble and dated "1830," is mounted on one wall of the facility; images of the Alamo and some of its defenders grace other walls. The building, which houses the tavern and the adjoining Trails End Restaurant, includes "Davy Crockett's Wilderness Arcade," a room full of classic video games. The taxidermied bear, which stood at the entrance for many years, was removed due to excessive handling by guests.

Sadly, a decision was made at Walt Disney World to remove the small assortment of Crockett items from its One Man's Dream: From Mickey Mouse to the Magic Kingdoms attraction in Hollywood's Studios. A film about Disney's life shown in the attraction's Walt Disney Theater included a one-second clip from "Davy Crockett Goes to Congress," but that film was replaced by other promotional films over the years. It would take nearly a decade for any *Davy Crockett* items to reappear at the site.[33]

Fess Parker, Walt Disney's *Davy Crockett*, died on March 18, 2010. Parker's passing was acknowledged in newspapers and periodicals across the country, and the entire May 2010 issue (no. 28) of *The Crockett Chronicle* was dedicated to him. Parker's death was officially recognized at the Alamo. Bruce Winders, the Curator and

Historian of the Alamo, set up a special memorial at the Shrine of Texas Liberty to honor him. "We wanted publicly to acknowledge the important cultural connection between the Alamo and Fess Parker," said Winders, who set up a memory book for visitors to sign. "We are going to send the book to his family." *Roundup* magazine, the official publication of the Western Writers of America, featured a photo of Parker on the cover of its August 2010 issue, which included the article, "Fess Parker: An Inspiration to a Generation." The article stated that "the Texan-born actor's frontier portrayal influenced some of the coonskin cap-wearing youngsters for the rest of their lives."[34]

Several Crockett biographies were published in 2011. W. W. Norton released Michael Wallis' *David Crockett: The Lion of the West,* which for some reason contained only two pages about Battle of the Alamo, and twice as many pages about slavery in Texas. Historian Bill Groneman pointed out in a *Crockett Chronicle* review that "Crockett had nothing to do [with slavery]." Additional errors, from a false association between Crockett and Bean rifles to the incorrect number of Alamo survivors, punctuated the text. Also that year, Geoff and Janet Benge wrote *Davy Crockett: Ever Westward,* a title in Emerald Books' Heroes of History collection, and Stephen Brennan edited *An Autobiography of Davy Crockett,* which was a combination of Crockett's *Narrative* and the subsequent *Tour to the North and Down East* title.

At "D-23: The Official Disney Fan Club" event, held at the Anaheim Convention Center in Anaheim, California on August 19-21, 2011, a new commercial Davy Crockett item was introduced: a nine-inch, plastic Vinylmation™ character created by artist Casey Jones. The limited run figure (only 1,000 were manufactured), which depicted a bearded Fess Parker from the "Keelboat

Race" and "River Pirates" episodes, featured movable parts and a removable coonskin cap that exposes Mickey Mouse ears resting on Crockett's head. The figure, which is not actually identified as Davy Crockett, sold for $44.95. According to the figure's packaging, "Vinylmation™ is a collectible vinyl series featuring original designs from Disney Theme Park Merchandise."

The life and legend of Crockett was explored in an amusing way in 2012 in Bob Thompson's *Born On A Mountaintop: On The Road With Davy Crockett and the Ghosts of the Wild Frontier*. The author's travels included interviews with historians; stops at historical sites, gift shops, and souvenir stands; and encounters with assorted "Crockettologists." However, some passages from *Fess Parker: TV's Frontier Hero* were included in the book without being properly cited.

That same year, James Donovan investigated and assessed all the sources relating to Crockett's death at the Alamo in *The Blood of Heroes: The 13-Day Struggle for the Alamo—and the Sacrifice that Forged a Nation*. "If these are examined critically, there is little evidence to support such a [capture and execution] scenario—certainly not enough to write it as history," wrote Donovan. "Each of the accounts has serious credibility problems."[35] The author did not rule out the possibility of Crockett's execution, but stated that "until stronger evidence is presented, let history show that he died fighting with his comrades."[36]

Another impressive book was Phil Collins' *The Alamo and Beyond: A Collector's Journey*, which included photographs of a rifle, bullet pouch, and a pair of brass powder flasks which allegedly belonged to Crockett, and a dated and signed copy of Crockett's *Narrative*. On the autobiography's first page, the following remarks are written, "Washington City, 19 March 1834. I David Crockett of

Tennessee do certify that this book was written by my self and the only genuine history of my life that was ever written. The first work [*The Life and Adventures of Colonel David Crockett of West Tennessee*] is a Counterfeit and was written with out authority. Given under my hand and seal. David Crockett."[37] Collins, whose successful multi-decade career included an impressive tenure with Genesis before he went out on his own as a solo artist, was a Davy Crockett fan since he saw Fess Parker's performance as a child in England in 1956.

Also in 2012, the Fess Parker Winery offered "Crockett," a highly-rated blend of Syrah, Petit Syrah, and Grenache, which was assembled from various family property sources, including Rodney's Vineyard in California's Santa Ynez Valley. Each dark-glass bottle is etched with "Crockett," the letters arranged vertically. Like other Fess Parker wines, the bottle's cork is embellished with the stamp of a coonskin cap.

A quirky comedy short, *A Man of Reputation,* which featured a Davy Crockett character played by Jack Wynne, debuted on November 12, 2015. When the film was scheduled to be part of the Third Street Film Festival at the Shaw Center for the Arts' Manship Theatre in Baton Rouge, Louisiana on December 28, the city's *Advocate* printed the following synopsis: "Tempers flare when legendary men, including Davy Crockett, cross paths in 19th century New Orleans."

Two years later, Karen Chutsky wrote *Young Davy Crockett: The Boy From Tennessee,* which is "told anectdotally (sic)... by one of his oldest living descendants." The book was criticized by members of the Direct Descendants and Kin of David Crockett for its inclusion of many artificially created characters and events, to say nothing of the text's mechanical mistakes.

In 2013, this author wrote *Davy Crockett from A to Z,* a book for young readers. Twenty-six alphabetical entries, from "Alamo" to "Zapadores," were illustrated by Wade Dillon, and Billy Bob Thornton, who played Davy Crockett in *The Alamo* (2004), provided the following statement on the back cover: "We are living in a time in which our knowledge of history is slowly but surely fading. It is our duty to teach our children the rich history of America. This book about the legendary hero David Crockett is a fine example."

For some unknown reason, Crockett was given a middle name, "Stern," in the TV documentary Bill O'Reilly's *Legends and Lies*, which aired on May 3, 2015. The program was plagued by several additional errors: Crockett wears a Civil War-era hat, carries a modern-day recreated flintlock shoulder arm, and follows an order given to him by Sam Houston to go the Alamo with "fifty-five" men.

In 2015, Richard Markey's *A Million Laughs: The Funny History of American Comedy* describes how Crockett used the comedic brag to help turn himself into America's first self-created political celebrity. Markey also pointed out that Crockett's death at the Alamo linked two seemingly unrelated elements. "Crockett's heroic death at the Battle of the Alamo in 1836 added a paradoxical quality to his legend, linking American comedy and heroic martyrdom in one celebrated figure, who was ever after both the *myth* made real and the *real* made myth," he said.

On July 1, 2015, President Barack Obama followed up a question about Social Security that was asked by Davy Crockett, an adult Tennessean, at a town hall meeting held at the Taylor Stratton Elementary School in Madison, Tennessee. "Davy Crockett!" said Obama. "You all remember that TV show? Actually, a lot of people are too young here." Then Obama sang, "Davy, Davy Crockett," and quipped, "I love that."

In July 2016, at the Direct Descendants and Kin of David Crockett family reunion in Fayetteville, Tennessee, sculpture James Shoop of St. Croix Falls, Wisconsin, debuted his new bronze bust of Crockett. The creation stood thirteen inches high and rested upon a wooden base that featured the following phrase: "Do not be uneasy about me, I am among my friends."

On December 6, 2016, a David Crockett Commemorative Bust was unveiled during a ceremony at Tennessee State Capitol's House of Representatives foyer. The impressive four-foot bronze figure was sculpted by Antonio Tobias Mendez, who was selected after submitting his design to the Tennessee Arts Commission on behalf of the Tennessee State Capitol Commission and the Tennessee General Assembly.[38]

Crockett was supposed to appear once again on the big screen when CineCoup, a Vancouver, Canada-based production company, began filming *The Legend of Davy Crockett*, which was to star Ty Olsson. However, a lack of funding and a change in artistic direction prevented the film's 2016 release.

Also, in 2016, a Crockett character, played by Allen Dillon, was added to the Battle for Texas: The Experience in San Antonio, Texas. The attraction, which bordered the Alamo battlefield and the Historic Menger Hotel, featured an extensive lineup of original Texas Revolution artifacts, artwork, recreated historical scenarios, costumed mannequins, interactive displays, and Dillon's colorful characterization. A photo of Dillon as the famous Alamo hero graced the cover of the 2017 issue of *The Crockett Chronicle*. Sadly, the Battle for Texas: The Experience closed in 2019.

In 2017, Emma E. Haldy wrote *Davy Crockett*, a title in the My Itty-Bitti Bio series, which was produced for the youngest readers. Bill Hayes, whose popular version of "The Ballad of Davy Crockett" spent five weeks atop *Billboard's* "Best Sellers in Stores" chart in 1955, appeared on *The Tonight Show Starring Jimmy Fallon* on June 27, 2017, and shared his recollection of recording the song back in 1954.

Notable Crockett celebrations in 2018, included the 60th anniversary celebration of the Crockett Tavern Museum in Morristown, Tennessee. Morristown Mayor Gary Chesney presented a proclamation acknowledging the event to Sally Baker, the site's manager and curator. The Direct Descendants and Kin of David Crockett held its bi-annual family and friends reunion in San Antonio, Texas, where over one hundred members of the organization had their official group photo taken in front of the Alamo Church.

Catering to the youngest fans of the "king of the wild frontier," *Baby Crockett*, an animated TV series created by Matt Solik, debuted in 2018, with Lana Rae Jarvis voicing the wild frontier toddler. According to DreamWorks Animation Television, the production is "about a baby who, alongside his raccoon friend Buddy, attempts to tame the wilderness with absolutely no knowledge or experience."

The legend of Davy Crockett continues to evolve, especially among those who enjoy unique meetings between the celebrated Tennessean and other earthly creatures. In 2018, the internet site Bigfootbase.com posed a question that was seemingly inspired by the Crockett almanacs: "Did Davy Crockett Ever Encounter Sasquatch?" The site posted a letter supposedly written by Crockett (it wasn't!) after he left Nacogdoches to Abner Burgin in which the former congressman explains his eye-to-eye confrontation with Bigfoot. The letter said that Crockett was clearing "some thicket" and had placed his axe "upon a the opposite end of the felled tree" when he saw the mysterious creature. The beast, instead of running away or attacking Crockett, gave him a warning. "It told me to return from Texas, to flee this Fort and to abandon this lost cause," noted Crockett in the letter.[39] The creature promptly took off after delivering the message. Crockett did have an encounter with a Big Foot, but it was the fictional Big Foot Mason of the "Davy Crockett Goes to Congress" episode from 1955. "Crockettology" has never been the exclusive territory of historians.

On August 17, 2018, Crockett's 232nd birthday was celebrated at the Alamo with a special evening program which included an outdoor showing of Walt Disney's *Davy Crockett, King of the Wild Frontier,* birthday cake, and a display of items which belonged the memorable Tennessean. A special appearance was also made by Jeff Bearden, the former mayor of Vernon, Texas and an experienced historical interpreter, who portrayed Crockett. Not far from the Alamo, at the Alamo Beer Company's outdoor beer garden, singer-songwriter K. R. Wood, who recorded *Davy Crockett's Fiddle Plays On: Live at the Alamo,* performed an extended set of tunes dedicated to Crockett.

The next day, a Davy Crockett Birthday Party was part of the East Tennessee History Fair that was held at the East Tennessee Historical Society's Museum of East Tennessee History in Knoxville. The historical society was founded in 1834 as the East Tennessee Historical and Antiquarian Society; the museum opened 1993. Among the museum's collections is the Crockett rifle owned by Joe Swann, an honorary board member of the East Tennessee Historical Society and a Crockett researcher.

Coinciding with the anniversary of Crockett's birth, two new four-by-five foot murals depicting stories about the intrepid backwoodsman were erected at the David Crockett Birthplace State Park in Limestone, Tennessee. Created by Gary Foreman and William Hamilton, "Eyewitness to a Tragedy" describes Crockett's recollection of the time when his four older brothers and a friend were in a canoe headed for a waterfall. Fortunately, the quintet was rescued by an adult who saw their plight. The colorful mural included a section from Crockett's autobiography and concludes with the frontiersman's quote about being left behind on the canoe adventure: "When they got out, I found the boys were more scared than I had been, and the only thing that comforted me was, the belief that it was a punishment on them for leaving me on shore." The other Foreman-Hamilton mural, "A Riverbank, Not a Mountain Top," helps remind visitors of the difference between the popular "born on a mountain top in Tennessee" lyric from "The Ballad of Davy Crockett" and Crockett's actual birthplace. The mural, along with over a dozen other Foreman-Hamilton panels, describes the history of the region and includes information about Crockett's early years.[40] The panels are part of Foreman's Native Sun Productions' Crockett Heritage Trail collection which spans several states. The state park also hosted historical interpreters and sutlers who helped recreate the early days of Crockett and his family for the benefit of the many visitors who attended.[41]

The line between the Crockett of history and the Crockett of popular culture crisscrossed when two early 19th century weapons, one owned by Crockett and the other used by Fess Parker, came up for auction at two different auction houses. On September 12, 2018, a knife that allegedly belonged to Crockett was placed at auction by the Ohio-based Cowan's Auctions. The Bowie-type blade was marked with Federalist Era patriotic motifs and featured a label on the blade that stated: "This knife was presented to and long in the possession of David Crockett. It was in Peale's Philadelphia Museum and marked 'Deposited by &c' (Original label lost.)" According to the auction house, a "May 1934 letter by Helen Chapman, a visitor to the Peale Museum in New York City, describes Crockett as being a guest of the museum," which was administered by Rembrandt Peale, who painted a portrait of Crockett that year. Cowan's explained that "it would seem likely that the knife was given as a token of respect and admiration from Crockett to America's most famous historical and horticultural institution." According to the auction house's website, the blade was expected to sell for between $100,000 and $150,000, but it eventually sold (with a buyer's premium) for $64,625.[42]

On September 26, 2018, Morphy Auctions, a firm with locations in Lancaster, Pennsylvania and Las Vegas, Nevada, offered an original late 18th century-early 19th century "Golden Age" .50-caliber flintlock rifle made by Lancaster gunsmith John Fondersmith and later used by Fess Parker in Disney's *Davy Crockett* series. The weapon was expected to sell for $20,000 to $40,000.[43] According to the auction house's website, the weapon sold (with a buyer's premium) for $40,950. The same evening of the auction, the first episode of CBS-TV's *Survivor* debuted. During the episode, which kicked off the series' 37th season, one of the contestants, Davie Rickenbacker, caught an octopus. As he emerged from the ocean, he held up his catch on a pole and shouted, "Davy Crockett, king of the wild frontier!"

For collectors, the numerous Walt Disney's Official Davy Crockett at the Alamo playsets issued by Louis Marx in the 1950s were celebrated in *Marx Alamo Playsets and Toys of the Alamo & Davy Crockett Craze of the 50's, 60's & 70's*, a comprehensive presentation of the colorful items written and photographed by Russell S. Kern in 2018. "What is important is that these sets, no matter how primitive, continue to teach history and develop our admiration for what is behind their meaning," noted the author in book's epilogue.[44]

Honey Grove, Texas, a place where Crockett traveled to on his way to San Antonio in 1836, celebrated the famous Alamo defender on September 29, 2018, with the Davy Crockett Festival. Sponsored by the community's chamber of commerce, the event took place at the town square and the civic center. Commercial vendors, live music and games were part of the all-day event.

The 51st Davy Crockett Days celebration was held on October 7-13, 2018, in Rutherford, Tennessee at the Davy Crockett Cabin Museum site, which features a replica cabin built with some of the original timbers from Crockett's last home. Crockett's mother's grave is situated nearby.

Comedy filmmaker David Zucker put his impressive Crockett collection up for auction on January 24, 2019. Among the rare items, which were offered through Sotheby's, were several 19th century books, numerous almanacs, posters, images, and letters, including the last one Crockett wrote before he departed Tennessee for Texas. The collection's estimated value was nearly $200,000.

In a January 17, 2019, interview with Kathleen White of Sotheby's.com, Zucker placed Crockett in a different pantheon of American heroes. "I'm sure he would make me laugh—he was more or less the Groucho Marx of his day," said Zucker. "In my mind, historically, he's in a succession of wit coming after Benjamin Franklin, and following him, Mark Twain, Will Rogers, Groucho Marx, Woody Allen. These are people who went far above; they were just zany." Zucker added that his proposed Crockett miniseries "is still a real possibility."

Upon completion of the single-day auction, most of the items in Zucker's collection were sold, although the last letter Crockett wrote in Tennessee, which carried an estimated initial bid of $70,000, was not. When asked about the letter's fate, Zucker replied, "my kids get them."[45]

Besides historical sites and genealogical organizations, the Crockett name survives in a number of ways. Tennessee and Texas, of course, have many parks, places, and businesses named after the famous frontiersman. Tennessee has riding stables, a hot rod race track, truck stops, schools, restaurants, a hospital, a bank, a golf course, a Masonic Lodge, a Boy Scout camp, and many other enterprises that bear the Crockett name. Texas has Lake Crockett, the David Crockett Spring, the Crockett National Forest, and a lineup of schools, businesses, streets, and events, such as the city of Crockett's "Davy Crockett Classic," a series of competitive bicycle races.

Other states acknowledge Crockett's name, too. Montana is the headquarters of the Boone and Crockett Club, a wildlife conservation through hunting organization, and Crockett's Bluff, Arkansas, is named after Crockett's grandson, Robert. Virginia is home to the Davy Crockett Coon Hunters Club, and then, of course, there's the Davy Crockett Ranch at Disneyland Paris. Sadly, however, the Davy Crockett saloon in San Francisco no longer exists; it went bankrupt in 1900.

The legend of Davy Crockett will continue to "Go Ahead!"

SECTION TWO NOTES

1. William Groneman III, "Colonel Crockett's Exploits and Adventures in Texas," *The Crockett Chronicle*, no. 26 (November 2009), 4.
2. William R. Chemerka, "Life of General Andrew Jackson: Crockett's Next Ghostwritten Book?," *The Crockett Chronicle*, no. 14 (November 2006), 8.
3. Dan Kilgore, *How Did Davy Die?* (College Station: Texas A&M Press, 1978), 42-44.
4. The town of Mechanickham, formed in 1836, the year Crockett died at the Alamo, was later renamed Gretna.
5. Roger A. Hall, *Performing the American Frontier, 1870-1906* (UK: University of Cambridge Press, 2001), 16; Laurence Hutton, *Curiosities of the American Stage* (New York: Harper & Brothers, 1891), 30.
6. *Utah Enquirer,* November 1, 1889. Mayo managed to occasionally perform in other productions during his run as Crockett.
7. Jim Boylston, "Crockett and Bunce: A Fable Examined," *The Crockett Chronicle*, no. 6 (November 2004), 10. The author pointed out that despite Ellis' assertion that Crockett was successful in defeating the legislation, it passed. Also Ellis fabricated a story about Crockett voting for similar legislation when the Tennessean wasn't even in congress.
8. Tim Massey, "Davy Crockett's Birthday Celebrations," *The Crockett Chronicle,* no. 22 (November 2008), 3-5. According to Massey, a Crockett descendant, "one account from the *Knoxville Journal* of the gathering stated 'to the people who gathered at Limestone Tennessee in 1889, Crockett represented the lost world of the closed opportunities of the West.' The speakers of the day also reflected this theme. N. B. Remine, vice president of the Davy Crockett Historical Society, spoke briefly about Crockett and other pioneers 'who roamed the misty avenues of unfriendly forests, subdued the dens of savagery, and opened up the western world.' Next the Honorable Alf Taylor, who was elected to Congress in 1889, was introduced. It was reported that 'this eloquent orator was at his best.'"

Major Pettibone was next on the program, and he introduced Robert H. Crockett, the grandson of the pioneer. The *Journal* records 'at first he was very much affected by his welcome and the position he occupied at the celebration, but he soon recovered himself and made a speech that for eloquence has never been surpassed, we believe, in East Tennessee. The theme was a great one, and the man was worthy of the theme. After asking indulgence from seeming egotism, he referred in thrilling and touching language to the deeds of his grandsire, culminating in the tragic Alamo, an event of which human heroism has reached no sublimer heights and of which it has been said…'Thermopylae had its messenger of defeat, the Alamo had none,' He closed with humor which was much appreciated. Following this, there was the Military Drill and the Sham Battle. The boys killed each other in great mimic style, and after exhausting their ammunition, the battle was declared a draw, much to the relief of the trembling umpires."

Although the artifacts on display were probably genuine, Gary Zaboly cautioned, in *An Altar For Their Sons: The Alamo and the Texas Revolution in Contemporary Newspaper Accounts* (Buffalo Gap, TX: State House Press, 2011): "In the many years since the battle of the Alamo, personal relics supposedly associated with one defender or another have occasionally surfaced, only a handful have had their historical ownership authenticated."

9. Frederick Jackson Turner, *The Frontier in American History,* (Mineola, NY: Dover Publications, Inc., 1996), 105.

10. McCardle painted the original version in 1875, which was destroyed in the Austin capitol fire of 1881.

11. *Bellingham* (Washington) *Herald,* May 18, 1905. Jeffries retired with an undefeated record of 19-0-2, but came out of retirement to fight Jack Johnson on July 4, 1910. Johnson won and Jeffries retired for good. Following his death in 1953, Jeffries' large barn in Burbank, California was dismantled and reassembled at the Knott's Berry Farm theme park in Buena Park, California, which is located fewer than ten miles away from Disneyland's Frontierland. Corbett appeared in an 1894 Kinetograph of a exhibition boxing match with Peter Courtney, which was produced by Thomas Edison's Manufacturing Company in West Orange, New Jersey. Later, besides his stage performances, Corbett became a film actor and appeared in several motion pictures, beginning in 1913, with *The Man from the Golden West* and ending in 1930, with *At the Round Table.*

12. Gary Cooper played the title role of *Sergeant York* in 1941, and subsequently won the Best Actor Oscar®. In 1952, Cooper starred in *Springfield Rifle*. One of the uncredited supporting players in the Western was Fess Parker, who later starred as Walt Disney's *Davy Crockett.*

13. Scates, S. E., *A School History of Tennessee* (Yonkers-on-Hudson, NY: 1925), 247; James Phelan, *School History of Tennessee* (Philadelphia: E. H. Butler and Company, 1889), 134.
14. *Springfield* (Massachusetts) *Republican*, Jan. 19, 1936. Some of the music was attributed to Mary Jane Hungerford.
15. Sheila Graham, "Hollywood," (Cleveland) *Plain Dealer*, December 14, 1939. In the April 9, 1941 edition of the Washington D. C. *Evening Star*, Graham said that Paramount paid $75,000 to Mayer for the rights.
16. Charles L. Fontenay, *Estes Kefauver: A Biography* (Knoxville, University of Tennessee Press, 1980), 148. The book's cover featured a photo of Kefauver wearing a coonskin cap.
17. Crockett's opponents in the 1829 election tallied the following vote percentages: Adam Alexander (34.3%), Joel Estes (1.6%), and James Clark (0.2%).
18. The *Parade* article included a number of exaggerations about the production ("500 extras") and myths about Crockett ("The real Davy had a regrettable tendency to wear tobacco-juice dribbles on his chin.") Interestingly, the last of Crockett's grandchildren, Ashley Wilson Crockett, 96, died on May 31, 1954, a few months before filming commenced. Disney's production team made a token effort to publicize the series while on location in North Carolina. A sign on the side of one of the grip trucks proclaimed: "A Great TV Show is Coming! Walt Disney's 'Davy Crockett' starring Fess Parker as Davy to be presented on 'Disneyland' Disney's Series on ABC-TV Premiering Oct. 27."
19. For a complete examination of "The Ballad of Davy Crockett" see William R. Chemerka and Allen J. Wiener, *Music of the Alamo: From 19th Century Ballads to Big-Screen Soundtracks* (Houston: Bright Sky Press, 2008).
20. The building was placed on the Register of Historic Places in 2014. The Direct Descendants and Kin of David Crockett have made official visits to the site, which added its first gift shop in 1997 (a new one was constructed in 2008), whenever bi-annual gatherings took place in east Tennessee.
21. William R. Chemerka, *Fess Parker: TV's Frontier Hero* (Albany: GA: BearManor Media, 2011), 205.
22. Due to some tie votes, the sum is greater than 100%.
23. William R. Chemerka, "David Zucker's Crockett Production: An Encouraging Update," *The Crockett Chronicle*, no. 31 (December 2013), 3-6.

24. William R. Chemerka, "Crockett Returning to Washington D. C. ?—Alamo Society to Provide Assistance," *The Alamo Journal*, no. 88 (October 1993), 8. At the time, the Crockett family organization had not added "Kin" to its name; it is now known as the Direct Descendants and Kin of David Crockett.

25. Michael Lind, *The Alamo: An Epic* (New York: Houghton Mifflin Company, 1997), 132. According to the author, a wounded Crockett is killed from multiple bayonet thrusts.

26. J. R. Edmondson, *The Alamo Story: From Early History to Current Conflicts* (Plano, TX: Republic of Texas Press, 2000), 399. In an interesting section of the book titled "Myths, Mysteries, and Misconceptions," the author suggests that "the odds are that Crockett died in a nondescript death in the battle, possibly shot down while retreating to the church, then bayoneted."

27. Stephen Harrigan, *The Gates of the Alamo* (New York: Alfred A. Knopf, 2000), 292-293.

28. *True West* (February/March, 2002), 35. Following an apology from the guest editor, the original article penned by this author was published in issue #124 of *The Alamo Journal* (March 2002).

29. The violin features an inscription: "This fiddle is my property. Davy Crockett. Franklin County, Tenn. Feb. 14, 1819." The April 5, 1936 edition of *The Houston Chronicle* featured a story about another violin that was supposedly owned by Crockett. The article said, "on one side of the head is carved 'D. Crockett.' On the other side is 'Tenn., 1835, D.C. Texas, 1836.'" According to the newspaper, the violin was sent to Mexico City along with other spoils of war confiscated at the Alamo. The violin was later acquired by an American soldier during the Mexican War who later sold it to a soldier from Texas. The violin was taken by a Union soldier in 1864, during the Civil War, but it was later found by John Houston Thurmond at a second-hand store in Parsons, Kansas. Thurmond was eighty-years-old in 1936. Lost amidst the Crockett Craze of the 1950s, Red River Dave (McEnery) played the violin on the 1955 Decca Records single "When Davy Crockett Met the San Antonio Rose." The record label notes that the song was "recorded with the authentic Davy Crockett fiddle, courtesy of the Witte Memorial Museum." On an historic note, Crockett never mentioned playing or owning a violin in extant documents, although several individuals, like Andrea C. Villanueva (better known as Madam Candelaria), said he played the fiddle "well" while in San Antonio.

30. *Variety,* November 21, 2002.

31. In 1836, Goliad defender John Sowers Brooks wrote home that the "Mexicans have made two successive attacks on the Alamo in both of which the gallant little garrison repulsed them with some loss. Probably Davy Crockett 'grinned' them off." Crockett was called Davy in such numerous contemporary newspaper accounts as the *Boston Traveler* in 1829; the *Pawtucket Chronicle and Manufacturers' and Artizans' Advocate* in 1830; the Richmond *Enquirer* in 1834; and the *Portsmouth Journal of Literature and Politics* in 1835. Robert Patton Crockett called his father Davy in a letter to the "keeper of the Alamo," *Daily Alta California,* September 22, 1889.

32. The authors explained their assessments of the various celluloid Davy Crocketts in issue no. 26 (November 2009) of *The Crockett Chronicle.* The question posed to them was: "What Crockett actors seem to have got it right from your book's perspective?"

    Wiener: "Fess Parker. No question. If you watch the original three *Disneyland* TV episodes in full, there is a clear progression from a somewhat comical 'Davy,' taken largely from pulp fiction, to a more nuanced character. Parker got the balance between the real, private Crockett and the more public campaigner, who grew into the legendary 'Davy,' just right. Although this is still a fictitious image of Crockett, it does capture Crockett's ability to switch the public persona on and off when he needed to, without ever compromising who he really was. I disagree with the idea that Crockett was somehow trapped by his public image. It did grow to a point beyond which he could fully control it, but he knew very well what it was and how to use it. Even in the 'Davy Crockett at the Alamo' episode, which is pretty somber, he does his best to keep up the defenders' spirits by using that image."

    Boylston: "I agree; Fess gets my vote, although many of the actors who have portrayed Crockett on film have correctly captured aspects of his character. John Wayne did a good job putting across Crockett's larger-than-life persona. Billy Bob Thornton humanized the character, but I sometimes felt that Thornton's Crockett was riddled with self-doubt. The real Crockett was confidant and comfortable in his own skin. His public image was largely of his own making, but it was primarily an exaggeration of Crockett's real personality, not a complete fabrication. People who knew Crockett through the media were often disappointed when they met him in person—they expected a wild man. Occasionally, Crockett obliged them, but he usually did so with a nudge and a wink. 'Davy' could be a bit over the top, and David wanted to make sure people were in on the joke."

33. The attraction One Man's Dream: From Mickey Mouse to the Magic Kingdoms reopened as Walt Disney Presents: From Mickey Mouse to the Magic Kingdoms and Beyond on September 8, 2017. Two *Davy Crockett* photos, a black and white image of Disney and Fess Parker, and an enlarged color shot from "Davy Crockett, Indian Fighter," were featured in a display titled "The Magic of Television: Big Heroes on the Small Screen." However, the next year the display was reorganized and the photo of Parker and Disney was removed. For a complete history of Davy Crockett at Walt Disney World see Bill Chemerka, "Davy Crockett: King of the Wild Frontier (land)," *Celebrations,* no. 10 (March/April 2010), 56-59.

34. William R. Chemerka, "Fess Parker: An Inspiration to a Generation," *Roundup*, vol. XVII, no. 6 (August 2010), 15. The article included comments by flintlock gunsmiths, writers, artists, historical interpreters, singer-songwriters, filmmakers, and other creative professionals who were influenced by Parker's portrayal in the *Davy Crockett* series. See also William R. Chemerka, *Fess Parker: TV's Frontier Hero* (Albany, GA: BearManor Media, 2011).

35. James Donovan, *The Blood of Heroes: The 13-Day Struggle for the Alamo—and the Sacrifice that Forged a Nation* (New York: Little, Brown and Co., 2012), 447.

36. Ibid., 453.

37. Phil Collins, *The Alamo and Beyond: A Collector's Journey* (Buffalo Gap, TX: State House Press, 2012), 71. Gary S. Zaboly provided the excellent illustrations and many of the annotated notes in the book.

38. The bronze bust was authorized by Tennessee Senate Joint Resolution 505, which was adopted on April 16, 2014: "Be it resolved by the Senate of the One Hundred Eighth General Assembly of the State of Tennessee, the House of Representatives concurring, that the State Capitol Commission is hereby requested to initiate the creation and placement of a monument to honor and commemorate legendary Tennessean, David Crockett." Mendez was an accomplished sculptor who had created the bronze of Teddy Roosevelt for the Theodore Roosevelt Inaugural National Historic Site in Buffalo, New York and the larger-than-life, full-figure of Boston Red Sox Hall of Famer Carl Yastrzemski at Fenway Park in Boston, among other figures.

39. A serious critique of the letter identifies a number of problems with it. For example, the letter featured excellent grammar, a skill that Crockett never mastered. The references to Crockett clearing "some thicket" and placing his axe "upon a the opposite end of the felled tree" suggested that he was clearing land, something he did not do in Texas, since he owned none. The document mentions that Crockett was already in the "Fort." Since there was no fort in Nacogdoches at the time (the La Casa Pierda, the town's mercantile house was later dubbed the Old Stone Fort) did the letter's "Fort" reference actually mean the Alamo in San Antonio? If a Crockett almanac would have been printed today, this lively story would have been included in it.

40. The Crockett Heritage Trail project, created by Gary Foreman and Carolyn Raine-Foreman's Native Sun Productions in 2012, "includes up-grading museums, highway markers, interpretive signage and programs, special events, a traveling exhibit, and new technology to help tell the larger story" of Crockett's life and times. Native Sun Productions also helped erect informative historical panels and displays at such Tennessee sites as Sycamore Shoals State Park in Elizabethton, Warrior's Path State Park in Kingsport, Cumberland Mountain State Park in Crossville, Chickasaw State Park in Henderson, Big Cypress Tree State Park in Greenfield, and Discovery Park of America in Union City. For additional information, go to: http://www.crockettheritagetrail.com

41. The David Crockett Birthplace State Park features an informative visitor center and a number of recreated wooden structures that were typical of those used in the late 18th and early 19th centuries. Besides the main cabin, which was moved closer to the park's entrance in 2017, the site includes two hunters cabins, a spring house, a corn crib, an outdoor kitchen, and a barn with two horse stalls. The park also contains an herb garden, pig pen, and chicken coop. According to park ranger Sean McKay, about 95% of the wooden structures were made with hand tools. Costumed historical interpreters periodically demonstrate such early American frontier skills as fire making. The visitor center is currently undergoing an expansion. The park also provides camp sites, walking trails, a swimming pool complex, a boat ramp, and other family-friendly features. In August, the park hosts its annual Crockett Days celebration.

42. Cowan's Auctions [www.cowanauctions.com]. According to the auction house. the knife was part of The Historic Firearms and Militaria Collection of

Peter Wainwright: "The Peale Museum operated in Philadelphia until 1841, when rising admission costs forced the closure of the institution as well as the sale of its entire collection, with the exception of the portraits. The minutes of the American Philosophical Society from 1833-1846 list no references to the knife. This indicates that the knife was personally presented to a member of the Peale family. The knife is recorded once again in 1887, when it passed to Colonel Archibald Loudon Snowden (1835-1910). Snowden rose to public prominence through his position as a registrar for the U.S. Mint. After the Civil War, Snowden continued his political career, serving as Chief Coiner from 1866 to 1877, then he was appointed by President Rutherford B. Hayes as Postmaster of Philadelphia. Two years later he accepted the position of Director of the Philadelphia Mint, retiring in 1885 with a national reputation. Snowden assisted in organizing of the 1887 Centennial celebration of the U.S. Constitution in Philadelphia. Snowden continued his career in politics, being named ambassador to Greece, Romania, and Serbia from 1889 to 1892, and from 1892 to 1893 as Minister to Spain. The provenance of the Crockett knife prior to Col. Snowden's possession is unclear. In his capacity as Marshal of the Centennial Celebration, he was in close contact with many of the organizations participating in the event, including the American Philosophical Society, by whom he was invited to an exclusive banquet attended by President Grover Cleveland. As Marshal, Snowden presented a toast, though there is no mention in the official record of any presentations to Snowden. Considering his position in the Constitution Centennial celebration coupled [with an] affidavit provided by the family stating that the Crockett knife was acquired by Snowden in 'approximately 1887,' it is more than likely that he was presented the knife as a token of gratitude for his service. The knife remained in Snowden's possession until his death in 1912, when it passed to his daughter Caroline Smith Snowden (1865-1960) who had married Stuyvesant Wainwright (1863–1930) in 1889. It has remained with the Wainwright family for 141 years."

43. The rifle was one of hundreds of valuable historic weapons, accoutrements, ephemera, utensils, furniture, art, and books that came from the estate of Walter O'Conner. The rifle had earlier been used in *The Fighting Kentuckian* (1949), which starred John Wayne, and *The Iroquois Trail* (1950), which starred Richard Montgomery. The auction house also offered a prop flintlock rifle, valued at between $8,000 and $12,000, which Fess Parker used in the *Daniel Boone* TV series.

44. Russell S. Kern, *Marx Alamo Playsets and Toys of the Alamo & Davy Crockett Craze of the 50's, 60's & 70's* (Colorado Springs, CO: Atomic Enterprises, 2018), 136. Along with the 1956 Topps *Walt Disney's Davy Crockett* picture cards, the Marx playsets remain as the most popular Crockett collectibles from the 1950s. However, according to the book, "Marx kept no public records" as to the number of playsets it sold." The book underestimates the number of Alamo defenders at 186. The Alamo has recognized 189 defenders for many years, although the actual number is probably higher.

45. Zucker to author, January 25, 2019.

SECTION THREE

Davy Crockett: Day by Day

JANUARY 1 – DECEMBER 31 CALENDAR

January

1. 1821 Crockett resigns as Town Commissioner of Lawrenceburg in order to seek a seat in the Tennessee General Assembly.

   1835 Crockett writes his publishers, Carey and Hart of Philadelphia: "Gentlemen, I here enclose you the title of the new book [*Col. Crockett's Tour to the North and Down East*]."

   1835 The first day of the first Crockett almanac, *Davy Crockett's Almanack of Wild Sports of the West, And Life in the Backwoods.*

2. 1821 Crockett serves on a jury which judges a dispute between Robert Mason and Bailey Brooks over the charge of armed trespass.

   1903 Crockett's "Pretty Betsey," the rifle presented to him in Philadelphia in 1834, is on display in Memphis, Tennessee. Crockett's grandson, Robert Hamilton Crockett, had used the weapon for hunting, but according to newspaper reports the rifle was going to be "retired."

   1988 A portrait of David Crockett, a coonskin cap, and a buckskin jacket adorn the apartment walls of character Frank Drebin (played by Leslie Nielsen) in *The Naked Gun: From the Files of Police Squad*, a Paramount Pictures film which debuts nationwide.

3. 1814 During the Creek War, Crockett and other Tennessee volunteers are on the march to Fort Strother, a stockade structure located at Ten

4. 1787 Birth of Mary Polly Finley, Crockett's first wife.

   1829 In a letter written in Washington City by the Honorable James Clark of Kentucky to Crockett about the frontier congressman's reported inappropriate behavior at a dinner held for President Andrew Jackson, the Bluegrass State representative stated that "in your letter of yesterday, you requested me to say if the ludicrous behavior account of your behavior when dining with the President, which you enclosed me, is true. I was at the same dinner, and know that the statement is absolutely destitute of every thing truth."

5. 1829 Crockett participates in debates over the Tennessee Land Bill in the United States House of Representatives. The proposed legislation involved the selling of western lands including some parcels which had already been improved upon by squatters, a group which Crockett represented and wanted to protect.

6. 1950 *Davy Crockett Indian Scout*, a United Artists film, starring George Montgomery as the legendary hero's nephew, debuts in movie theaters nationwide. Cast member Robert Barrat, who plays the part of James Lone Eagle, portrayed Crockett in *Man of Conquest*, a 1939 Republic Pictures release.

7. 1832 In a letter written from his home in Weakley County, Tennessee to Richard Smith, an officer in the Second Bank of the United States, Crockett asks for a modification on his loan with the financial institution. The favor that he requests is included with a reminder of his support for the bank. "I did come out in the late election in favor of the renewal of your charter and the thing [William Fitzgerald] that had the name of beating me took the Jackson ground against it," explained Crockett.

8. 1835 Crockett writes his publishers, Carey and Hart of Philadelphia: "I was with Mr. [William] Clark this morning and he [read] me what he had finished of the book [*Col. Crockett's Tour to the North and Down East*] and I have no doubt of its filling your actpectation (sic) it must sell."

January Calendar

9. 1836 Crockett departs Nacogdoches, Texas for St. Augustine, Texas where he expressed his desire to participate as a member in a forthcoming convention. "I have but little doubt of being elected a member to form a Constitution of this province," wrote Crockett to his son-in-law and daughter, Wiley and Margaret Flowers. "Do not be uneasy about me, I am among my friends."

   1950 Ted Malone, a nationally syndicated radio storyteller, features a story on the ABC network about how Davy Crockett "grinned the bark off a tree" and then used the feat for political capital.

10. 1834 In a letter written in Washington City to his oldest son, John Wesley, Crockett criticizes President Andrew Jackson, explains the benefits of the land bill to his Tennessee constituents, and describes two important events in the making. "I am engaged in writing a history of my life and have completed one hundred and ten pages," he said. "I may take a trip through the eastern States during the session of Congress and sell the book."

11. 1844 The *Boston Evening Transcript* reported: "At the Apollo Saloon, near the National Theatre, are to be seen a ball pouch worn by Davy Crockett at the battle of the Alamo."

12. 1836 At Nacogdoches, Texas, Crockett is sworn into Capt. William B. Harrison's Volunteer Auxiliary Corps company during the Texas Revolution. Despite his status as a colonel in the 57th Tennessee State Militia, Crockett elects to serve as a private in the Texas unit. A document later issued by the Republic of Texas identifies January 8, 1836 as the beginning of his service.

   1846 William Finley Crockett, the second child born to David and Polly, dies. He was thirty-six years old.

   1899 Rev. James R. Winchester delivers an address titled "David Crockett" at the Tennessee Society's annual banquet. The minister called Crockett the "pioneer statesman and warrior of Tennessee."

13. 1989 "Davy Crockett: Guardian Spirit," the second of five Walt Disney Davy Crockett production episodes, starring Tim Dunigan in the title role, debuts on NBC television.

14. 1910 In the *Albuquerque Journal* Samuel C. Mott, the manager of heavyweight champion James Jeffries' stage career, praises the boxer, who portrayed Crockett in the Frank Murdock-Frank Mayo play *Davy Crockett; Or, Be Sure Yo're Right, Then Go Ahead.* "Never failed to make a hit in the wolf scene," said Mott, "where Davy Crockett holds the door while the brutes try to get in the cabin."

    1956 Tennessee Ernie Ford's version of "The Ballad of Davy Crockett" enters the British record charts at the number eleven position.

15. 1829 In a circular directed at the "Independent Voters In The Ninth Congressional District In The State of Tennessee," Crockett explains why he offered a legislative amendment which would benefit the poor squatters against the authority of the General Assembly: "To make a short story of the whole affair, I wished you to have your homes directly from the hands of Congress, and then you could, with certainty, call them your own."

16. 1829 In a letter written by Tennessee congressman James Knox Polk to Davison McMillen of Fayetteville, Tennessee, the representative displays his contempt for Crockett's position on the Tennessee Land Bill.

17. 1834 In a letter written in Washington City to G. W. McLean, Crockett is critical of President Andrew Jackson's transfer of government deposits from the Second Bank of the United States to select state banks. "We are still engaged in discussing the great question of Jackson's kingly power in the removal of the Deposits," said Crockett. "I have no doubt of the deposits ordered back by the houses of Congress and I have as little doubt that Jackson will veto the measure, and if he does I hope Congress will teach him a lesson that will be of use to the next Tyrant that fills that chair."

18. 1890 The *Charlotte News* reports that "workmen were excavating the central Alamo plaza,[a] place within fifty yards of the famous structure which was the death place of Crockett." The excavation was one of a number of future archaeological digs that took place on the Alamo battlefield over the next 130 years.

19. 1834 Crockett writes his son, John, and informs him that he is "writing a history of my life." Months later, Philadelphia publishers Carey and Hart produced *A Narrative of the Life of David Crockett of the State of Tennessee*. The book became a best seller, and by 1837, Carey and Hart had published twenty-four editions.

20. 1828   In a letter later published in the *Jackson Gazette*, Crockett says, "Mr. [James Knox] Polk and myself are getting along very well with our vacant land bill, and I have no doubt but we shall effect a relinquishment early this session."

21. 1814   Crockett, serving as a mounted rifleman General Andrew Jackson's army during the Creek War, arrives at Emuckfaw Creek, in what is now Alabama, and establishes a camp with his fellow soldiers in anticipation of a possible attack by nearby warriors.

22. 1814   In the predawn darkness, Creek warriors attack Crockett and the rest of General Andrew Jackson's command near Emuckfaw Creek, in what is now Alabama. "The only guide we had in shooting was to notice the flash of their guns, and then shoot as directly at the place as we could guess," said Crockett in his 1834 autobiography. "In this scrape we had four men killed, and several wounded; but whether we killed any of the Indians or not we never could tell, for it is their custom always to carry off their dead, if they can possibly do so."

23. 1836   Crockett and fellow members of the Volunteer Auxiliary Corps are provisioned in Washington-on-the-Brazos, during the Texas Revolution. One month later, Crockett was at the Alamo during the first day of the siege.

24. 1814   During the Creek War, Crockett, as a member of Captain Russell's company of mounted riflemen, participates in the Battle of Enotachopco, in what is now Alabama. "We moved on till we come to a large creek which we had to cross; and about half of our men had crossed, when the Indians commenced firing on our left wing, and they kept it up very warmly," said Crockett in his 1834 autobiography. "I know I was mighty glad when it was over, and the savages quit us, for I had begun to think there was one behind every tree in the woods."

25. 1956   "Davy Crockett's Keelboat Race," starring Fess Parker in the title role, airs for the second time on Walt Disney's ABC-TV program *Disneyland*. The popular episode made its debut on November 16, 1955. Jeff York co-stars as Mike Fink, the legendary "king of the river."

26. 1955 "Davy Crockett Goes to Congress," starring Fess Parker in the title role, airs as the second episode in Walt Disney's *Davy Crockett* trilogy on ABC-TV's *Disneyland*. The episode traces Crockett's life from 1815 to 1835.

    1987 *The Alamo: 13 Days to Glory* debuts on NBC-TV with Brian Keith starring as Crockett. The actor was sixty-five years old, more than fifteen years older than Crockett was during the thirteen-day siege of the Alamo.

27. 1878 Concerned about the nation's ongoing depression, which began several years earlier, the *Memphis Daily Appeal* recommends a cautious fiscal approach for Tennessee: "We must work under Davy Crockett's motto. We must be sure we are right before we go ahead."

    1992 Fess Parker, star of Walt Disney's *Davy Crockett, King of the Wild Frontier*, leaves his hand prints and a dated signature in the cement walkway outside of the Theater of the Stars at Hollywood Studios in Walt Disney World.

28. 1834 Crockett concludes his autobiography with a statement of political independence and a criticism of Andrew Jackson by mentioning this date on page 210 of his work. "*A Narrative of the Life of David Crockett of Tennessee* was published less than two months later.

29. 1836 The *New York Sun* reports that "David Crockett has gone to Texas, and he says that he will have Santa Anna's head, and wear it for a watch seal."

30. 1835 Crockett participates in subduing Richard Lawrence after the assassin's attempt on President Andrew Jackson in Washington. Jackson was leaving a funeral for Warren Ransom Davis, a congressman from South Carolina who served with Crockett in the Twentieth and Twenty-first Congresses, when Lawrence pulled the trigger on two pistols that failed to fire.

31. 1860 Elizabeth Patton Crockett, David's second wife, dies. Her grave marker reads: "Mrs. Elizabeth Crockett/Wife of/David Crockett/Born in Buncomb Co. NC/May 22, 1788/Married to David Crockett/In Lawrence Co. Tenn. 1815/Died in Johnson Co. Now Hood Co,/Jan. 31, 1860, Age 72 Years"

FEBRUARY

1. 1819 Crockett is selected by the Lawrenceburg court to participate in "a court of Quorum for the trail of all Jury cases by ballots."

   1834 In the dated preface of his autobiography, Crockett asks readers to "just read for yourself, and my ears for a heel-tap if before you get through you don't say, with many a good-natured smile and hearty laugh, 'This is truly the very thing itself—the exact image of its Author.'"

2. 1936 John W. Thomason's illustration, *Crockett Taken Before Santa Anna*, is on display at the Fort Worth Woman's Club. The colorful image appeared two years earlier as "Crockett led before Santa Anna" in his book *The Adventures of Davy Crockett—Told Mostly by Himself*.

3. 1881 In an article about Susanna Dickinson, a non-combatant at the Alamo during the thirteen-day siege in 1836, the *Galveston News* reports that following the battle, she "beheld the flames that consumed her husband [Almaron] and of Crockett and Travis, and was instructed by Santa Anna to describe the horrible scene to Houston and his followers."

4. 1836 Crockett, his nephew William Patton, and Daniel Cloud are among the Tennessee Mounted Volunteers riding to San Antonio, Texas. The group, led by Captain William B. Harrison, are within a week's ride of the town.

5. 1828 In a letter to James Blackburn, written in Washington City, Crockett describes his recent bout of Bilious fever. "I have enjoyed the worst health since I arrived here that I ever did in my life," noted Crockett, who added that he "was taken down and lay four weeks."

   1900 Anaconda, Montana's *Anaconda Standard* praises actor Harry Sedley, who is starring in *Davy Crockett; Or, Be Sure Yo're Right, Then Go Ahead* at Sutton's Theater.

6. 1840 A letter written by William C. White, an American living in Mexico, to the *Austin City Gazette*, describes an encounter in a mine, four years after the Battle of the Alamo. A man allegedly approached White and said, "My name is David Crockett—I am from Tennessee, and have a family there—they think I am dead, and so does everyone else; but they are mistaken." White said that the man gave him a let-

ter which he asked to be sent to his family in Tennessee. According to White, Crockett was "sent together with two other men to Loredo, from which place they had been removed; with a part of the army that moved to Monterrey—and when the troops marched from Monterrey to Mexico, they went to Guadelejera (sic), and placed in a mine by the Alcalde, at which place they have been every since."

7. 1834 Crockett is given the nickname "Son of the West" by Philadelphia publishers Carey and Hart in a commercial broadside which promotes the forthcoming release of *A Narrative of the Life of Col. David Crockett of Tennessee*.

8. 1836 Crockett arrives in San Antonio during the Texas Revolution. William C. Binkley in his 1936 publication *Official Correspondence of the Texas Revolution, 1835-1836* writes that Crockett "seems to have arrived on February 7th or 8th."

9. 1836 The *Arkansas Gazette* reports that Crockett interrupted his journey to Texas and participated in a buffalo hunt after reaching the Red River. "Davy is as fond of hunting as fighting," states the newspaper.

10. 1836 A fandango is held in Crockett's honor following his arrival in San Antonio.

    1925 *The Kansas City Star* features an article titled "Davy Crockett, Dead Shot Pioneer, Who Went to Congress." The article coincided with 100th anniversary of Crockett's first run for Congress.

11. 1828 In a letter written in Washington City to James L. Totten, a Tennessee state legislator, Crockett comments favorably about Andrew Jackson and his forthcoming Presidential election campaign. "So with General Jackson the harder they rub him the brighter he shines," says Crockett.

12. 1831 In a letter written in Washington City to the Editor of Jackson, Tennessee's *Southern Statesman*, Crockett reminds all of his purpose in Congress: "It is well known to you and to them, that ever since I have been in Congress, I have been engaged in one continuous struggle, to secure to the honest poor of my district, to their wives and helpless children, their humble homes, and to afford them the means of substance, and shelter from the pitiless storm."

13. 1835 The *Vermont Phoenix* reprints an article from the *Boston Gazette* which acknowledged Crockett's ability to charm all classes of society: "Davy, with all his rudeness, is not destitute of an occasional grace of manner, and action, or something else, which commends him to the smiles of the fair, and some of the anecdotes he relates to them are abundantly ludicrous and amusing."

14. 1819 Crockett allegedly inscribes a violin with the following: "This fiddle is my property. Davy Crockett. Franklin County, Tenn. Feb. 14, 1819." The instrument is housed at the Witte Museum in San Antonio, Texas, and has been used on a few modern recordings, including Red River Dave's single "When Davy Crockett Met the San Antonio Rose" in 1955, Dean Shostak's *Davy Crockett's Fiddle* in 2002, and K. R. Wood's *Davy Crockett's Fiddle Plays On: Live at the Alamo* in 2008.

15. 1841 Representative John Wesley Crockett, the famous frontiersman's son, and fellow congressman Isaac Edwin Crary of Michigan, are successful in having their bill, H.R. 607, a land bill similar to the unsuccessful H.R. 528, passed in the House of Representatives.

16. 1828 The *Jackson Gazette* publishes parts of a letter written by Crockett in which he expresses the harmonic legislative relationship between him and fellow Tennessee congressman James Knox Polk.

17. 1829 In a letter from James K. Polk to Pryor Lea, the Tennessee congressman is critical of Crockett who "did vote with the administration men to lay on the table, the resolution of Mr. Wickliffe, which proposed that all elections in the Ho. Rept. should hereafter be viva voce, and not by ballot."

18. 1825 The *Knoxville Register* announces: "The following gentlemen are candidates for Congress in the 9th district in this state; Adam R. Alexander, David Crockett, James Terrel, Harry H. Brown, Th. H. Person."

    1894 The *Idaho Statesman* prints the recollections of Mrs. Ibbie Gordon who said she met Crockett in "the winter of 1834." Gordon said, "It has always disgusted me to read these accounts of Crockett that characterize him as an ignorant backwoodsman. Neither in dress, conversation nor bearing could he have created the impression that he was ignorant or uncouth. He was a man of wide practical information and was dignified and entertaining. His language was about as good as any we hear nowadays."

1956 Max Bygraves' version of "The Ballad of Davy Crockett" enters the British record charts. It is the fourth recording of the Blackburn-Bruns song that registered in the British Top Twenty.

19. 1834 New York's *Commercial Advertiser* announces that "Colonel Crockett is about publishing his autobiography, which is to appear, in a few days, from the press of Carey & Hart of Philadelphia."

1955 *Billboard* magazine states that Bill Hayes' 45-rpm recording of "The Ballad of Davy Crockett" should "hit the national lists shortly." The song eventually reached number one on the "Best Sellers in Stores" chart and remained there for five weeks

20. 1835 While serving in the Second Session of the Twenty-third Congress, Crockett attempts to bring up H.R.126, a land bill, which he introduced on January 2, 1834; however, the bill fails to be brought up for debate by a vote of 77-52.

21. 1835 The *Cincinnati Mirror and Western Gazette of Literature and Science* includes an observer's description of Crockett: "[He] was about six feet high—stoutly built—his hands and feet were particularly small for a man of his appearance. His complexion was swarthy; his cheek bones high; his nose large, and designed to favor as an Indian's. His hair was long, dark, and curly looking rather uncombed than carefully attended to. His pantaloons, which were fashionably cut, developed an extremely handsome limb. And his loose calico hunting shirt, ruffled around collar, cape, cuffs, and skirt, full and flowing. Set off his person as the rough and untutored woodsman, to particular advantage."

22. 1834 The *New York Mirror* prints an article titled "Davy Crockett's Own Book," which was about *A Narrative of the Life of David Crockett of Tennessee*. The article says that "His fame rolls on, increasing, like an avalanche."

23. 1836 The *New Hampshire Gazette* erroneously reports that "David Crockett is no more! He died on his way to Texas. Alas, poor Yorick!" The article appeared on the first day of the thirteen-day siege of the Alamo when Crockett was very much alive.

| | 1936 | In a centennial report about the Siege and Battle of the Alamo, *The Dallas Morning News* says, "Crockett was then 50 years old and to the defenders of the Alamo the most famous person in their midst. Travis in one of his letters proudly refers to the presence of the 'Hon. David Crockett.'" |

1955 "Davy Crockett at the Alamo," the third and final episode of the *Davy Crockett* trilogy, debuts on ABC-TV's *Disneyland*.

24. 1836 The *Rhode Island Republican* erroneously reports that Crockett died in Texas on February 17, six days before the siege of the Alamo began.

25. 1836 During the siege of the Alamo, in a letter to Maj. Gen. Sam Houston, Alamo commander Lt. Col. William B. Travis describes Crockett as being "seen at all points, animating the men to do their duty."

26. 1834 According to the Worcester *Massachusetts Spy*, Crockett described the House of Representatives' Committee of Way and Means as a nine-pin: "Large at the middle, and small at both ends." Crockett's "middle" were Benjamin Gorham of Massachusetts, Horace Binney of Pennsylvania, and Richard Henry Wilde of Georgia. The "ends" were James Knox Polk of Tennessee and Henry Hubbard of New Hampshire.

1955 Bill Hayes' recording of "The Ballad of Davy Crockett" enters *Billboard* magazine's "Best Sellers in Stores" chart at the number sixteen position.

27. 1836 Bellefontaine, Ohio's *Western Aurora And Farmers and Mechanics Advocate* prints an article titled "Crockett's Successor," which included the following statement: "It is well known that Davy Crockett did not regret his defeat as a candidate for Congress so much as he did his being beaten by one Adam Huntsman."

28. 1831 A sixteen-page David Crockett Circular describes the Tennessean's criticism of Congressional spending and President Andrew Jackson's treatment of American Indians. "I wish that the waste of public money and neglect of promises made by General Jackson were the only charges that could be made against his Administration," said Crockett, who represented his state's Ninth Congressional District.

"My heart bleeds when I reflect on his cruelty to the poor unprotected Indians."

1834   In a letter written in Washington City to Mary Barney, the former editor of the anti-Jackson *National Magazine, or Ladies Emporium*, Crockett speculates about the ongoing conflict between two United States Senators, George Poindexter of Mississippi and John Forsyth of Georgia. "We had a controversy in the Senate this morning between two of the Honourables Mr. Poindexter and Mr. Forsyth," wrote Crockett. "It is believed it will end in a duel."

29. 1836   According to the diary entry mentioned in *The Life of David Crockett: The Original Humorist and Irrepressible Backwoodsman*, Crockett writes that he shot five Mexican artillerists who attempted to fire their gun at the Alamo. "And then the whole party gave it up as a bad job, and hurried off to the camp, leaving the cannon ready charged where they had planted it," remarked Crockett.

MARCH

1. 1997   The Keene Gallery in San Antonio, Texas debuts its Thom Ross painting exhibit, which includes such canvases as *Davy Crockett and His Fiddle* and *Davy at the Doorway*.

2. 1986   Walter Blair's "'Bout Time 'ol Davy Crockett Got Borned Again" article appears in the *Chicago Sun-Times*. His piece coincided with the sesquicentennial of the Siege and Battle of the Alamo.

    2002   The "Sunrise in his Pocket: The Life, Legend and Legacy of Davy Crockett" exhibit opens to the general public at the Bob Bullock Texas State History Museum in Austin, Texas. The museum hosted a symposium, offered a new set of Crockett collectibles in its gift shop, and featured an edited version of the Gary Foreman-directed History Channel production *Boone & Crockett: The Hunter Heroes*, which was shown continuously on a video monitor. The exhibit, which Fess Parker, star of *Davy Crockett, King of the Wild Frontier* visited, ran until August 18, 2002.

3. 1830   Crockett writes a letter to Secretary of State Martin Van Buren and criticizes him over not being consulted about a constituent's loss of business activity. "I have recently been much surprised upon the re-

ception of a letter from one of my constituents, informing me that without knowing why or wherefore, the printing of the Laws of the United States had been taken from him and bestowed upon another," wrote Crockett. "You have removed a man who was the first Editor of a newspaper within that District, and a warm friend of the present Chief Magistrate, and appointed one who had junior claims."

4. 1836 The *Mississippi Free Trader and Natchez Gazette* reports that "Col. Crockett visited St. Augustine [Texas] and met with a very warm and cordial reception from the citizens of that place, who earnestly solicited him to become a candidate to represent them in the next convention."

    2007 Fess Parker, star of Walt Disney's *Davy Crockett, King of the Wild Frontier*, receives the Walter E. Disney Lifetime Achievement award from the Carolwood Historical Society. The award was later displayed on a wall in Parker's Los Olivos, California office.

5. 1873 The *San Francisco Bulletin* publishes an article titled "David Crockett: His True Character Very Different from the Vulgar Ideal of Him"

    2004 Fess Parker donates the 19th century flintlock rifle that was given to him at a 1955 Philadelphia ceremony to the Alamo. The event recalled the Young Whigs' presentation of a new rifle that was given to Crockett in Philadelphia in 1834.

6. 1836 Crockett dies at the Alamo.

    1988 *Alamo...The Price of Freedom* premieres as an invitation-only event in San Antonio, Texas. Merrill Connally, at age sixty-six, becomes the oldest motion picture actor to portray Davy Crockett.

7. 1955 At the Emmy Awards ceremony held at the Moulin Rouge Nightclub in Hollywood, Fess Parker, Disney's *Davy Crockett*, is upstaged by fellow actor George Gobel, who wins TV's "Most Outstanding New Personality" award.

8. 1834 In a letter written in Washington City to Philadelphia book publishers Carey and Hart, Crockett introduces them to Mr. Lewis, a merchant who lived in the congressman's district. "He may wish to purchase some of the books that you are publishing—I mean my narrative," said Crockett.

9. 1941 The *Seattle Daily Times* announces that Erma Davis, a member of the University of Washington faculty, will deliver an address about "Davy Crockett" at a forthcoming folk and patriotic musical function in the city.

    1955 Four versions of "The Ballad of Davy Crockett" are listed on *Billboard* magazine's "Best Sellers in Stores" chart: Bill Hayes (# 2), Fess Parker (# 7), Tennessee Ernie Ford (# 8), and Walter Schumann (# 29).

10. 1948 The *San Antonio Light* reports that prior to filming *Three Godfathers*, John Wayne, director John Ford arrived in San Antonio to begin some film location scouting. During a visit to the Alamo, Wayne mentions to the press that he is interested in making an Alamo movie; Ford indicates that Wayne would play Crockett.

11. 1828 In a letter written in Washington City to Captain Robert Seat, Crockett tells his friend about the difficulty in passing tariff reform legislation. "There is so much party feeling...here that it is with great difficulty to do anything," says the Tennessean.

12. 1831 Trenton, New Jersey's *Emporium and True American* reports that "Davy Crockett, the half horse, half alligator, from the wilds of Tennessee, as the Coalition papers used to call him, has recently declared on the floor of Congress that 'Jackson is not a Jackson man,' and his enemies are in ecstasies. Davy, like some other wild men, has had his head turned by getting into the white house, and the best of the joke will be, that when he goes home to his constituents he will find to his sorrow that for once in his life he has 'barked up the wrong tree.'"

    1955 Fess Parker's version of "The Ballad of Davy Crockett" debuts on *Billboard* magazine's "Best Sellers in Stores" chart in the number sixteen position; Bill Hayes' recording of the tune climbs to number six.

13. 1836 Susanna Dickinson, an Alamo survivor, reports the death of her husband, Almaron; Crockett; Travis; Bowie; and the rest of the garrison to General Sam Houston.

14. 1828 In a letter written in Washington City to the Editor of the *Jackson Gazette*, Crockett explains his desire to introduce his vacant land bill. "I am doing the best I can to promote the welfare and interest of my district," said Crockett.

15. 1999 In an *People* magazine interview, filmmaker Steven Spielberg acknowledges the importance of Crockett's "Be sure you're right, then go ahead" motto. "That was the Davy Crockett motto and I've lived by it all my life," said Spielberg.

16. 1828 In a letter written in Washington City to Dr. Cahern, Crockett expresses his disappointment in how specific pieces of proposed legislation can affect the operation of the House of Representatives. "I have no news, we are doing nothing here worth your attention only discussing the Tariff," remarked Crockett. "I have no idea when we will get rid of it. It keeps down all other business."

    1863 The *Indiana State Sentinel* stated: "Everybody, young and old, has heard of David Crockett, and some of his printed sayings are matters of every day reference."

17. 1940 In a review of Richard M. Dorson's *David Crockett: American Frontier Legend,* Kentucky's *Lexington Leader* noted that "David Crockett, Tennessean member of Congress, was in person an interesting enough individual but Davy Crockett, frontier comedian, is the handiwork of many hands."

    1970 Fess Parker appears as Davy Crockett in comedy sketch titled "He Died With His Boots On Cause He Had Cold Feet To Start or He Died With His Boots Off, That's Why He Stubbed His Toe" on CBS-TV's *The Red Skelton Show*.

18. 1994 Portraits of Crockett are mounted on the apartment walls of character Lt. Frank Drebin, played by actor Leslie Nielsen, in *Naked Gun 33 1/3: The Final Insult*, a Parmount Pictures production directed by Peter Segal and co-produced by David Zucker, which opens in theaters nationwide.

19. 1834 The *Vermont Advocate* reports that "Davy Crockett announces that he 'neither seeks nor declines office.' He is perfectly willing that all of his friends, who will support him for President, 'go ahead.'"

    1955 Bill Hayes' "The Ballad if Davy Crockett" reaches the number three position on *Billboard* magazine's "Best Sellers in Stores" chart. The roster of recordings also includes Fess Parker's version at number eleven. Tennessee Ernie Ford's rendition of the song enters the chart at number nineteen.

	2005	"Davy Crockett's Tall Tales," an amusement ride, opens on Alamo Plaza in San Antonio, Texas. The ride depicts various episodes in Crockett's life but concentrates on his association with a bear called Death Hug. The ride closed several years later.
20.	1959	Fess Parker makes an uncredited cameo appearance as Davy Crockett during a Western shoot-out sequence in *Alias Jesse James,* a Bob Hope comedy which debuts in theaters nationwide.
21.	1821	Crockett begins a three-month horse drove to the home of Robert Patton, his father-in-law, who lived in Swannanoa, North Carolina.
	1829	Crockett criticizes fellow congressman Pryor Lea in a letter, which is reprinted in the *Jackson Gazette*. "It pained me to the heart to find out that I had been so much disappointed in you, and that while I had cherished you in my affections as a friend, you were planning my destruction as a foe," said Crockett.
22.	1834	The *Boston Morning Post* prints an advertisement promoting "Oratorical Imitations and Improvisations," a one-man show starring John C. Mossie, who specialized in an imitation of Crockett.
23.	1873	The *Chicago Daily Tribune* announces that "Mr. Frank Mayo, one of the finest actors on the American stage, will appear in the powerful and successful drama, written expressly for him by Frank Murdock, and entitled 'Davy Crockett; or, Be Sure You're Right, Then Go Ahead.' at the city's Academy of Music for a week-long stand.
	1879	Rebecca Elvira Crockett, the second child born to David and Elizabeth, dies. She was sixty-years old.
24.	1833	The Twenty-first Congress of the United States begins; Crockett represents the Ninth District as an Anti-Jacksonian.
25.	1834	In a letter written in Washington City to Philadelphia book publishers Carey and Hart, Crockett explains the financial impact of his last election campaign. "I was beaten the election before last and it give me a back set in money matters," he remarked. "An election costs a man a great deal in my country."
26.	1955	Bill Hayes' "The Ballad of Davy Crockett" tops *Billboard* magazine's "Best Sellers in Stores" chart. Fess Parker's version of the song climbs to the number seven position; Tennessee Ernie Ford's cover of the same tune reaches number seventeen.

	2004	The *USA Today* prints "Hats Off to 'Davy,' Fess Parker: 50th Anniversary of 'Crockett' Legend." The article describes his TV and film career, his winery, and hotel building plans.
27.	1815	Crockett ends his military service during the Creek War as a fourth sergeant.
	1818	Crockett is elected colonel of the 57th Regiment of Militia in Lawrence County.
	1836	The *New York Sunday Morning News* reports that "Colonel Crockett whose death was reported some time since, is said to be alive and kicking. He has expressed his determination to grin all the Mexicans out of Texas."
28.	1836	The *Louisiana Advertiser* describes Crockett's fate at the Alamo: "Col. Crockett is among the slain...[He] fell like a tiger."
	1836	The *Stamford Sentinel* reports that "Col. David Crockett is yet alive and kicking. Information has been received from him very recently. He had been a Coon hunting among the Rocky Mountains, and is expected home soon."
29.	1961	*The Alamo*, starring John Wayne as Crockett, opens in wide-screen theaters in Los Angeles. The film is an edited version of the 1960 original.
30.	2004	Fess Parker, star of Walt Disney's *Davy Crockett, King of the Wild Frontier*, is the guest of honor at the "Fess Parker—Celebrating an American Icon" at the Smithsonian Institution's Museum of American History.
31.	1899	In an article about the Battle of the Alamo, based on the alleged recollection of Madam Candelaria, Indiana's *Evansville Journal* states that "David Crockett was a native of Tennessee and a typical frontiersman, famous as a mighty huntsman."
	1956	Fess Parker, star of Walt Disney's *Davy Crockett, King of the Wild Frontier*, arrives in London, England on a promotional tour.

APRIL

1. 1818   Crockett serves as a Lawrenceburg, Tennessee town commissioner and hears five depositions brought before him.

2. 1876   The *Chicago Tribune* mentions Frank Mayo's recent Washington D.C. performance as *Davy Crockett* in an article about some of the nation's most popular actors, including Edwin Booth, brother of John Wilkes Booth, who had played Hamlet in Cincinnati.

   1955   Bill Hayes' "The Ballad of Davy Crockett" remains at the top of *Billboard* magazine's "Best Sellers in Stores chart. Fess Parker's version of the song climbs to the number six position. Tennessee Ernie Ford's recording of the tune falls to the tenth spot.

3. 1847   Honolulu's *The Polynesian* prints an account of an exchange between some Americans and Pope Gregory XVI in Rome: "He wanted to know if David Crockett was a real or fictitious being, and considered him the most original character, except Falstaff."

4. 1822   Crockett has a debt judgment against him extended to include his other assets.

   1836   The *Farmer's Cabinet* reports that "Crockett, so far famed in the United States, is said to have performed wonders of chivalry [at the Alamo.]"

5. 1836   The *Monroe Democrat* erroneously states: "We are happy to state, on the authority of a letter from Tennessee, that the report of the death of the eccentric Davy Crockett is not true."

6. 1800   Crockett travels to Baltimore with Adam Myers, a wagoner. Crockett was fascinated by the ships in the harbor. "While I was there, I went, one day, down to the wharf, and was much delighted to see the big ships, and their sails all flying," noted Crockett in his autobiography.

7. 1836   The *New York Mercury* reports: "that Davy Crockett is among the heroes who volunteered to defend the [Alamo], well knowing that in case of capture, which is by no means improbable, they will all be massacred."

8. 1876   Massachusetts' *Springfield Republican* reports that "Robert H. Crockett, grandson of the famous Davy Crockett, will take with him to Philadelphia the rifle presented to his grandfather in that city, 41 years ago." The rifle was actually presented forty-two years earlier.

	1994	In a memo written by motion picture director David Zucker to the editor of *The Crockett Chronicle*, a journal dedicated to the life and legend of David Crockett, the filmmaker acknowledges making some historical corrections to his screenplay about the legendary frontier hero. Unfortunately, the film was never made.
9.	1834	Crockett writes to his friend Hiram Favor that he will be touring the northeastern states. "I have had a desire to travel through your country mearly [sic] as a curiosity as I have been raised entirely in a frontear [sic] country and that it is natural for me to have a desire to become acquainted with the customs and habits of your country," wrote Crockett.
	1955	Bill Hayes' "The Ballad of Davy Crockett" remains at the top of *Billboard* magazine's "Best Sellers in Stores" chart. Fess Parker's recording of the song is at number seven, and Tennessee Ernie Ford's adaptation is at number nine.
	2004	Disney's *The Alamo* debuts in the United States with Billy Bob Thornton starring as David Crockett. In one scene, Thornton's Crockett admits to Jim Bowie that problems arise when people view him as a larger-than-life personality rather than a common man. "If it was just me, simple old David from Tennessee, I might drop over that wall some night, take my chances. But that Davy Crockett feller—they're all watchin' him," he said.
10.	2000	Scott Wickware portrays Crockett in *Dear America: A Line in the Sand*, a Scholastic Productions short which debuts on HBO. Wickware's Crockett wears a coonskin cap and sports a drooping handlebar mustache.
11.	1836	The *New York Evening Post* reports Crockett's fate at the Alamo: "We regret to say, that Col. David Crockett and his companion, also the gallant Col. Benham (sic), of South Carolina, were of the number who cried for quarter, but were told there was no mercy for them. Then they continued fighting until the whole were butchered."
12.	1836	The *Richmond Enquirer* identifies Crockett as one of "a number of officers who distinguished themselves" in a "gallant repulse" of an attacking Mexican force at the Alamo.
13.	1955	Due to popular demand, Walt Disney rebroadcasts "Davy Crockett, Indian Fighter" on ABC-TV's *Disneyland*. The program originally aired on December 15, 1954.

14. 1834 In a letter to Jacob Dixon, Crockett makes references to "banking and faro dealing," which suggests that the frontier congressman may have engaged in gambling activities.

15. 1830 In a letter written in Washington City to the *Jackson Gazette*, Crockett points out his support of squatters' rights by inserting language in proposed legislation affecting the sale of federal government lands. "I done this to prevent the State from selecting lands that are not settled, to get a higher price than 12 ½ cents per acre—my object is to provide for the occupants, and my opinion is that if I pass the bill now before Congress, I will effect the object," said Crockett.

    1848 The *Boston Semi-Weekly Atlas* quips, "As David Crockett said of President [John Quincy] Adams' olives and champaigne (sic)—'I like your pickles, but curse your cider,'—I may say, the Mexican belles are beautiful enough, but confound their fandangoes."

16. 1955 Bill Hayes' "The Ballad of Davy Crockett" remains at the top of *Billboard* magazine's "Best Sellers in Stores" chart for the fourth straight week. Fess Parker's recording of the song is at number six, and Tennessee Ernie Ford's version of the tune is at number nine.

    1995 John Schneider portrays Crockett in *James A. Michener's "Texas,"* a two-part TV mini-series which debuts on ABC-TV. Schneider, thirty-four at the time of filming, was fifteen years younger than Crockett was when the famous Tennessean was at the Alamo.

17. 1836 *The New York Times* reports that "Davy Crockett is fighting like a wildcat in the cause of the Texians [at the Alamo]."

    1939 Ernie Pyle's syndicated column in the *Miami Herald* provides an update on Ashley Wilson Crockett, the famous frontiersman's grandson, who was living in Granbury, Texas. According to Pyle, Crockett, 82, lives with his daughter and son-in-law. "There aren't any Davy Crockett relics around, though," noted Pyle, who added that four decades earlier Ashley Crockett made his only visit to the Alamo.

18. 1829 In a letter to Gales and Seaton, Crockett states that "Governor Houston has parted with his wife and resigned the governor's appointment. He told me that he was going to leave the country and

go up the Arkansas [River] and live with the Indians, as he calls them his adopted brothers."

    2004   David Herman is the voice of the animated Davy Crockett in an episode of the Fox network's *King of The Hill* titled "How I Learned to Stop Worrying and Love the Alamo."

19. 1936   *The Houston Chronicle* calls Crockett "the 'Poor Richard' of backwoods America, an acknowledgment of the almanac and autobiography connection between the frontier congressman and Benjamin Franklin.

    1956   Fess Parker, star of Walt Disney's *Davy Crockett, King of the Wild Frontier*, arrives in Cardiff, England, during his promotional tour of Europe.

    1986   The *Knoxville Journal* publishes Doug Morris' "Don't Go Trashing Davy Crockett," a followup to the newspaper's April 17, 1986 article, "Professor Shoots Holes in Crockett Myth."

20. 1956   Fess Parker, star of Walt Disney's *Davy Crockett, King of the Wild Frontier*, returns to London, England, during his promotional tour of Europe.

21. 1910   *Davy Crockett*, a black and white silent film featuring Hobart Bosworth, debuts.

    1958   The Crockett Tavern Museum, a reconstructed log cabin based on an original Crockett home, opens in Morristown, Tennessee.

22. 1822   Representative David Crockett returns to an "extraordinary session" of the Tennessee General Assembly, which was called by Governor William Carroll.

23. 1955   Bill Hayes' "The Ballad of Davy Crockett" rests at the top of *Billboard* magazine's "Best Sellers in Stores" chart for the fifth week in a row. Fess Parker's recording of the song remains at number six, and Tennessee Ernie Ford's rendition is at number seven.

    1992   A character in *The Simpsons'* episode "The Otto Show" sees Homer Simpson, who is wearing an old fringed jacket, and exclaims, "There goes Davy Crockett and his baldskin cap."

24. 1828   During Crockett's first session of the Twentieth Congress, H.R. 27, a land bill, is debated but eventually tabled on May 1, 1828.

25. 1831 *The Lion of the West*, starring James Hackett as the Crockett-like Nimrod Wildfire, opens in New York City.

    1834 Crockett begins his tour of the northeastern states. The sojourn will later be described in *An Account of Col. Crockett's Tour to the North and Down East*, which was written by Crockett and William Clark.

    1955 *Life* magazine publishes "U. S. Again Is Subdued By Davy," a multi-page article on the historical Crockett and Walt Disney's *Davy Crockett* craze.

26. 1834 Crockett takes his first railroad ride, a seventeen mile journey in Delaware, while traveling to Philadelphia. Upon arrival at his destination, he delivers an informal speech to a crowd that had gathered at the United States Hotel, where he was staying. "My visit to your city is rather accidental," he said. "I had no expectation of attracting any uncommon attention. I am traveling for my health, without the least wish of exciting the people in such times of high political feeling."

    1836 The *Albany Evening Journal* reprints the following report about the Battle of the Alamo: "The famous Davy Crockett was in the fort, and when the Mexicans entered, was sick in bed. He however called for his arms, with which he killed fourteen Mexicans, and then throwing them down resigned himself to his fate."

27. 1836 The *Memphis Enquirer* prints a tribute to Crockett, following his death at the Alamo: "A general expression of deep sympathy pervades the press, over the lamentable fall of Col. Crockett. Though not a great, he was an honest, noble, generous, brave and good man. No stranger left him in hunger or naked, if he had an ear of corn or a sixpence to divide with his suffering brother. His political life rendered him obnoxious to his opposition, whose weapons of distraction were sped at him even while pouring out his blood in the cause of oppressed humanity, upon the walls of the Alamo."

28. 1958 George Dunn portrays Crockett in "A Night in Tennessee," an episode in *The Adventures of Jim Bowie* TV series.

29. 1834 During his tour of the northeastern states, Crockett departs Philadelphia and sails on the Delaware River on the *New Philadelphia* to Camden, New Jersey where he boards the Camden and Amboy

		Railroad for a steam locomotive ride to South Amboy, New Jersey. He later takes a boat to Manhattan.
	1836	The *Gloucester Democrat* issued the following about the Battle of the Alamo: "A writer from Texas says, that when fort Bexar was taken, Col. Davy Crockett was sick in bed, but he just got up, took his rifle and killed fourteen Mexicans, and then agreed to be shot."
30.	1955	Due to popular demand, Walt Disney rebroadcasts "Davy Crockett Goes to Congress" on ABC-TV's *Disneyland*. The original episode aired on January 26, 1955. The April 30-May 6, 1955 issue of *TV Guide* features a photo of Fess Parker and Buddy Ebsen on the cover.
	1955	After five weeks at the top of *Billboard* magazine's "Best Sellers in Stores" chart, Bill Hayes' "The Ballad of Davy Crockett" falls to the number two position; however, the song is at the top of the "Most Played in Juke Boxes" chart and the "Most Played by [Disc] Jockeys' roster. Tennessee Ernie Ford's adaptation reaches the number six position; Fess Parker's version of the song occupies the number seven slot.
	2005	The Alamo Society hosts its first Fandango at the Crockett Tavern in Walt Disney World's Fort Wilderness Campground in honor of the 50th anniversary of *Davy Crockett, King of the Wild Frontier's* theatrical release.

MAY

1.	1836	The *New York Sunday Morning News* prints "David Crockett is Dead" and follows with an extensive tribute, which includes the following passages: "He was brave, and had the ardent soul of a warrior. He knew that military renown was more rapidly acquired, if acquired at all, than any other. One bold adventure has fixed the soldier's fate—either sent him to sleep in the bed of honour or raised him to fame and power. Reasoning thus, he went 'ahead.' Nor was his destiny long doubtful; he met the enemy and boldly died."
2.	1834	Crockett participates in a rifle frolic in Jersey City, New Jersey. His clothing is adorned with a cameo pin which features an image of George Washington. "He shot well on that occasion, but complained that the gun was different from those he had been accustomed to," said Guy Maxwell Hinchman, an observer.

1836 The *New York Sun* publishes an erroneous report about Crockett's fate at the Alamo. "We are much gratified in being able to inform our readers that Col. Crockett, the hero and patriot, it is said is not dead yet," stated the newspaper. "This cheering news is brought by a gentleman now in this city, directly from Texas, and who left the Colonel, as he states, three weeks ago, at the house of his brother-in-law in Texas, where the Colonel was lying quite ill, but gradually though slowly recovering from his wounds. The gentleman who brings this news is known to a number of our citizens, who believe him to be a man of veracity. He states that Crockett was left upon the battle ground at San Antonio covered with wounds, and as the Mexicans supposed, dead. That after the Mexicans had abandoned the place, Crockett was discovered by some of his acquaintances to be lying among the slain, still exhibiting signs of life. He was immediately taken care of, and conveyed to comfortable lodgings where his wounds were dressed."

3. 1831 Crockett signs a sixty-day promissory note for $600 to R. E. B. Taylor. The document was sold an auction in 2003 for $9,500.

1836 The *Arkansas Gazette* reports on Crockett's weapons inventory and their effectiveness during the Siege and Battle of the Alamo: "David Crockett had fortified himself with sixteen guns well charged, and a monument of slain foes encompassed his lifeless body."

1930 *Davy Crockett* is performed by Hank Simmons and his *Show Boat* company on the Columbia broadcast system. An ad in the *Cincinnati Post,* which promoted radio station program on WKRC, describes Crockett as "a backwoodsman who could neither read nor write" and "a great hero who was unconscious of his heroism."

4. 1818 Crockett serves as a Giles County, Tennessee court referee.

1890 The *Springfield Republican* reports that "Frank Mayo's audience at the performance of 'Davy Crockett' at the Opera house last evening was very good sized and of superior quality. Mr. Mayo's work in the role needs no extended notice."

5. 1836 The *New York Evening Star* states that "the brave Travis, Bowie and Crockett, made the [Alamo] seem to Santa Anna's eye peopled with innumerable hosts."

May Calendar

	2014	The *Fort Worth Star-Telegram* challenges its most educated readers when it prints a quiz that includes the following question: "Which of these famous historical figures was not at the Battle of the Alamo: A) David Crockett, B) Jim Bowie, C) William B. Travis, D) John Wayne." The newspaper didn't even provide a hint.
6.	1834	The *Boston Evening Transcript* reports that Crockett is sitting for Boston artist Chester Harding.
	1840	The *Gloucester Telegraph* reports that John W. Crockett, the famous frontiersman's eldest son, "has started to Mexico, with a view to regain his father [from his captivity in the mines]." The Mexico mine story was repeated in *Ben Hardin's Crockett Almanac of 1842*. In the almanacs, Hardin, a fictitious sailor, was Crockett's sidekick.
	1955	The *Corpus Christi Times* reports that David Crockett, 55, the son of Ashley Wilson Crockett and the great-grandson of David Crockett, has been getting numerous phone calls at his accounting office about the legendary frontiersman ever since the Walt Disney *Davy Crockett* series debuted on TV. According to the newspaper, many of the calls are from children who ask him to sing "The Ballad of Davy Crockett," and, without hesitation, he complies. "They must find my name in the phone book," said the accountant.
7.	1834	Crockett visits the water-powered mills at Lowell, Massachusetts during his tour of the northeastern states.
8.	1834	Crockett recalls how he was perceived by those in attendance at Tremont Theatre in Boston. "Having been invited to the theatre, I went over and sat a short time to be looked at. I was very genteel and quiet, and so I suppose I disappointed some of them, who expected to see a half horse half alligator sort of a fellow," said Crockett.
	1904	In a front page article titled "True Story of the Alamo Hero," Council Bluffs, Iowa's *Daily Nonpareil* states that "American history pulsates with the brilliant achievement of her sons, and of all the early pioneers and patriots who offered their lives that the spirit of freedom might not perish, there is no name deserving of higher veneration than David Crockett."
9.	1955	In advance of the release of Walt Disney's *Davy Crockett, King of the Wild Frontier*, the feature film that was created from edited portions of the three *Davy Crockett* TV episodes, a syndicated newspaper ar-

ticle states: "As American as his pioneer counterpart is Fess Parker, the Davy Crockett of movie land."

10. 1860 The York, South Carolina *Yorkville Enquirer* publishes a tribute piece to "Col. David Crockett" which mentions that his name "brings to mind a variety of stories of how he 'chawed alligators,' 'grinned the bark off knotty trees' or 'strode a swift streak of lightning' and other performances and adventures of this class."

    1877 The 1,000th production of *Davy Crockett; Or, be Sure You're Right, Then Go Ahead*, starring Frank Mayo, is performed in Rochester, New York.

11. 1955 Due to popular demand, Walt Disney rebroadcasts "Davy Crockett at the Alamo" on ABC-TV's *Disneyland*. The original episode aired on February 23, 1955.

12. 1907 In an interview published in the *San Antonio Express*, Alamo survivor Enrique Esparza describes Crockett during the Siege and Battle of the Alamo. "Crockett seemed to be the leading spirit," said Esparza. "He was everywhere. He went to every exposed point and personally directed the fighting. Travis was chief in command but he depended more on the judgment of Crockett and that brave man's intrepidity than upon his own."

    1997 Gordon Sterne portrays a character named Davy Crockett in episode "#1.1" in the British TV miniseries *Melissa*.

13. 1834 During his tour of the northeastern states, Crockett arrives in Baltimore, where he had first visited in 1800.

    1845 Massachusetts' *Springfield Republican* reports that Seth R. Snow of the packet whaler *David Crockett* was killed by a whale off the coast of Race Point in Provincetown when the creature turned upon one of the whale boats, "utterly demolishing it, killing instantly, Mr. Snow, leaving the others afloat in the water."

14. 1834 Philadelphia's *Commercial Intelligencer and Literary and Political Journal* reports that "David Crockett is not only a man of parts himself, but he awakens genius in others. The light from his jolly face plays into the soul of a bystander, and rouses it to harmony, like the smile of the ancient sun, on the Egyptian Memnon. His

humor is infectious, one cannot be long about him without feeling the premonitory symptoms of a joke."

    2006   Thomas R. Bond's *Davy Crockett: American Hero*, an American Mutoscope & Biograph Co. film, fails to start pre-production. Lee Horsely was slated to play Crockett. The film was never made.

15. 1939   *Man of Conquest*, a biographical film about Sam Houston, debuts in theaters nationwide. The Republic Pictures production features Robert Barrat as Crockett.

16. 1819   Crockett submits his findings while serving as a census taker in Lawrenceburg, Tennessee.

    1836   The *Boston Courier* mentions Crockett in an article about the possibility of going to war with Mexico. "If we must have a war with Mexico, let us be prepared for it—let us go into it calmly and deliberately—let us not leap into it hap-hazard to gratify the appeals of General Houston, and others, or to lay the ghost of Davy Crockett," noted the newspaper.

17. 1997   The *Gullywhumper*, one of Walt Disney World's Mike Fink Keel Boats, named after a similar vessel featured in Walt Disney's "Davy Crockett's Keelboat Race," tips over with guests aboard. The unsteady keel boat and its companion craft, the *Bertha Mae*, were permanently removed from service.

18. 1889   The *Boston Daily Advertiser* announces that "the distinguished actor Frank Mayo comes next week to the stage of the Boston Theatre in his charming backwoods idyll, Davy Crockett. The drama holds the interest of the audience throughout."

    1915   *Davy Crockett*, a black and white silent comedy, debuts.

19. 1830   Crockett delivers a speech in Congress explaining his opposition to the Indian Removal Bill.

    1831   Crockett sells some of his property to pay off a debt which originated from a legal suit.

    1971   The Davy Crockett's Explorer Canoes attraction debuts at Disneyland. Each canoe is steered by a coonskin cap-wearing cast member and powered by the participating guests who handle the paddles. The attraction existed since July 4, 1956 as the Indian War Canoes but was renamed in 1971.

20. 1830   In a letter written in Washington City, and later published in the *United States Telegraph* on May 25, 1830, Crockett asks the newspaper to correct the following published statement concerning the Indian Removal Bill: "Mr. Crockett also spoke in opposition to it, stating that, although four counties of his Congressional district, adjoined the Chickasaw nation of Indians, he was opposed in conscience to the measure; and such being the case, he cared not what his constituents thought of his conduct." Crockett replied with, "I request it, Sir, as an act of justice, that the error be corrected, as I never hurl defiance at those whose servant I am. I said that my conscience should be my guide, regardless of the opposition of any colleagues, or any other consequence as to myself, and that I believed if my constituents were here, they would justify my vote."

    1934   Ashley Wilson Crockett, son of Robert Patton Crockett and grandson of David Crockett, delivers an address at the gravesite of Elizabeth Patton Crockett, David Crockett's second wife, at the Acton Cemetery in Granbury, Texas.

21. 1815   Crockett is elected a lieutenant in the 32nd Regiment of the Tennessee State Militia.

22. 1788   Elizabeth Patton, Crockett's second wife, is born. Twenty-seven years later, Patton and Crockett marry, following the death of his first wife, Polly Finley Crockett.

    1860   The *Memphis Daily Advance* reports that one of the city's fire department hose carriages, the *Davy Crockett*, "was draped in mourning, the bells muffled" in honor of William A. Kelly, a fire fighter who lost his life in a recent blaze.

23. 1831   The *New-Hampshire Patriot and State Gazette* adds to the early development of the Crockett legend when it noted that "Davy is upwards of six feet high, erect in his posture, and has a nose extremely red, after taking some spirits. He possesses vast bodily powers, great activity, and can leap the Ohio, wade the Mississippi, and carry one steam and two flat boats on his back. He can vault across a streak of lightning, ride it down a honey locust; grease his heels, skate down a rainbow and whip his weight in wild cats and panthers."

May Calendar

24. 1941   The *Fort Worth Star-Telegram* reports that Ashley Wilson Crockett, the eighty-three-year-old grandson of David Crockett, filed to run for the United States Senate, in a special election scheduled for June 28, 1941. According to the newspaper, over twenty candidates filed for the position, which was occupied at the time by Andrew Jackson Houston, 86, the son of Sam Houston, who had been appointed to the Senate following the death of incumbent Morris Shepard. However, W. Lee O'Daniel won the special election in 1941, and was later elected to a full term in 1942. A victory by the octogenarian would have marked the third time that a Crockett served in Congress. In the 1920s, O'Daniel and his band, the Light Crust Doughboys, were radio favorites of Fess Parker, who later became Walt Disney's *Davy Crockett, King of the Wild Frontier*.

    1953   Davy Crockett is depicted in "The Defense of the Alamo," an episode of You Are There, a TV program which featured modern reporters who were placed back in time at important historical events.

25. 1825   A fictional letter is written by George Russel, Davy Crockett's sidekick, about a shooting match between Crockett and Big Foot Mason in which the famous backwoodsman fired two consecutive shots in the same small bullseye target. The letter rests upon a obscure shelf in one of the dining rooms at the Pecos Bill Tall Tale Inn & Cafe in Walt Disney World's Frontierland.

    1911   *The Immortal Alamo*, a Star Film Company production, is released in the United States with Francis Ford allegedly starring as Davy Crockett. However, it is not certain that Ford actually played the part in the lost film.

    1955   *Davy Crockett, King of the Wild Frontier*, starring Fess Parker, debuts in American movie theaters. The theatrical release is an edited version of the three original television episodes ("Davy Crockett, Indian Fighter," "Davy Crockett goes to Congress," and "Davy Crockett at the Alamo") which aired on ABC-TV's *Disneyland*.

26. 1829   In a letter to John Bryan, a former member of Congress from North Carolina, Crockett optimistically describes his chances in the next congressional election. "I have no doubt of getting a much larger majority in the very next race," said Crockett.

	1859	Honolulu Hawaii's *Pacific Commercial Advertiser* includes an anecdote about Crockett's observations about dining habits in Washington: "Members of the House, said he, dine not at the good old fashioned hour of noon, but at 3 o'clock in the afternoon; Senators at 5; and the Cabinet at 7 p. m. 'And the President,' inquired one of his auditory, 'when does he dine?' Oh, said Mr. Crockett, he doesn't take dinner till the next day."
27.	2006	The Second Annual Alamo Society Fandango is held at the Crockett Tavern in Walt Disney World's Fort Wilderness. John Lee Hancock, director of *The Alamo* (2004) and Fess Parker, star of *Davy Crockett, King of the Wild Frontier*, write welcome messages in the programs. "So happy you will be having a Crockett get together," wrote Parker. "Davy would say of Florida today: Good thing the Grizzlies are not as plentiful as the alligators!"
28.	1955	Bill Hayes' "The Ballad of Davy Crockett" remains at number four on *Billboard* magazine's "Best Sellers in Stores" chart. Fess Parker's recording of the song is at number six, and Tennessee Ernie Ford's version is at number seven.
29.	1955	Fess Parker, star of Walt Disney's *Davy Crockett TV series,* appears in Morristown, Tennessee. The city is celebrating its centennial, and the community's Princess Theater is showing *Davy Crockett, King of the Wild Frontier.*
30.	1836	The *National Banner and Nashville Whig* reports Crockett's fate at the Alamo: "We had hoped to see Davy coming out of the war, at its termination, with new honors bound thickly round his brow. But alas, he has passed from among us, and been gathered to his fathers in the full meridian of his glory. We never expect to look upon his like again. He was indeed one out of a thousand—ay, of a million. Poor Davy Crockett."
31.	1954	Ashley Wilson Crockett, 96, the last surviving grandchild of David Crockett, dies in Granbury, Texas. He was born in Texas after his parents, Robert Patton Crockett and Matilda Porter Crockett, moved there from Tennessee. His death came only several months before filming began on "Davy Crockett, Indian Fighter," the first episode in Walt Disney's *Davy Crockett* series.

1959   *The Dallas Morning News* prints an article titled "Davy Crockett is Big Business," a pre-production tie-in to the forthcoming big screen production of *The Alamo*, which stars John Wayne as the famous Tennessean.

JUNE

1. 1914   *The Siege and Fall of the Alamo*, a black and white silent film, which features Ray Myers as Crockett, is released.

2. 1962   The second annual David Crockett Festival is held at Cherokee Park on Cherokee Lake in Morristown, Tennessee. *The Knoxville News-Sentinel* states: "all afternoon will be a feast of barbecued ham."

3. 1955   The *Cincinnati Post* announces: "Get out them shootin' irons, podner—Davy Crockett's Comin' to town!" The newspaper article was reporting on the forthcoming visit of Fess Parker, star of Walt Disney's *Davy Crockett, King of the Wild Frontier*.

4. 1909   *Davy Crockett—In Hearts United*, a black and white silent film starring Charles K. French as the title character, debuts.

5. 1937   *The Painted Stallion*, a 12-episode Republic Pictures serial, debuts. Jack Perrin portrays Crockett in episodes five through twelve.

6. 1801   Crockett is working in Virginia for Elijah Griffith, "a hatter by trade" who become so much in debt he "left the country." In his autobiography, Crockett recalled that his employer had left him "without money, and with but very few clothes, and them very indifferent ones."

7. 2015   *Too Many Crocketts*, a Western comedy, stars Jeff Justice as Dave Crockett, a so-called descendant of Davy Crockett, who is portrayed by Thomas Partain.

8. 1802   Crockett works for John Canady in order to pay off some of his father's debts. "I never visited my father's house during the whole time of this engagement, though he lived only fifteen miles off," wrote Crockett in his autobiography.

    1955   Georgia's *Columbus Daily Enquirer* features an ad from Hofflin and Greentree, a clothing store, that stated: "Davy Crockett's Complete Frontier Shop! Unusual and Official Davy Crockett items!" The unusual item was a Davy Crockett flashlight, which carried a one dollar price tag.

9. 1834 In a letter written in Washington City to William Hack, Crockett explains his vote against the need for a Congressional bank committee which was formed to examine the Bank of the United States after President Andrew Jackson withdrew federal funds from it. "It looked to me just like taking a man up and hanging him and then [asking] a jury to try whether he was guilty or not," said Crockett.

1896 The *Sacramento Daily Union* reports the death of actor Frank Mayo: "Began his Life in California as a Newsboy—Made Himself Famous Throughout the Country as a Melodramatic Actor in the Texas Drama of 'Davy Crockett.'"

10. 1955 Fess Parker, star of Walt Disney's *Davy Crockett, King of the Wild Frontier*, visits Dallas, Texas during his national promotional tour as the famous frontier hero.

11. 1815 Death of Mary Polly Finley, Crockett's first wife. She was twenty-eight years old.

1989 "Davy Crockett: A Letter to Polly," the third of five Walt Disney NBC-TV production Davy Crockett episodes starring Tim Dunigan in the title role, debuts.

12. 1880 The *Salt Lake Tribune* prints remarks about Crockett made to actor Frank Mayo in Texas by Susanna Hannig, who was married Alamo defender Almaron Dickinson during the Siege and Battle of the Alamo. "Mrs. Hannig said that Crockett was the bravest man she ever saw; that his chief occupations were fiddling and swearing, and his sole ambition was to fight Mexicans," stated the newspaper.

13. 1835 The *Downing Gazette*, an anti-Andrew Jackson publication, includes an "extract from a speech lately delivered by Col. Crocket." (sic)

14. 1884 In an article about the Alamo and its grounds, the *Cincinnati Commercial Tribune* describes one building and mentions Crockett: "A little back but joining on the end of the convent, stands the massive building in which Crockett and his band retired and made their last stand."

15. 2008 *Davy Crockett Battles the Kung Fu Vampires*, an SMU student film, starring Andrew Sensenig as Crockett, is available for screening. Crockett is created "using stem cells and blood samples" from a coonskin cap.

16. 1831   In a letter to Jackson, Tennessee's *Southern Statesman*, Crockett responds to the newspaper's coverage of one of his speeches regarding William Fitzgerald, a political opponent. "I discover he has come out with an answer to that which I never did say—that which appeared in the Southern Statesman, as my speech in Huntington, where it purported that Fitzgerald was called on to do his duty and refused," stated Crockett. "I never said that."

     1910   The Davy Crockett Hook & Ladder Company in Poughkeepsie, New York wins the "Best Appearance" award in the Hudson Valley Volunteer Firemen's Association annual convention parade.

     1912   The *San Antonio Express* publishes William Alexander Ridgeway's "The Only Man Alive Who Knew Davy Crockett." The article was about Enrique Esparza, age seventy-three, who as a child was inside the Alamo during the historic thirteen-day siege and battle. His father, Gregorio, one of the Alamo defenders, died on March 6, 1836. "You ask me if I remember it," said Esparza in an interview five years earlier. "I tell you yes. It is burned into my brain and indelibly seared there. Neither age nor infirmity could make me forget."

17. 1955   Fess Parker, star of Walt Disney's *Davy Crockett, King of the Wild Frontier*, visits Philadelphia during his national promotional tour, participates in a 22-car motorcade through the city, and receives a 19th century flintlock rifle presented to him by the National Rifle Association.

18. 1899   The Seattle *Daily Intelligencer* stated that "in the last fifteen years all of the eminent actors and actresses have passed away [including] Frank Mayo whose Davy Crockett made the world akin."

     1955   Bill Hayes' "The Ballad of Davy Crockett" is at the number nine position on *Billboard* magazine's "Best Sellers in Stores" chart. Fess Parker's version of the tune is at number ten, and Tennessee Ernie Ford's recording is at number sixteen.

     1989   "Davy Crockett: Warrior's Farewell," the fifth and final episode of Disney's new Davy Crockett series, starring Tim Dunigan, debuts on NBC-TV.

19. 1827   Crockett campaigns in McNairy County, Tennessee, in his quest for a seat in the United States House of Representatives.

	1904	The *Omaha World-Herald* publishes "How David Crockett Lived, Fought, and Died," a large three-column article.
20.	1835	The *New York Mirror* announces the showing of John Gadsby Chapman's portrait of Crockett at the National Academy of Design in New York.
	1960	*Knoxville News-Sentinel* columnist Mrs. Walter Ferguson, writing in her "A Woman's Viewpoint," laments about the lost art of diaries. "Since David Crockett lived, the art of letter-writing has died," wrote Ferguson. "People no longer keep diaries. Future historians will find it hard to get the source material that makes the past come alive." She adds that Crockett "left us a thrilling account of his life in his autobiography, which is in the form of a daily journal. Whether it is factual, or half factual, doesn't matter. It gives us the 'feel' of a day that is gone."
21.	1955	The nationally syndicated comic strip *In the Days of Davy Crockett* features the following text which focused on the Texas Revolution: "Commander of the Alamo during the great siege was a husky six-foot fellow name of William Barret Travis, He was only 27 years old but not too proud to ask advice from veteran fighters like Davy Crockett."
	2015	In a syndicated news story published in the *Fort Worth Star-Telegram* about Walt Disney merchandising, Disney CEO Bob Iger says, "Davy Crockett was an idol of mine. I remember as a kid having a Davy Crockett lunchbox, and I had to have one." He subsequently secured one on eBay.
22.	1834	Crockett sits again for painter John Gadsby Chapman in Washington. The Tennessee congressman first sat for Chapman the previous month.
23.	1838	In a reprint of an article from the April 28, 1838 edition of the *Texas Telegraph and Register*, the *Niles' Weekly Register* prints an account of Crockett taking the Oath of Allegiance to Texas soon after his arrival there.

24. 1833 In a letter written by S. Burch, Chief Clerk of the House of Representatives, to Crockett, the government official explains the following: "The Clerk of the House of Representatives has nothing whatsoever to do with the payments of the members of Congress. The law provides that they shall be paid by the Speaker of the House of Representatives; and there is nothing in the office of the clerk that shows how the money is disbursed, or to whom paid, or the amount paid."

25. 1955 Bill Hayes' "The Ballad of Davy Crockett" occupies the number twelve position on *Billboard* magazine's "Best Sellers in Stores" chart. Fess Parker's version of the song is at number thirteen, and Tennessee Ernie Ford's adaptation is at number nineteen.

26. 1830 Tennessee's *Jackson Gazette* comments on Crockett's opposition to the Indian Removal Act: "He had his constituents to settle with, he was aware; and should like to please them as well as other gentlemen; but he had also a settlement to make at the bar of his God, and what his conscience dictated to be just and right he would do, be the consequences what they might."

27. 2017 Bill Hayes, who recorded the chart-topping "The Ballad of Davy Crockett" in 1955, appears on *The Tonight Show with Jimmy Fallon* and explains that he recorded the song in one take on December 16, 1954, one day after "Davy Crockett, Indian Fighter" aired on ABC-TV's *Disneyland*.

28. 1991 Director David Zucker is costumed as Davy Crockett during a cameo appearance in *The Naked Gun 2½: The Smell of Fear*, which opens in theaters nationwide. Zucker and artist-author Robert Weil, who is costumed as George Russel, appear briefly firing flintlock weapons in a modern-day police shoot out scene. In other scenes, large portraits of Crockett appear in two locations in the film's White House scenes.

29. 1956 James Griffith portrays Crockett in *The First Texan*, an Allied Artists production about the life of Sam Houston.

30. 1834 Representative David Crockett completes his first session in the Twenty-Third Congress of the United States.

JULY

1. 1834   The Young Whigs of Philadelphia present Crockett with a rifle made by gunsmith Richard Constable. Crockett names the weapon "Pretty Betsey."

   1956   Bill Hayes' "The Ballad of Davy Crockett" enters the British record charts at the number thirteen position, and eventually reaches number two.

2. 1834   Crockett travels to Camden, New Jersey where he fires "Pretty Betsey" for the first time.

   1955   Bill Hayes' "The Ballad of Davy Crockett" is at the number fourteen position on *Billboard* magazine's "Best Sellers in Stores" chart. Fess Parker's version of the song, which sold over one million copies, is at number sixteen, its final position after seventeen weeks on the chart. Tennessee Ernie Ford's recording is at number twenty-one.

3. 1836   The *New York Evening-Post* reports on a number of Crockett's possessions which were brought to New York City, following the Battle of the Alamo: "Captain Kimball has brought on the rifle, powder horn, bullet pouch, &c., of Colonel David Crockett, given him by Captain David of the Mexican army, who obtained them from Colonel Bradburn, of the Mexican army."

4. 1834   Crockett delivers a speech in Philadelphia during his tour of the northeastern states.

   1956   *Frontier Woman: Daughter of Davy Crockett*, starring Cindy Carson as Polly Crockett, debuts in American theaters.

   1956   The Indian War Canoes attraction, later called Davy Crockett's Explorer Canoes, opens at Disneyland in Anaheim, California.

5. 1834   After a tumultuous reception in Philadelphia the day before, Crockett abstains from public events; however, he receives a gift of Dupont gunpowder.

   1986   Dorothy Gibson's "Davy Crockett *Did* Wear a Coonskin Cap" appears in *The Washington Post*.

6. 1890   Matilda Crockett, the third child born to David and Elizabeth, dies. She was sixty-eight years old.

7. 2001   *Boone & Crockett: The Hunter Heroes* debuts on the History Channel.

Mark Baker portrays Crockett in the Gary Foreman-directed Native Sun Productions documentary.

8. 1955 In the *Hudson All-American Go-Getter*, the Hudson auto company's newsletter, Fess Parker, star of Walt Disney's *Davy Crockett, King of the Wild Frontier*, says, "Sure hope I prove to be a good Hudson salesman." The company was promoting his national tour.

9. 1955 Bill Hayes' "The Ballad of Davy Crockett," which has sold over one million copies, is at number fifteen on *Billboard* magazine's "Best Sellers in Stores" chart, its final position after spending twenty weeks on the chart. Tennessee Ernie Ford's version of the song, which also sold over one million copies, is at number twenty-five, its final position, after seventeen weeks on the chart. Both recordings remain on *Billboard's* "Most Played in Jukeboxes" chart.

10. 1807 Crockett's first child, John Wesley, is born.

11. 1829 In a letter published in the *Jackson Gazette*, Crockett comments about "a matter that took place between [him and] Col. A. R. Alexander" that was distorted by Bartholomew G. Stewart, who had served as a county commissioner and judge in Madison County, Tennessee. "I have understood that Mr. Stewart has stated that I had tried to injure Col. Alexander, by telling a lie on him, in relation to a monied matter in Washington City," wrote Crockett. "I now think it is my duty to make a fair statement on the subject."

12. 1899 A front-page statement of purpose, Hardinsburg, Kentucky's *Breckenridge News* reads: "Like Davy Crockett, the Breckenridge News would rather be honest and be politically damned than be hypocritically immortalized."

13. 1833 In a letter written to Jackson, Tennessee's *Southern Statesman*, Crockett attacks William Fitzgerald, a political opponent, for abusing travel allowances issued by the House of Representatives. "I do hope Mr. Fitzgerald cannot with impunity lie the people out of their votes a second time," he noted. "I will dismiss this subject as the certificates of my neighbors annexed to my circular will prove him a liar and ought to convict him before any Court or Jury."

14. 1828 Crockett is placed on a Weakley County, Tennessee jury to "view and mark a road the nearest way and on the best ground from Dresden to meet a road at [the] Gibson County line."

	1835	The *Albany Argus* sums up the movement to nominate Senator Hugh Lawson White as the Whig candidate for President in a short "Question and Answer" article: "Who nominated Judge White for the presidency? Answer: One state legislature, ten members Congress, and Davy Crockett."
15.	1834	Newark, New Jersey's *The Sentinel of Freedom* publishes a front page story that includes Crockett as one "of our most eminent statesmen." The article described Crockett's recent appearance in Philadelphia.
	1941	*The Son of Davy Crockett*, starring Bill Elliott as Dave Crockett, debuts in theaters nationwide.
16.	1916	*Davy Crockett*, a black and white silent film starring Dustin Farnum, debuts.
17.	1890	The Johnson City, Tennessee *Comet* announces that the "Davy Crockett Historical Society met at Limestone on the 15th [of July] and unanimously decided to have a grand celebration at Strong's Springs, the birth-place of the 'Hero of the Alamo,' on the 15th of August, it being the birth-day of the illustrious Tennessean." Crockett, though, was born on August 17.
	1955	Fess Parker, star of Walt Disney's *Davy Crockett* series, is the featured celebrity in Disneyland's opening day ceremonies in Anaheim, California.
	1962	The first Davy Crockett Weapon System, a tactical nuclear weapon device, is tested at the Nevada Proving Grounds before an observation team that included U.S. Attorney General Robert F. Kennedy. The test of the nation's lightest nuke marked the last time a nuclear device was detonated in the open air.
18.	1956	*Davy Crockett and the River Pirates*, starring Fess Parker, debuts in American movie theaters. The theatrical release is an edited version of the two television episodes, "Davy Crockett's Keelboat Race" and "Davy Crockett and the River Pirates."
19.	1857	The clipper ship *David Crockett* completes its New York to San Francisco run in a record-setting 122 days.
20.	1833	Jackson, Tennessee's *Southern Statesman* publishes a letter written by Crockett in which he attacks Adam Huntsman, a political opponent, for writing about the frontier congressman's alleged franking

abuses. "I can only say, that Black Hawk [Huntsman] is not the man that I thought he was," wrote Crockett. "I did think that piece emanated from some poor little possum headed lawyer. I have cut open many possums' heads to hunt for brains and I never found any; therefore, I considered some little pin hook lawyer without brains was the author of that piece, and that old Black Hawk believing in his mental powers, took it on himself."

21. 1949 The *Morristown Daily Gazette and Mail* incorrectly states that the location of the rebuilt Crockett Tavern in Morristown, Tennessee is the same as the original structure which Crockett's father constructed in the late 18th century. The new structure, which will eventually be called the Crockett Tavern Museum, is located approximately 100 yards away from a well that existed near the original tavern.

22. 1822 Representative David Crockett joins the commencement of the Tennessee General Assembly.

    1845 The *Baltimore Sun* reprints an article from the Arkansas *Southern Shield* in which Mississippi's Laman Webster was dubbed "a second Davy Crockett" because between June 1, 1844 and April 1, 1845, he claimed he killed 106 bears, one more than the total Crockett claimed during the winter of 1825-1826.

23. 1892 Lancaster, Pennsylvania's *Daily Examiner* reports that an "estimated...40,000 people will attend the Davy Crockett memorial exercises" in Rutherford, Tennessee on August 17, the 106th birthday anniversary of the famous Alamo defender.

    1955 Tennessee Ernie Ford's recording of "The Ballad of Davy Crockett" is at the number sixteen position on *Billboard* magazine's "Most Played in Juke Boxes" chart, its last listing after fifteen weeks on the twenty-song roster.

24. 1987 A scene from *Alamo...The Price of Freedom,* which features Merrill Connally as Crockett, and other Texians evacuating the town of San Antonio for the protection of the Alamo, is filmed at Alamo Village in Brackettville, Texas.

25. 1942 *The Daily Illinois Journal* lists "Davy Crockett Plows a Furrow Straight" in its radio listings.

	1955	After participating in the televised opening of Disneyland on July 17, Fess Parker returns to location on the Ohio River in Kentucky for the filming of "Davy Crockett's Keelboat Race."
26.	1875	The *Wheeling Register* compares West Virginia Governor John J. Jacob to Crockett: "The governor I take to be a man after the Davy Crockett...who first knows he is right and then goes ahead."
	1955	Fess Parker, costumed as *Davy Crockett,* and Walt Disney appear on the cover of *Look* magazine.
27.	1878	The clipper ship *David Crockett* arrives in San Francisco harbor after departing New York 117 days earlier.
28.	1994	Filmmaker David Zucker completes a "Third Draft (revised) Davy Crockett" screenplay.
29.	1841	The *Jamestown Journal* publishes comments by George W. Kendell, the editor of the *Picayune*, which stated that Crockett was one of a number of Alamo defenders who etched his name on the San Antonio mission's wall.
30.	1822	Crockett votes against a motion in the Tennessee General Assembly which would have extended the date beyond which certain land warrants would no longer be honored.
	1936	The *Corpus Christi Caller* reports that "practically all the bones of three men, believed by some to be those of William B. Travis, James Bowie and David Crockett, were exhumed yesterday and today in two graves about 15 feet behind the present alter of the [San Fernando] cathedral. They were buried there under the original altar by Capt. Juan Seguín after the battle of San Jacinto. The bones discovered ranged from charred bits the size of the eraser of a pencil to a jawbone with all of the teeth intact."
31.	1835	In an article about the railroad line between Albany and Saratoga Springs, the *New York Commercial Advertiser* notes that "the locomotive 'Davy Crockett' with the appropriate motto to 'Go Ahead' performs his duty admirably, and quite in character with the 'Backwoods' legislator."
	1987	Scenes depicting a fiddle duel between Crockett, portrayed by Merrill Connally, and John MacGregor, portrayed by Frank Frizell,

are filmed during the making of *Alamo... The Price of Freedom*. However, the scene was never used in the film.

AUGUST

1. 1926 Sunset Productions' *Davy Crockett at the Fall of the Alamo* debuts in the United States with Cullen Landis in the title role.

   1950 The San Antonio Chamber of Commerce presents a portrait of Davy Crockett, which was painted by Harry Dunn, to the Daughters of the Republic of Texas during a ceremony at the Alamo. A photo of the painting originally appeared with an article titled "There Was a Man—Davy Crockett" in the August issue of *Esquire* magazine,

2. 1821 Matilda Crockett, the third child born to David and Elizabeth, is born.

3. 1955 Republic Pictures' *The Last Command*, a film about the Battle of the Alamo, debuts in the United States with Arthur Hunnicutt playing Davy Crockett.

4. 1954 Fess Parker signs a sixteen-page "Agreement" with Walt Disney Productions for three motion pictures about Davy Crockett, which would later air on television during the 1954-1955 season on the ABC-TV network.

5. 1960 United Artists' *The Alamo*, starring John Wayne as Davy Crockett, is shown to a preview audience at the Aladdin Theatre in Denver, Colorado.

6. 1824 In a letter to C. McAllister, Crockett makes inquiries about the sale of cotton. From Nashville, Crockett writes that he wished "to be kept advised of the price of cotton."

7. 1806 Crockett's romantic pursuit of Mary Polly Finley is approved by her father but disapproved by her mother. "She looked at me as savage as a meat axe," wrote Crockett about his future mother-in-law in his autobiography.

8. 1822 Crockett votes with the majority in the Tennessee House of Representatives which approves a Senate measure to provide for "an extension of time for the filing of claims to the 1st day of October next."

   1955 *Time* magazine reports that the Boston Museum of Fine Arts is displaying John Neagle's "1828" portrait of Crockett alongside a life-size image of Fess Parker as Disney's *Davy Crockett*. The 1834 painting was later attributed to Chester Harding.

9. 1950 Hollywood columnist Hedda Hopper reports that Johnny "Tarzan" Weissmuller will be cast as Davy Crockett in *The Alamo,* a motion picture that will star John Wayne.

 1998 *New York Daily News* writer David Hinckley suggests that director Stephen Spielberg's recently released film, *Saving Private Ryan,* was influenced by Walt Disney's *Davy Crockett* series. "With *Private Ryan,* it's impossible not to notice a resemblance, eerie beyond coincidence, to 'Davy Crockett at the Alamo,' a TV drama aired by Disney on Feb. 23, 1955," wrote Hinckley.

 2003 The first issue of *The Crockett Chronicle,* a quarterly dedicated to the life and legend of David Crockett, is published. Fess Parker, star of Walt Disney's *Davy Crockett, King of the Wild Frontier,* has his own question-and-answer column, "Talkin' With Fess," in the publication.

10. 1835 In a letter to Washington's *Daily National Intelligencer,* Crockett places much of the blame for his recent election defeat on President Andrew Jackson and his allies. "I had to contend against the whole popularity of Andrew Jackson and Governor Carroll, and the whole strength of the Union Bank," he claimed. "I have been told by good men that the managers of that bank offered twenty-five dollars a vote for Mr. Huntsman. I had no bank aid me."

11. 1835 In a letter written to Philadelphia book publishers Carey and Hart, Crockett describes how President Andrew Jackson played a role in his recent Congressional defeat. "The Genl [Jackson] come out openly to Election against me," he said. "I now say the oldest man living never heard of the president of a great nation to come down open Electionaring for his successor."

12. 1806 Crockett obtains a marriage license in the Dandridge Courthouse in order to wed Mary Polly Finley. Thomas Doggett, Crockett's friend, countersigned the document.

13. 2011 *K-911,* a modern police drama video production, which features Tim Dunigan as Chief David Crockett, is released. Dunigan portrayed Davy Crockett in five Disney-produced NBC-TV episodes which aired in 1988 and 1989.

14. 1805 Crockett, along with some members of his family and friends, travel to the home of Mary Polly Finley in preparation for the marriage ceremony.

15. 1890 The cornerstone of a monument honoring Crockett is laid during a ceremony at Strong's Springs, Tennessee, near the site of Crockett's birthplace.

    1899 The *Fort Worth Daily Register* notes that "David Crockett, or Davy Crockett, as he is better known, was one of the most famous pioneers in the history of this country." The newspaper prints a biography of Crockett in the issue.

    1986 The Davy Crockett Birthplace State Historical Area in Limestone, Tennessee begins a three-day celebration acknowledging the bicentennial of Crockett's birth.

16. 1806 Crockett marries Mary Polly Finley. Colonel Henry Bradford, a Jefferson County Justice of the Peace, performs the ceremony.

    1924 Fess Parker, the star of Walt Disney's *Davy Crockett* TV series, is born in Fort Worth, Texas.

17. 1786 David Crockett is born near the mouth of Limestone Creek and the Nolichucky River in the State of Franklin in what is now eastern Tennessee.

    1986 Jack Hurst's "Legendary Davy Crockett a Good Ole Boy at Heart" appears in the *Chicago Tribune*. The article coincided with the bicentennial of Crockett's birth.

18. 1831 In a letter written from his home in Weakley County, Tennessee to James Davidson, Crockett discusses politics and his status among his contemporaries in government. "I am a very plain man," he noted. "I never had six months education in my life. I was raised in [obscurity] without either wealth or education. I have made my self to every station in life that I have ever filled through my own exertions."

19. 1899 The *Philadelphia Inquirer* reports on the Crockett birthday celebration held at his at his birthplace: "Speeches were made by Governor Taylor, Congressman Alf Taylor, E. L. Wells of Ohio, and Col. R. H. Crockett, a grandson of the old backwoodsman. An immense crowd was present and a fund was started to build a monument."

	1890	The cornerstone of the Crockett monument in Lawrenceburg, Tennessee is laid.
	1954	Writer Tom Blackburn revises the "I Get Into Politics" teleplay, the second part of Walt Disney's *Davy Crockett* TV trilogy. The episode is eventually titled "Davy Crockett Goes to Congress."
20.	1806	After spending a few days at his father's home, Crockett and his new bride, Polly, travel to her parents home where they receive a warm welcome from the "old Irish mother" who exhibited "the finest humour in the world." The newlyweds were given two cows as wedding gifts,
21.	1930	A dramatic presentation of "Davy Crockett" is performed on San Francisco's KGO radio station.
	1953	Trevor Bardette portrays Crockett in *Man From the Alamo*, a Universal International motion picture, which debuts in theaters nationwide.
	1995	New Jersey's *Daily Record* features a front page teaser, "Fans Bring Wild Frontier to E. Hanover [NJ]," about a Davy Crockett birthday party which was attended by Crockett fans from six states. The main article is titled "Davy Crockett Craze Lives on for Madison teacher [William Chemerka] and friends."
22.	1831	In a letter written in Weakley County, Tennessee to Dr. Calvin Jones, Crockett seeks to lease land from him, but also added some political notes. "I have always supported measures and principals, and not men," said Crockett. "I have acted fearless and independent and I never will regret my course. I would rather be politically buried than to be hypocritically immortalized."
	1837	A $240 Republic of Texas voucher is made out to the estate of David Crockett for his service in the Texas Revolution.
23.	1872	The play *Davy Crockett; Or, be Sure You're Right, Then Go Ahead*, starring Frank Mayo, debuts in Rochester, New York.
24.	1835	The *Commercial Bulletin and Missouri Literary Register* states that the voting results for Tennessee's Twelfth Congressional District election confirm that "David Crockett, of hunting famed renowned, has been *beaten* on his own *beaten* track, and by one of his own kith, bone and persuasion [Adam Huntsman]."

25. 1835 The *Arkansas Gazette* calls Crockett a "buffoon" after he failed to win reelection against Adam Huntsman in the Tennessee's Twelfth Congressional district.

26. 1836 The *Missouri Argus* prints a letter written by Dr. J. H. Barnard, who tended the Goliad garrison and, later, the victorious Mexican army. "The Americans fought to the last, and were killed to a man," stated Barnard. "There were several friends who were saved, and who informed me that the men with the full prospect of death before themselves, were always lively and cheerful, particularly Crockett, who kept up their spirits by his wit and humor. The night before the storming [March 5, 1836], he called for his clothes that had been washed, stating that he expected to be killed the next day, and wished to die in clean clothes."

    1892 Tennessee's *Bolivar Bulletin* reports that at the Davy Crockett birthday celebration at Strong's Springs "in a drunken row Andy Rix was shot and killed by an unknown man. Two boys, who were standing near, were also hit from shot from the gun, and it is thought that one of them will die."

27. 1836 *Niles' Weekly Register* reports that Crockett "in company with several other gentlemen" arrived at Lost Prairie, Arkansas, before traveling on to Texas.

28. 1835 The *Arkansas Advocate* prints a story about a campaign incident between Crockett and Adam Huntsman, his opponent in the Congressional election: "We learn from one of the Tennessee papers, that while Col. Crockett, was addressing the people in Wesley, a pert political opponent, with the view of confounding him, handed him a 'coon skin asking him if it was good fur. The speaker, instead of flying into a passion, deliberately took the skin, blew it, examined it, and turning to the owner, dryly remarked, 'No sir, 'tis not good fur; my dogs wouldn't run such a 'coon, nor bark at a man that was fool enough to carry such a skin.' The poor fellow skunk away, and has not been heard of since."

29. 1806 Following their wedding, Crockett and his wife, Polly, rent a small farm and cabin in Jefferson County, Tennessee.

30. 1813 Creek warriors massacre most of the inhabitants of Fort Mims, in what is now Alabama. The tragic event is the main reason why Crockett volunteers to fight in the developing Creek War.

1900 New York's *The World* reports: "Here is a dulcimer which belonged to the great pioneer Davy Crockett. It was made by a French army officer who served under Lafayette. It is now owned by Geo. F. Crockett of Philadelphia, a second cousin of the original owner." Crockett was best associated with the violin, although he never mentioned anything about the instrument in his autobiography. The Crockett-dulcimer association is unique but highly unlikely.

1990 A Walt Disney's *Davy Crockett, King of the Wild Frontier* book bag is piled alongside other items outside an Atlantic City hotel entrance scene in *The Lemon Sisters*, which opens in theaters nationwide.

31. 1956 Walt Disney's *Davy Crockett, King of the Wild Frontier*, starring Fess Parker, opens in theaters in Finland as *Davy Crockett, erämaan kunigas*.

SEPTEMBER

1. 2012 Texas' *Hood County News* reports that "two descendants of David (Davy) Crockett were in Granbury last week as they continued their research—and show a one-of-a-kind photograph" of Elizabeth Patton Crockett and daughter, Rebecca Elvira Crockett," the only existing picture of Crockett's wife and daughter.

2. 1835 In a letter dated August 10, 1835, and published in Washington's *Daily National Intelligencer*, Crockett states that political corruption played an important role in his congressional election loss to Adam Huntsman. "I expected to have a fair race, but when the time came, and the polls opened, I found all Huntsman judges, and, in nearly all cases, Huntsman officers to hold the election," he pointed out. "In fact, I am astonished that I came as near beating him as I did."

1847 In an abridged article about the history of Texas, the *Boston Bee* prints: "With Travis, fell Jim Bowie, the celebrated David Crockett, [Robert] Evans, and others in this modern Thermopylae."

3. 1955 The *New Yorker* features an article about the national Davy Crockett

Craze titled "Be Sure You're Right, Then Go Ahead," written by E. J. Kahn, Jr.

4. 1860 The *San Francisco Bulletin* reports that the 12th District Court heard a case in which one party accused another of over driving the horse "Davy Crockett" to its death. The plaintiff asked for $1,000 for the loss of the horse, but the jury awarded $425.

2004 Musician Dean Shostak plays Crockett's fiddle at the San Jacinto Museum of History. Shostak, who recorded the *Davy Crockett's Fiddle* CD in 2002, used the historical instrument which bears the inside description, "This fiddle is my property. Davy Crockett. Franklin County, Tenn. Feb. 14, 1819."

5. 1807 A land survey at Rattle Snake Spring in Tennessee is completed on land owned by Elijah Patton, the father of James Patton whose wife, Elizabeth, later married Crockett following James' death on November 23, 1813, during the Creek War.

1894 The Crockett Clan holds its first reunion in Humboldt, Tennessee.

1894 The *Worcester Daily Spy* prints an obituary for Judge A. H. Douglass, which originally appeared in a Memphis newspaper the day before. The newspaper claimed that the judge, who died at age eighty-four, "was an old Indian fighter and soldier with Davy Crockett in the early part of the century." Since Crockett ended his participation in the Creek War in 1814, and the War of 1812 a year later, young Douglass would have been no more than a four-year-old "Indian fighter."

6. 1826 Crockett is called for jury duty in Gibson County, Tennessee.

7. 1833 The *Niles' Weekly Register* states: "We have been often times asked 'what sort of man is colonel Crockett?' and the general reply was 'just such a one as you would desire to meet with, if any accident or misfortune happened to you on the highway.'"

1836 Writing in New York's *Jamestown Journal*, Isaac N. Jones states the following about Crockett: "His military career was short. But though I deeply lament his death, I cannot restrain my American smile at the recollection of the fact that he died as a United States soldier should die, covered with his slain enemy, and, even in death presenting to them in his clenched hands, the weapons of their destruction,"

8.	1954	Filming commences on "Davy Crockett, Indian Fighter," the first episode in Walt Disney's *Davy Crockett* TV trilogy, in Tennessee. "We mostly crawled around the rocks in a stealthy way looking for the Indians," recalled Fess Parker, who was on location at the Qualla Boundary, the home of the Eastern Band of Cherokee Indians, adjacent to the Great Smoky Mountains National Park.
	1994	John Hull's *Death of Crockett*, an acrylic on canvas, is displayed at the Grace Borgenicht Gallery in New York City.
9.	1835	Following the voting in Tennessee's 12th Congressional District, Maine's *Eastern Argus* newspaper states that "Davy Crockett...has been *treed* by his opponent [Adam] Huntsman."
10.	1813	Crockett and other Tennessee volunteers march to Beaty's Spring, near Huntsville, in what is now Alabama during the Creek War.
11.	1813	Crockett and his fellow volunteers march to Winchester and join Captain Francis Jones and his Company of Mounted Riflemen during the Creek War.
12.	1835	*New Hampshire's Portsmouth Journal of Literature and Politics* suggests that "all sorts of means" were used by Andrew Jackson and others to defeat Crockett in the election for Tennessee's Twelfth Congressional District. The publication adds that "Davy is a hard customer" who "we hope will be more fortunate in the next heat."
13.	1930	A Bowie knife allegedly belonging to Crockett is stolen from the Chicago Historical Society.
	1955	Danny Thomas' TV character, Danny Williams, in an episode of *Make Room For Daddy*, is costumed as the frontier hero in an attempt to better understand his son's (played by Rusty Hamer) interest in the national Davy Crockett Craze.
14.	1922	A sculpted figure of Crockett, standing on a large stone base, is dedicated in a ceremony in Lawrenceburg, Tennessee.
15.	1823	Victorious in the Tennessee House of Representatives election, Crockett represents Carroll, Henderson, Humphreys, Madison, and Perry Counties in the first session of Tennessee's Fifteenth General Assembly in Murfreesboro.

	1826	In the *Jackson Gazette,* Crockett announces his campaign for a seat in Twentieth United States Congress, representing Tennessee's Ninth District,
16.	1816	Robert Patton Crockett, the first child born to David and Elizabeth, is born.
17.	1821	Crockett, representing Hickman and Lawrence Counties, attends the opening session of the first session of Tennessee's Fourteenth General Assembly in Murfreesboro, Tennessee.
18.	1839	The *Norwich Aurora* erroneously reports that "Col. David Crockett, is yet alive, and in Mexico, working in the mines." The Connecticut newspaper explained that the report originated from two Alamo survivors who had escaped from the mines.
19.	1821	Crockett serves on the Tennessee General Assembly's committee of Proposition and Grievances which recommends that "the owner of lands in the Western district should be exempted from the payment of a double tax for the year of 1820."
20.	1824	Representative David Crockett attends the opening of the second session of Tennessee's Fifteenth General Assembly in Murfreesboro.
	1925	New Orleans' *Times-Picayune* reports that "a little more than a generation ago, the education of no theatergoer was considered complete until he had seen Frank Mayo's performance of *Davy Crockett*, says *Equity*, the organ of the Actors' Equity Association."
	1987	The Showtime cable TV network debuts "Davy Crockett," an episode of *Shelley Duvall's Tall Tales & Legends* series. Singer-songwriter Mac Davis stars as Crockett.
21.	1835	The *Hartford Times* notes that "Davy Crockett says, (and most of the Whig editors give currency to the report) that the President sent thousands of the Globe and other papers, into his district, to electioneer against him, and in favor of [Adam] Huntsman, his successful rival."
	1997	The Disney Channel schedules a broadcast of "Davy Crockett, Indian Fighter."
22.	2004	The *San Antonio Express-News* reports that bronze bust of Crockett, which was created by Texas artist William Easley in 1989, was stolen from its place in San Antonio's Crockett Park. The sculpture was later found in a pawn shop.

23. 1870 In a lengthy tribute to Crockett, the *Jamestown Journal* states that "he was dead before we were born, but we have had his life and his history, his tragically heroic death and his wonderful feats in bear hunting in 'the shakes' about Reelfoot Lake and the Cyprus swamps and canebrakes of the bottom recounted to us, in fancy, by his old pioneer comrades and admirers (now mostly in their graves) until to doubt them would be 'a sin to Crockett.'"

    1889 Death of Robert Patton Crockett, the son of David and his second wife, Elizabeth. He was seventy-two years old.

24. 1813 Crockett is officially mustered for a ninety-day term in service in Captain Francis Jones' Company of Tennessee Mounted Volunteers during the Creek War.

    1937 Sunset Productions' *Heroes of the Alamo* premieres in San Antonio, Texas with Lane Chandler starring as Crockett.

    1964 Wearing a Davy Crockett-like coonskin cap, Fess Parker debuts as *Daniel Boone* on NBC-TV.

25. 1821 Representative David Crockett votes to exempt West Tennessee landowners from paying additional taxes.

26. 1829 In a lengthy undated letter published in the *Jackson Gazette*, Crockett explains that he did not pay off the debt of another man who, in return for paying off the debt, promised to build the canebrake congressman a mill, because the structure's condition was unsatisfactory and placed in the wrong location. According to Crockett, the mill was nothing more than "a mere Rattle box unfit for any other use than to scare the crows with, for which purpose it unfortunately stood in the wrong place."

27. 1821 Crockett votes with the majority in the Tennessee General Assembly to recommend that the call for a Constitutional Convention be put to a vote in the next general election.

28. 1814 Crockett reenlists in General Andrew Jackson's army during the War of 1812.

29. 1821 Crockett's grist mill, distillery, and powder mill are destroyed in a flood. In his autobiography, Crockett described the event as "a very severe misfortune."

30. 1889 The *Times-Picayune* prints a report from Granberry, Texas that "Colonel Robert Patterson Crockett died at his residence, on Rucker's Creek, last Thursday, in the 73rd year of his age. His death removes the only remaining son of Davy Crockett."

OCTOBER

1. 1821 General William Carroll, a Creek War veteran, is sworn in as Governor of Tennessee, thanks to a majority vote of the Tennessee General Assembly, which included a ballot cast by Crockett.

   2012 The *Seattle Times* identifies the "430 foot *Davy Crockett*" as "the state's worst derelict vessel" among hundreds of abandoned ships and boats on Washington's waterways.

2. 1817 Crockett explores a western area of Tennessee that would eventually become Lawrence County.

3. 1876 Wilmington, Delaware's *The Morning Herald* announces two forthcoming performances of *Davy Crockett,* starring Frank Mayo, at the city's Grand Opera House on October 6 and 7.

   1915 The Fine Arts Company's *The Martyrs of the Alamo* premieres in New York with Alfred D. Sears portraying Davy Crockett.

4. 1877 In a travel article about Austin, Texas, the *New York Observer* states that "a portrait of [Stephen] Austin hangs opposite, and near the door leans a painting of Davy Crockett, dressed in hunting costume, and accompanied by his faithful hounds."

5. 1822 Crockett is presented with several judgments for debts associated with his destroyed mills.

   1907 President Theodore Roosevelt delivers a speech in Memphis, Tennessee and states: "Like Davy Crockett, the great Tennessean, I favor his motto, 'Be sure you are right, then go ahead,'"

6. 1835 The *Vermont Gazette* reports that "Davy has become disgusted with this country since his defeat [in the Congressional election for Tennessee's Twelfth Congressional District], an has determined to move to Texas, lock, stock, and barrel."

7. 1813 Crockett participates in a scouting mission under the command of Maj. John H. Gibson during the Creek War.

8. 1813 Maj. John H. Gibson divides his small scouting party, which includes Crockett, in two groups during the Creek War. Crockett and four other volunteers maneuver near present day Browns Creek in Marshall County, Alabama.

9. 1821 Crockett introduces a bill in the Tennessee General Assembly dealing with the number of land grants that could be included in a warrant.

10. 1985 Richard Young portrays Crockett in "Alamo Jobe," an episode of NBC-TV's *Amazing Stories* program. The half-hour production, which was based on a story written by Steven Spielberg, tells the tale of a young Alamo defender, Jobe H. Farnum, played by Kelly Reno, who time travels from 1836 to 1985, and back again. The production contained stock footage from John Wayne's *The Alamo* (1960).

11. 1821 A resolution in the Tennessee General Assembly calling for a vote on a proposed Constitutional Convention, which Crockett supported, is tabled.

12. 1829 A twenty-five acre parcel of land in Weakley County, Tennessee is surveyed. It was later sold by Crockett on May 19, 1831.

    1876 The New York *Daily Graphic* reports that Frank Mayo has portrayed *Davy Crockett* on stage "831 times."

13. 1950 A bronze statue of Crockett presented by the Tennessee Historical Commission is unveiled at the Gibson County courtyard in Trenton, Tennessee. The unveiling ceremony's keynote speaker, Temple Houston Morrow, a grandson of Sam Houston, says of Crockett: "That one day his voice would be heard in the halls of Congress, and later he would be numbered among the immortals of the ages." Ashley Wilson Crockett, 92, Crockett's last surviving grandson, was scheduled to attend but was unable to participate due to illness.

14. 1813 Crockett and other mounted scouts, commanded by Col. John Coffee, are on a scouting mission along the Black Warrior River during the Creek War.

15. 1862 Clearfield, Pennsylvania's *Rafismun's Journal* states that "we shall never forget, and always feel proud of the fact, that we knew so great an every-day Plato as Davy Crockett."

	1931	Vocalist Chubby Parker records "Davey Crockett" on New York's Conqueror Records. The 78-rpm single is the first commercial recording of a Crockett song.
	1936	President Franklin D. Roosevelt proclaims the Davy Crockett National Forest in Houston and Trinity Counties, Texas.
	1955	*TV Guide's* cover features a headline that reads "Davy Crockett Rides Again," an article which promoted the forthcoming "Davy Crockett's Keelboat Race" episode on ABC-TV's *Disneyland*.
16.	1833	Philadelphia's *Galaxy of Comicalities*, a satirical publication, features an article titled "Crockett teaching a Landlord how to Grin!" It marked the first time that Crockett's image appeared in print.
17.	1858	The clipper ship *David Crockett* begins a record-setting 95-day journey from San Francisco to New York.
18.	1853	The clipper ship *David Crockett* is launched on the Mystic River in Connecticut.
	2008	A bronze plaque at the Crockett Tavern Museum in Morristown, Tennessee is dedicated by the Samuel Doak Chapter of the National Society of the Daughters of the American Revolution. The plaque reads: "Crockett Tavern Museum. Site of the boyhood home of David Crockett, frontiersman and congressman, where his parents, John and Rebecca, ran a 1790s wagoner's inn and tavern. Crockett Tavern Museum operated by the Hamblen County Chapter APTA, has provided heritage education for 50 years since April 21, 1958."
19.	1809	Crockett participates in a flintlock rifle shooting contest at a local frolic and wins an entire beef.
	1952	The *San Antonio Express* reports that "clamoring for a secure foothold atop the cenotaph in Alamo Plaza, one youngster found himself stepping on the sculpted head of Davy Crockett at the same time [presidential candidate Adlai] Stevenson was speaking about the honor and dignity which the defenders of the Alamo deserved."
20.	1816	Crockett and a few neighbors named Robinson, Frazier, and Rich explore Creek territory in what is now northern Alabama.
21.	1805	A marriage contract is drawn up for Crockett and Margaret Elder. However, the relationship soon ended.

22. 1821 Crockett withdraws his land grant bill of October 9, in order to amend it.

    1991 With a band playing "The Ballad of Davy Crockett," Fess Parker receives a Disney Legend award at ceremonies held at the Walt Disney Studios in Burbank, California.

23. 1838 John Gadsby Chapman's painting of Crockett is on display at the Apollo Association's showing in Washington D.C.

24. 1960 United Artists' *The Alamo* premieres at San Antonio's Woodlawn Theatre, starring John Wayne as Colonel Davy Crockett.

25. 1993 The Davy Crockett School in Dallas, Texas is declared an historical landmark, but two decades later the building is transformed into The Principal Residences, an upscale apartment complex.

    1996 A large portrait of David Crockett is featured on one of the walls at the fictional Wellington School in the comedy *High School High*, which opens in theaters nationwide.

26. 1820 In a letter to John C. McLemore, a Tennessee road commissioner, Crockett requests a land warrant for claimed property that he lacked title to. "I don't expect I can pay you the [w]hole amount until next Spring," wrote Crockett.

27. 1954 Fess Parker is introduced by director Norman Foster as *Davy Crockett* during a musical segment on the first episode of ABC-TV's *Disneyland*.

28. 1813 Crockett and his fellow Company of Mounted Riflemen arrive at Wills Creek and establish a camp during the Creek War.

    1875 The *Daily Illinois State Journal* describes Frank Mayo's one-night performance as *Davy Crockett* at the Springfield, Illinois Opera House as "the great dramatic event of the season."

29. 1813 Crockett and his fellow Company of Mounted Riflemen are placed under the command of Col. John Alcorn, who replaced Col. John Coffee, during the Creek War.

30. 1823 As a member of the Tennessee General Assembly, Crockett delivers a speech against a bill which would have prohibited candidates from offering alcoholic beverages to voters during election campaigns.

31. 1835   In a letter to Andrew J. Hutchings from President Andrew Jackson, the chief executive criticizes the "miserable caucus" of "Crockett and Co." after the frontiersman lost his Congressional election bid.

    1910   "Davy Crockett Wrecked" reads the headline in Pennsylvania's *Lancaster Daily Examiner*. The newspaper reported that "the 'Davy Crockett' fast passenger train on the San Antonio and Arkansas Pass railroad, east-bound, was wrecked near Yoakum, Texas, early today. A bridge over a small ravine gave way, derailing the entire train with the exception of the Pullman. Several passengers were bruised but none seriously hurt."

NOVEMBER

1. 1819   Crockett resigns as a local justice of the peace in order to seek a seat in the Tennessee General Assembly.

   1835   Following his defeat for reelection in Congress, Crockett tells an audience at the Union Hotel in Memphis, Tennessee, "Since you have chosen to elect a man with a timber toe to succeed me, you may all go to hell and I will go to Texas."

2. 1818   Crockett is named by the Lawrenceburg, Tennessee court to serve as a custodian of funds for a child born out of wedlock.

3. 1813   Crockett participates in the Battle of Tallushatchee during the Creek War.

4. 1901   The *Duluth News Tribune* describes one of Crockett's rifles, which was given to C. W. Callaghan, proprietor of the Hotel Maryland, by Robert Blair of Wytheville, Virginia: "a flintlock of about 40 caliber. It is 5½ feet long, and the barrel is nearly a half inch thick. The workmanship, all by hand, is excellent."

5. 1985   In a scene identified as November 5, 1955, from the motion picture *Back to the Future*, Fess Parker's version of "The Ballad of Davy Crockett" is heard playing on a jukebox. The film, which stars Michael J. Fox, opens in theaters nation wide.

6. 1821   Crockett introduces a bill in the Tennessee General Assembly designed to protect squatters who resided in certain areas affected by the Congressional Reservation Line.

7. 1835 Crockett travels through the "Big Prairie" area of Arkansas before proceeding to Texas.

   1896 Jackson, Michigan's *Jackson Citizen Patriot* reports that "David Crockett's Masonic apron is now in the possession of Mrs. E. M. Taylor, of Paducah, Kentucky. It is in excellent condition and treasured highly. It was given to Mr. Taylor by a descendant of a friend, one of the old-time settlers, and an associate of Crockett."

8. 1814 Crockett arrives in Pensacola, in what is now Florida, following the capture of the port city the day before by Gen. Andrew Jackson's forces during the War of 1812.

9. 1813 Crockett participates in the Battle of Talladega during the Creek War.

   1881 A fire in Texas's State Capitol building destroys John Gadsby Chapman's portrait of David Crockett and Samuel Stillman Osgood's painting of the Tennessean.

10. 1813 Following the Battle of Talladega, Crockett and his fellow volunteers remain at Fort Talladega. "We now remained at the fort for a few days, but no provision came yet," wrote Crockett in his autobiography. "The weather also began to get very cold; and our clothes were nearly worn out, and horses getting very feeble and poor"

11. 1911 The Lancaster, Pennsylvania *New Era* prints a story about Crockett's 1833 encounter with actor James Hackett, who portrayed the Crockett-like Nimrod Wildfire in the play *The Lion of the West*: "After some time the curtain rose, and Hackett appeared in a hat covered in a wild-cat skin, who, after bowing to the audience, turned towards Crockett, bowing again and again. The compliment was reciprocated by the Colonel, to the great amusement of the spectators."

    1926 Austin P. Foster, Assistant Tennessee State Librarian and Archivist, in a presentation about Crockett, before the James Robertson Chapter of the Daughters of the American Revolution in Nashville, says that he was "the most unique character in American history, the quaintest, frankest and most honest of all men in public life."

12. 1835 Crockett and a small group of followers arrive in Little Rock, Arkansas, on the way to Texas.

13. 1835   The *Arkansas Advocate* reports that "we have seen the Honorable David Crockett—who arrived in this place [Little Rock] last evening, on his way to Texas, where he contemplates ending his days."

14. 1960   A large photograph of John Wayne as Crockett dominates a trade ad for "The Spirit of the Alamo," an ABC-TV special about the making of *The Alamo* (1960).

15. 1833   The *Baltimore Gazette and Daily Advertiser* publishes a lengthy excerpt from *Sketches and Eccentricities of Colonel David Crockett of West Tennessee*, which included the following passage about a bear hunt: "I knew I had him, so I just sat down and rested a little; and then, to keep my dogs quiet, I got up, and old Betsey thundered at him. I shot him right through the heart, and he fell without a struggle. I run up and stuck my knife into him several times up to the hilt, just because he devilled me so much; but I had hardly pulled it out before I was sorry, for he had fought all day like a man, and would not have got clear but for me."

    1853   The *New York Evening-Post* posts reports that "at the pier on the east side of Coenties slip lies a very beautiful clipper ship, called David Crockett. Her bow is very ornamented with a full-length figure of the celebrated Col. Crockett, with musket in hand, indicating that he is 'going ahead.'"

    1953   The *Omaha World Herald* reports that director Kendrick Wilson of the Omaha Community Playhouse is having auditions for *Davy Crockett*. "[The play] was a hit back in 1875, and Mr. Wilson has pledged himself to see that it's a hit in 1954 as well," notes the article.

16. 1859   Palestine, Texas' *Trinity Advocate* states: "No two characters could be more dissimilar than those of [Daniel] Webster and [David] Crockett. One had penetrated to the profoundest depth of law, statesmanship and diplomacy. The other had penetrated to the profoundest depths of the forest, and was passionate lover of its wild delights."

    1955   "Davy Crockett's Keelboat Race," starring Fess Parker, debuts on ABC-TV's *Disneyland*. The episode is TV's first prequel production since it represents a fictionalized chapter in Crockett's life before the stories that were featured in the three original episodes.

17.	1821	Crockett departs for home after the Tennessee General Assembly adjourns.
	1835	The *Arkansas Gazette* reports that "Colonel [Crockett] and his party, all completely armed and well mounted, departed on Friday morning for Texas, in which country, we understand, they intend establishing their future abode, and in the defense of which, we hope they may cover themselves in glory."
18.	1833	In a letter to the Gentlemen of Abingdon, Virginia, Crockett accepts a dinner invitation. "I am at a loss, gentlemen, for language to express my gratitude to you for this mark of respect," he wrote.
19.	1834	In Elizabethtown, Kentucky, Crockett is a guest at the home of Thomas Chilton who had assisted Crockett in writing his autobiography.
20.	1988	"Davy Crockett: Rainbow in the Thunder," the first of five Walt Disney-produced Davy Crockett episodes starring Tim Dunigan in the title role, debuts on NBC-TV. Johnny Cash plays an elder Crockett in the episode.
	1976	*Davy Crockett on the Mississippi*, an animated TV movie debuts, featuring the voice of Ned Wilson as the title character.
21.	1915	The Fine Arts Company's *The Martyrs of the Alamo* is released following its New York premiere (on Oct. 3) with Alfred D. Sears starring as Crockett.
22.	1813	Crockett and other Tennessee volunteers at Fort Strother participate in a mutiny over the lack of food and supplies during the Creek War. The volunteers depart for home, but later return to the army.
	1986	An uncredited Guy Arnold portrays the dead body of Crockett in the TV movie *Houston: The Legend of Texas* (aka *Gone to Texas*).
23.	1813	James Patton dies of his wounds during the Creek War. Following the death of Polly Crockett in 1815, David Crockett marries Patton's widow, Elizabeth.
24.	1852	John Wesley Crockett, David and Polly's first born, dies. He was forty-seven years old.
25.	1809	William Finley Crockett, David and Polly's second child, is born.
	1812	Margaret Finley Crockett, David and Polly's third child, is born.

	1817	Crockett is selected as a justice of the peace in Giles County, Tennessee.
26.	1831	The *New York Mirror* praises actor James Hackett for his characterization of the Crockett-like Nimrod Wildfire in the play *The Lion of the West*. "The irresistibly comic style in which Mr. Hackett represented the 'half-horse, half-alligator' original cannot be forgotten by those who witnessed the performance," stated the newspaper.
27.	1866	The *San Francisco Evening Bulletin* prints an anecdotal story about Crockett appearing at a grand White House social function during the Jackson administration: "Crockett, with coonskin cap and linsey-woolsey hunting shirt, fringed leggings and buckskin moccasins—not unconsciously, but studiously in character, advanced to the great door to enter. 'Room for the Honorable David Crockett, of the Representatives of the United States,' cried the officious usher. 'Davy Crockett will make room for himself!' exclaimed the eccentric guest in a tone of tremendous volume and gravity, as he marched into the company."
28.	1835	The *New York Transcript* reports that Crockett is "on his way to Texas where he is going to join the American forces against the Mexicans."
	1944	The USS *Crockett* (APA-148), an attack transport ship, is launched. It will be commissioned on January 18, 1945, and will serve until October 15, 1946.
29.	1823	Crockett completes his first session as a Tennessee State legislator in the First Session of the Fifteenth General Assembly in Murfreesboro.
	1876	The San Francisco *Evening Post* announces the "last four nights of the popular young actor Mr. Frank Mayo" as *Davy Crockett* at the city's California Theater.
30.	1834	Crockett returns to Washington after spending time in Kentucky where he delivered a few campaign speeches. Understandably, Crockett was well aware that Kentucky citizens could not vote for him but he realized that his comments would later appear in Tennessee newspapers.
	1888	The Grand Rapids *Evening Leader* praises "Mr. Edwin F. Mayo, known to fame for his great impersonation of the backwoods hero Davy Crockett." Edwin F. Mayo is the son of Frank Mayo, who originated the role.

DECEMBER

1. 1833 Crockett deliberately dates a January 12, 1835 letter as December 1, 1833 correspondence in the Washington D. C. *Daily National Intelligencer* in an effort to embellish a lengthy parody in which the frontier congressman declines an offer to run for President of the United States. "I'm a very candid man, and when my mind is fixed upon a matter, you might as well try to stop gunpowder half blown up, as stop me," he wrote. "I can't agree to be President."

2. 1940 In an update about the forthcoming Alamo Cenotaph dedication ceremony, the *Dallas Morning News* describes the sculpted figure of Crockett: "Besides Travis stands the usually cheerful Crockett in scout or hunter garb."

3. 1807 Franklin County, Tennessee is created by an act of the General Assembly of the State of Tennessee. Crockett resides in the county from 1812 to 1817.

   1902 In an article about one of Crockett's rifles on display in the office of Tennessee's Secretary of State, Texas' *Shiner Gazette* called the weapon "a relic of one of the greatest characters this nation has ever produced."

4. 1835 Crockett, his nephew William Patton, and two friends, Lindsay Tinkle and Abner Burgin, pass through Clarkesville, Texas, and head west into the interior.

5. 1833 In a letter written on November 18, and published in Washington's *United States Telegraph* to the Gentlemen of Abingdon, Virginia, Crockett accepts a dinner invitation. "I will do myself the pleasure to dine with you at the appointed hour," said Crockett.

6. 1835 The *New York Sunday Morning News* reports that "Davy Crockett has actually gone to Texas, with 'his rifle, and a hundred rounds.'"

7. 1827 Crockett arrives in Washington D.C., having been elected to the House of Representatives in the Twentieth United States Congress. Crockett represents Tennessee's Ninth Congressional District.

   1876 Ravenna, Ohio's *Democratic Press* publishes a fictional tale about Crockett in which the candidate missed a campaign debate by being deliberately misguided to a place on the Salt River. The newspaper said that Crockett, "the famous Kentucky Congressman," lost the election because some voters believed he was "afraid" to show up. "Hence the phrase, 'Up Salt River,' meaning that party is hopelessly defeated," noted the newspaper article.

    1922   New Jersey's *Trenton Times* prints comments made by Charles Matthew Adams who said, "The thrilling tale of David Crockett should be an inspiration to every boy. To know his life story is to understand his famous saying in its fullest meaning, for he is one of the great heroes of Texas and American history."

8. 1813   Crockett and other member of the Tennessee Mounted Volunteers rendezvous at Huntsville, in what is now Alabama, during the Creek War.

9. 1966   Davy Crockett is mentioned as having been killed on March 5, 1836, a day before he actually died, in "The Alamo," an episode of the ABC-TV science fiction series *The Time Tunnel*.

    1972   Vincent Van Patten voices the Possessed Davy Crockett Mannequin character in "The Phantom of the Country Music Hall," an episode of the animated CBS-TV series *The Animated Scooby-Doo Movies*.

10. 1835   Crockett, his nephew William Patton, and two friends, Lindsay Tinkle and Abner Burgin, are on a hunting sojourn in east Texas.

11. 1835   New York's *Albany Journal* reports that "Colonel Crockett who has recently gone to Texas is probably one of the best shots in the world. One hundred men like Crockett would be of immense service to the Texians at this time—if you could only make them believe that enemies were *bears*, instead of men."

12. 1829   The "Crockett" post office site is created in Gibson, Tennessee. Crockett used the location as his official home mailing address while serving in the Twenty-first Congress and the Twenty-third Congress.

13. 1828   In a letter written in Washington City to the Editor of the *Jackson Gazette*, Crockett explains the need for legislation that would protect Tennessee squatters' rights from state authority. "I choose to obey my constituents, who have placed me in office, and whose servant I am," stated Crockett. "I am decidedly opposed to placing it in the power of the Tennessee Legislature, or any, tribunal, to

speculate on their labor; to avoid which, I am inclined to give each one a home to shelter his wife and little ones."

14. 1955 "Davy Crockett and the River Pirates," starring Fess Parker," debuts on ABC-TV's *Disneyland*. In this follow-up to "Davy Crockett's Keelboat Race," Crockett joins forces with adversary Mike Fink and his crew to fight river pirates.

15. 1890 The *Kansas City Times* publishes "Career of Davy Crockett: Incidents From the Life of a Most Remarkable Man."

    1939 *The Sacramento Bee* reports that in San Antonio, "two packages have just come to the Alamo for David Crockett, bear hunter and Tennessee Congressman, [who] died a hero in the Alamo in 1836. Postmaster Dan Quill said the packages were mailed recently from an Indianapolis publishing house." The article did not identify the contents of the packages.

    1954 "Davy Crockett, Indian Fighter," starring Fess Parker in the title role, airs as the first episode in Walt Disney's memorable *Davy Crockett* trilogy on ABC-TV's *Disneyland*.

    2004 The "Crockett and Russel Hat Company" sign is dedicated at Disneyland's Pioneer Mercantile building in Disneyland in honor of the fiftieth anniversary of TV's "Davy Crockett, Indian Fighter." Fess Parker and his family attend the ceremony.

16. 1954 Bill Hayes records "The Ballad of Davy Crockett" in one take for Cadence Records. The single will eventually reach the top position on *Billboard* magazine's "Best Sellers in Stores" chart.

    1836 The *Arkansas Advocate* reprints a review of *Colonel Crockett's Exploits and Adventures in Texas*, which was ghostwritten by Richard Penn Smith. "David has greased the lightning and ridden it through the cane brake," stated the reviewer, who echoed Crockett's mythical persona. "He has breasted the rushing current of the father of waters, towing a dozen steamboats with his teeth. He has whipped his weight in cougars —grinned whole menageries into convulsions— and screamed the earthquake into silence."

17. 1827 In a letter to James L. Totten, a Tennessee state legislator, Crockett discusses the creation of post office routes that would connect several towns, including Troy, Mills Point, and Dresden.

	1870	Boston's *Massachusetts Ploughman and New England Journal of Agriculture* prints a front page biography of Crockett in which his early campaign style was described. "His remarkable speeches and odd sayings, and his great reputation as a bear hunter, all told so powerfully in his favor that his more intelligent competitors were 'no-whar,'" noted the publication.
18.	1988	"Davy Crockett: A Natural Man," the fourth of five Walt Disney production Davy Crockett episodes starring Tim Dunigan in the title role, debuts on NBC-TV.
	2005	The *Knoxville New Sentinel* proclaims Crockett as the third most famous East Tennessean of all time. Dolly Parton was voted number one and Sgt. Alvin York was the runner up.
	2013	The Crockett Tavern Museum in Morristown, Tennessee is placed on the Register of Historic Places.
19.	1834	In a letter from Nicholas Biddle, President of the Second Bank of the United States, to Crockett, the financial institution officer informs the frontier congressman that a "note has been discounted and the old draft paid."
20.	1835	Crockett continues on a buffalo hunt in east Texas. He expects to rendezvous with others at the falls of the Brazos River on Christmas.
	1845	The Tennessee General Assembly passes an act which creates Crockett County from parts of Dyer, Gibson, Haywood, and Madison counties.
	1902	In a recollection piece in Lexington, Missouri's *Intelligencer,* a stage hand said that during a performance of the Murdock-Mayo play *Davy Crockett,* lead actor Lester Lonergan kicked one of the prop wolf heads so hard that "the head was crushed like an egg shell." After the curtain was dropped, the property man confronted the actor and said, "Why, you infernal fool, you have ruined the finest wolf I ever had."
21.	1834	Crockett writes to his publishers, Carey and Hart of Philadelphia, that he "commenced on the new book [*Col. Crockett's Tour to the North and Down East*] and have taken 31 pages to Mr. [William] Clark to correct and have twelve more written ready for him."

22. 1830　In a letter written in Washington City to James Kirke Paulding, the playwright who created *The Lion of the West*, a parody about Nimrod Wildfire, a character associated with Crockett, the frontier congressman explained that he held no disfavor towards the production. "I thank you however for your civility in assuring me that you had no reference to my peculiarities," said Crockett.

23. 1955　Fess Parker, costumed as Davy Crockett, appears on Walt Disney's *Mickey Mouse Club* ABC-TV program. The program was filmed on sound stage number three at the Disney Studios, the same building where "Davy Crockett at the Alamo" was filmed a year earlier.

24. 1813　Crockett's ninety-day enlistment in the Creek War ends. He was paid $65.59. Crockett would later return to the army the following autumn.

25. 1818　Rebecca Elvira Crockett, the second child born to David and Elizabeth, is born.

26. 1833　In a letter written in Washington City to John McClean, Crockett criticizes President Andrew Jackson's attack on the Second Bank of the United States. "It appears if Jackson is determined to destroy the United States Bank or sacrifice the Government," stated Crockett.

　　 1862　The *Sacramento Daily Union* states: "There was never a better motto than the homely one of David Crockett, 'Be sure you're right, then go ahead.'"

27. 1834　In a letter to John Ash, Crockett criticizes the popularity of President Andrew Jackson. "It appears as if Jackson can do anything he pleases, and the people will say he is right," wrote Crockett.

28. 1888　In "Sailing Southern Seas," an article written by Wm. H. S. Atkinson in South Dakota's *Wessington Springs Herald*, the author suggests that steamships navigating unknown Asian waters should "be slow and sure, or in the words of the immortal Davy Crockett, 'Be sure you're right, then go ahead.'"

　　 1956　Walt Disney's *Davy Crockett, King of the Wild Frontier*, starring Fess Parker, opens in Japan.

29. 1825　Crockett is on a bear hunt that took place during the last week of the year.

	1936	The *Houston Chronicle* announces that "a contract will be let January 5 for the erection of the Davy Crockett Memorial Building in the city park here." The structure's plans included space for 600-seat auditorium, a library, a small museum, and a kitchenette.
30.	1870	The *Leavenworth Bulletin* reports that "John Bell Crockett, grandson of Davy Crockett, was on Wednesday found murdered in his trading-boat" at Brandy's Landing near Memphis. His head had been "horribly crushed with an iron bar" and his boat "plundered."
31.	1833	In a letter written on December 30, and printed in the Washington D.C. *Daily National Intelligencer*, Crockett announces the following about his forthcoming autobiography: "I shall put to press a Narrative of my Life; in which I will carefully endeavor to avoid those refinements of literature which would disrobe my narrative of its greatest interest —and shall strive to represent myself, as I really am, a *plain, blunt, Western man*, relying on honesty and the woods, and not on learning and the law, for a living."
	1938	A large granite monument to Crockett is dedicated in Ozana, Crockett County, Texas. At the base of the structure is a modified version of Crockett's motto, "Be Sure You Are Right Then Go Ahead."

Epilogue

David Crockett was a one-of-a-kind American folk hero—military volunteer, backwoods storyteller, frontier *speechifyer*, gentleman from the cane, champion of the poor, fighter for Native American rights, bear hunter, stage legislator, congressman, Alamo defender.

Above all, poverty and debt were more characteristic of Crockett than the coonskin cap and long rifle. Failed business enterprises were common events throughout his life, but he never made excuses for his troubles; he simply went ahead. In a way, the financial struggles strengthened him and allowed him to better understand those he sought to represent in the legislative halls of government.

Crockett was not clothed in primitive buckskins or coarse linens when he arrived in Washington D.C., but he faithfully represented frontier America, a region of the country that would inexorably shift westward with every passing decade. To some, Crockett became a living symbol of the nation's heartland, an untamed world of wild beasts, native American warriors, and challenging landscapes. His tour of the northeastern states in 1834 was a major event which was celebrated by thousands and enthusiastically reported in scores of newspapers.

He wasn't the ideal husband or father, since he spent more time away from home than with his family. He was clearly in love with his first wife, Polly, but had more of a practical relationship with his second wife, Elizabeth, who did all of the child-rearing and household maintenance by herself while he was away hunting, campaigning, or serving in the Tennessee General Assembly and the United States House of Representatives. Yet his constant, restless search for new parcels of land were always done to benefit his family.

After his death at the Alamo, the Republic of Texas issued Elizabeth a bounty of 1,280 acres, as a result of her husband "being honorably discharged from the army by death." She later moved to Texas in 1853 with her son Robert and daughter Matilda. She died on January 31, 1860, and was buried in what is now the Acton State Historic Site, Texas' smallest historic park. A monument was erected in her honor at the site in 1913. Mary Polly Finley Crockett is buried in a cemetery named after her in Franklin County, Tennessee.

Although Crockett became a celebrity in his own lifetime, his death at the Alamo elevated him to the heroic ranks of other famous Americans who also gave their lives in the cause of liberty. Crockett's stand for freedom and democratic ideals against overwhelming odds during the Texas Revolution was memorable, and his earlier stand against the Jackson political machine, especially its policies against the southeastern tribes, was courageous and noble. No wonder the *Niles' Weekly Register* appropriately called him "a man of strong mind and of great goodness of heart."

Perhaps, Council Bluffs, Iowa's *Daily Nonpareil* stated it best in 1904: "American history pulsates with the brilliant achievement of her sons, and of all the early pioneers and patriots who offered their lives that the spirit of freedom might not perish, there is no name deserving of higher veneration than David Crockett." Twenty-two years later, Austin P. Foster, Assistant Tennessee State Librarian and Archivist, added to Crockett's legacy when he said that the backwoodsman was "the most unique character in American history, the quaintest, frankest and most honest of all men in public life."

Crockett developed into a legendary figure, a super hero of sorts, in the hands of writers, especially those who wrote the sensational stories in the 19th century almanacs. In every decade, since the 1830s, Crockett has been celebrated and memorialized numerous times in prose and poetry; staged productions; radio, film, and television; music and art; newspapers and periodicals; and in fanciful tall tales.

David Crockett *was;* Davy Crockett *is.* And his legend will continue—much, no doubt, to his delight and amusement.

Appendix A

David Crockett Biography, Collection of the U.S. House of Representatives

Crockett, David, (father of John Wesley Crockett), a Representative from Tennessee; born at the confluence of Limestone Creek and Nolichuckey River in the State of Franklin, present day Greene County, Tenn., August 17, 1786; attended the common schools; served in Creek campaign, 1813-1814; member of the Tennessee state house of representatives, 1821-1823; unsuccessful candidate for election to the Nineteenth Congress in 1825; elected as a Jacksonian to the Twentieth Congress (March 4, 1827-March 3, 1829); changed from a Jacksonian to an Anti-Jacksonian; elected as an Anti-Jacksonian to the Twenty-first Congress (March 4, 1829-March 3, 1831); unsuccessful candidate for reelection to the Twenty-second Congress in 1830; elected as an Anti-Jacksonian to the Twenty-third Congress (March 4, 1833-March 3, 1835); unsuccessful candidate for reelection to the Twenty-fourth Congress in 1834; fought at the Battle of the Alamo, San Antonio, Tex., 1836; died about March 6, 1836; remains cremated.

Notes and clarifications on the biographical entry:

The "common schools" statement is a bit of a generalization, since Crockett attended Benjamin Kitchen's "little country school" for four days in the autumn of 1799, and was later taught by John Canady's son four days a week during a six-month period in 1804.

The so-called "Creek campaign, 1813-1814" was the Creek War, 1813-1814 (also known as the Creek Indian War or the Red Stick War).

Crockett died at the Alamo on March 6, 1836, not "about March 6, 1836."

The expression "remains cremated" suggests a respected formality; however, Crockett's body and those of the other Alamo defenders were tossed on simple funeral pyres.

Appendix B
David Crockett's Legislative Career

On June 1, 1796, Tennessee was admitted to the union as the 16th state. Its first state constitution, approved by the United States Congress, included a bicameral legislature. Article One, Section One, stated: "The Legislative Authority of this State shall be vested in a General Assembly, which shall consist of a Senate and House of Representatives, both dependent on the People." The first constitution was in effect until 1835, when it was replaced.

Murfreesboro, Tennessee, Fourteenth General Assembly, House of Representatives

Speaker: James Fentress

First Session: September 17, 1821-November 17, 1821

An "extraordinary session" was proclaimed by Governor William Carroll following the burning of the capital's log courthouse. The General Assembly met at the First Presbyterian Church from July 22, to August 24, 1822. Crockett and his fellow representatives were assigned to meet on the first floor; the senate met on the second floor.

Murfreesboro, Tennessee, Fifteenth General Assembly, House of Representatives
Speaker: James Fentress

> First Session: September 15, 1823-November 29, 1823
> Second Session: September 20, 1824-October 22, 1824

Twentieth Congress of the United States
Speaker: Andrew Stevenson (Virginia)

> First Session: December 3, 1827-May 26, 1828
> Second Session: December 1, 1828-March 3, 1829

Tennessee delegation:

> 1st District: John Blair (Jacksonian)
> 2nd District: Pryor Lea (Jacksonian)
> 3rd District: James C. Mitchell (Jacksonian)
> 4th District: Jacob C. Isacks (Jacksonian)
> 5th District: Robert Desha (Jacksonian)
> 6th District: James K. Polk (Jacksonian)
> 7th District: John Bell (Jacksonian)
> 8th District: John H. Marable (Jacksonian)
> 9th District: David Crockett (Jacksonian)

Twenty-first Congress of the United States
Speaker: Andrew Stevenson (Virginia)

> First Session: December 7, 1829-May 31, 1830
> Second Session: December 6, 1830-March 3, 1831

Tennessee delegation:

1st District: John Blair (Jacksonian)
2nd District: Pryor Lea (Jacksonian)
3rd District: James I. Standifer (Jacksonian)
4th District: Jacob C. Isacks (Jacksonian)
5th District: Robert Desha (Jacksonian)
6th District: James K. Polk (Jacksonian)
7th District: John Bell (Jacksonian)
8th District: Cave Johnson (Jacksonian)
9th District: David Crockett (Anti-Jacksonian)

Twenty-third Congress of the United States
Speaker: John Bell (Tennessee)

First Session: December 2, 1833-June 30, 1834
Second Session: December 1, 1834-March 4, 1835

Tennessee delegation:

1st District: John Blair (Jacksonian)
2nd District: Samuel Bunch (Jacksonian)
3rd District: Luke Lea (Jacksonian)
4th District: James I. Standifer (Jacksonian)
5th District: John B. Forester (Jacksonian)
6th District: Balie Peyton (Jacksonian)
7th District: John Bell (Jacksonian)
8th District: David W. Dickinson (Jacksonian)
9th District: James K. Polk (Jacksonian)
10th District: William M. Inge (Jacksonian)

11ᵗʰ District: Cave Johnson (Jacksonian)
12ᵗʰ District: David Crockett (Anti-Jacksonian)
13ᵗʰ District: William C. Dunlap (Jacksonian)

Appendix C:
Davy Crockett; Or, Be Sure You're Right, Then Go Ahead Cast.

Davy Crockett; Or, Be Sure You're Right, Then Go Ahead, the 19th century play written by Frank Murdock and Frank Mayo, was sometimes promoted as *Davy Crockett—An Idyl of the Backwoods*. The productions also changed cast lineups, sometimes omitting characters and, at other times, adding some. Here is an example (from an undated promotional flyer):

Davy Crockett	Mr. Frank Mayo
Major Roylston	Mr. W. B. Arnold
Neil Crampton	Mr. Edwin Frank
Oscar Crampton	Mr. H. A. Weaver, Jr.
Big Dan	Mr. J. Holmes
Yonkers	Mr. Joseph Richards
Briggs	Mr. Edward Secor
Watson	Mr. Joseph Brooks
Quickwitch	Mr. T. H. Conley
Parson Ainsworth	Mr. Samuel R. Reed
Eleanor Vaughan	Miss Affie Weaver

Dame Crockett	Mrs. J. L. Sanford
Bob Crockett	Clara Thropp
Little Sal	Baby Thropp

Frank Mayo wasn't the only member of his family who had an association with the play. Georgia's *Macon Telegraph* reported in its February 16, 1913 issue, that twenty-five years ago, "Edwin F. Mayo, son of Frank Mayo, presents his father's famous play, 'Davy Crockett,' at the Academy of Music."

On November 21, 1922, San Diego's *Evening Tribune* published a recollection provided from Frank Mayo's grandson: "At the age of five I was playing little Davy in my grandfather's play 'Davy Crockett.' I played with him till he died two years later, and then my mother sent me to the Peekskill Military Academy, where I remained until I graduated. I had no idea of becoming an actor." Mayo went on to appear in over 350 motion pictures.

Appendix D: Topps *Walt Disney's Davy Crockett* Picture Cards, 1956.

Card #20-A in the second series is particularly rare. The card, titled "Ambush," features a photo of Crockett, Russel and some volunteers preparing to attack Red Stick's camp. The back of the card's title should repeat "Ambush," but actually reads "Look Out, Georgie!" The bottom of the card reads: "See card #21A – A Shot Rings Out." The mistake in the limited run second series was corrected making the replacement card more rare than the original.

The Orange-Back Series

#1	King Of The Wild Frontier *	#41	Vote For Davy!
#2	Call To War	#42	Serving His Country
#3	Off To Battle	#43	Congressman Crockett *
#4	Sentry! Where's Crockett	#44	You're Cheating, Mister
#5	Bear Meat For Dinner	#45	Reach, Crockett
#6	Davy In Command	#46	Off To Texas
#7	Alerted For Danger	#47	Trouble Ahead
#8	Preparing For War	#48	Davy's Victory

Davy Crockett Day by Day:

#9	Dance Of Death	#49	In Enemy Territory
#10	Ready To Strike	#50	Davy Arrives
#11	A Daring Raid	#51	Col. Crockett Reporting
#12	Flying Lead	#52	A Desperate Decision
#13	Moving Targets	#53	A Near Miss
#14	Indian Attack	#54	The Alamo's Answer
#15	Biting The Dust	#55	Things Look Bad
#16	Every Man For Himself	#56	Ready For Night Attack
#17	Tomahawk Terror	#57	No Relief In Sight
#18	Fight For Life	#58	Night Bombardment
#19	Picking 'Em Off	#59	Bad News
#20	Hand Fighting	#60	A Startling Report
#21	Savage Chief	#61	We'll Never Surrender
#22	Davy In Danger	#62	A Tough Choice
#23	Hall Or We'll Shoot	#63	Keeping Spirits High
#24	Home Sweet Home	#64	Checking The Defenses
#25	Indian Territory	#65	Plans For Defense
#26	On Guard *	#66	Reload – Quick!
#27	Indian Torture	#67	Storming The Walls
#28	Davy Senses Trouble *	#68	Heavy Artillery
#29	Face To Face With Death	#69	Help!
#30	Arms Of Steel	#70	Defenses Crumble
#31	Fists Flying	#71	Fists Against Guns
#32	Breaking The Hold	#72	Every Shot Counts
#33	Fighting – Indian Style	#73	Fighting To The End
#34	Davy Is Challenged	#74	Flashing Steel
#35	Bullseye!	#75	Travis Hit
#36	Don't Move, Crockett	#76	A Bullet Finds Its Mark
#37	Dirty Fighting	#77	Blazing Rifles
#38	The Knockout	#78	Fight To The Finish
#39	Now Get Going	#79	Russel Falls
#40	Tragedy Strikes	#80	Bowie's Last Stand *

Cards #1-33 are from "Davy Crockett, Indian Fighter"
Cards #34-43 are from "Davy Crockett Goes to Congress"
Cards #44-80 are from "Davy Crockett at the Alamo"
Cards marked with an * indicate a publicity still, not a scene from an episode. Card #1 is the only vertical card in the series, and graded as a rare PSA Mint 9, carries the highest current market price of approximately $3,000.

The Green-Back Series:

#1A	Buckskin Buddy		#41A	Davy's New Adventure
#2A	Dangerous Mission		#42A	Norton's Scheme
#3A	Catching A Bear		#43A	Doublecrossed
#4A	Out Of My Way		#44A	Heading South
#5A	Old Hickory		#45A	Davy Has Company
#6A	You're Wrong, Crockett		#46A	Comanche!
#7A	Setting The Trap		#47A	Rough And Tumble
#8A	A Fearful Site		#48A	Sign Language
#9A	The Warning		#49A	"Capture Crockett"
#10A	Deadly Arrow		#50A	The Alamo
#11A	Davy's Gamble		#51A	How's Are Chances?
#12A	Go Get 'Em, Davy		#52A	The Fighting Major
#13A	Sharpshooting		#53A	Bowie's "Toothpicks"
#14A	Davy In Action		#54A	Blasting The Alamo
#15A	Quick On The Trigger		#55A	Driving 'Em Back
#16A	Fighting Fury		#56A	Looking For Trouble
#17A	Blazing Bullets		#57A	Ol' Betsy's Victim
#18A	Shower Of Lead		#58A	Georgie, Come Back!
#19A	Suicide Attack		#59A	Rough Ride
#20A	Ambush		#60A	Furious Assault
#21A	A Shot Rings Out		#61A	On The Run
#22A	A Close Call		#62A	Brief Rest

#23A	Prepare To Fire!	#63A	Davy's Song
#24A	Happy Vacation	#64A	Outsmarting The Gambler
#25A	Disobeying Orders	#65A	Time's Running Out
#26A	Sneak Attack	#66A	Ready To Charge
#27A	Jaws Of Death	#67A	Direct Hit *
#28A	An Enemy Falls	#68A	Wall Of Bullets
#29A	Vicious Battle	#69A	Over The Top
#30A	Fight For Life	#70A	Keeping 'Em Off
#31A	Finish 'Em, Davy!	#71A	Take That!
#32A	Give Up?	#72A	Breaking Through
#33A	Peace	#73A	Enemy Reinforcements
#34A	Taking Careful Aim	#74A	Straight For Davy
#35A	Strange Neighbor	#75A	Surrounded
#36A	Davy's Down	#76A	5,000 Against 200
#37A	Flying Tackle	#77A	Slashing Sword
#38A	Good-Bye, Crockett!	#78A	Blazing Pistols
#39A	A Surprising Offer	#79A	Fighting Finish
#40A	The Reunion	#80A	Texas Triumph

Cards #1A-33A are from "Davy Crockett, Indian Fighter"

Cards #34A-43A are from "Davy Crockett Goes to Congress"

Cards #44A-80A are from "Davy Crockett at the Alamo"

Card #67A is a scene from *Man From the Alamo* (1953). It is one of two brief scenes from the film that were edited into the Disney production.

Appendix E
Western Writers of America's "All-Time Greatest Western TV Series, Movies and Miniseries" 2009 Poll Winners, Top Ten.

1. *Lonesome Dove* (1989)
2. *Centennial* (1978)
3. *The Sacketts* (1979)
4. *Conagher* (1991)
5. *Monte Walsh* (2003)
6. *Davy Crockett* (1954-1955)
7. *Last Stand at Saber River* (1997)
8. *Broken Trail* (2006)
9. *Riders of the Purple Sage* (1996)
10. *Into the West* (2005)

Appendix F
Billboard Magazine's Top Singles of the Year, 1955. Based on the "Best Sellers in Stores" Chart.

1. Perez Prado — "Cherry Pink and Apple Blossom White"
2. Bill Haley & his Comets — "Rock Around the Clock"
3. Mitch Miller — "The Yellow Rose of Texas"
4. Roger Williams — "Autumn Leaves"
5. Lex Baxter — "Unchained Melody"
6. Bill Hayes — "The Ballad of Davy Crockett"
7. The Four Aces — "Love is a Many-Splendored Thing"
8. The McGuire Sisters — "Sincerely"
9. Pat Boone — "Ain't That a Shame"
10. Georgia Gibbs — "The Wallflower (Dance With Me, Henry)"

22. Fess Parker — "The Ballad of Davy Crockett"

24. Tennessee Ernie Ford — "The Ballad of Davy Crockett"

Appendix G
Top Ten Best Davy Crockett Movie Lines

Source: "Davy Crockett in the Movies," *The Crockett Chronicle*, no. 33 (August 2015).

A select list of memorable dialogue from the most famous actors who have played the part of the frontier hero on the big screen (arranged chronologically):

Fess Parker: *Davy Crockett, King of the Wild Frontier*, 1955
(the theatrical release of the edited three
original television episodes)

"You sure spoiled things good. Now I gotta do it the old fashioned way."

"Never went to a shootin' match in my life without gettin' at least one shot off."

"Well, with old Betsy here n' this Arkansas toothpick of yourn,' how can we lose?"

Arthur Hunnicutt: *The Last Command*, 1955

"If you're expectin' fightin,' you can't exactly say it's only twenty nine 'cause these is Tennesseans, and that makes a difference."

"They'll eat snakes before they get in here."

"Keep prayin,' Parson. Hard."

John Wayne: *The Alamo,* 1960

"Republic. I like the sound of the word. It means people can live free, talk free, go or come, buy or sell, be drunk or sober, however they choose. Some words give you a feeling. Republic is one of those words that makes me tight in the throat, the same tightness a man gets when his baby takes his first step or his first baby shaves and makes his first sound like a man. Some words can give you a feeling that makes your heart warm. Republic is one of those words."

"You do the one and you're living; you do the other and you may be walkin' around but you're as dead as a beaver hat."

"Not thinkin.' Just rememberin.'

Billy Bob Thornton: *The Alamo,* 2004

"Amazing what a little harmony will do, ain't it?"

Bibliography

Books

Abbott, John S. C. *David Crockett: His Life and Adventures.* New York: Dodd, Mead and Co., 1874.

_____. *The Terror of the Indians; or, The Adventures of D. Crockett with Illustrations.* London: Ward Lock and Co., 1879.

_____. *David Crockett.* New York: Dodd, Mead and Co., 1898.

Adler, David A. *A Picture Book of Davy Crockett.* New York: Holiday House, 1996.

Allen, Charles Fletcher. *David Crockett, Scout, Small Boy, Pilgrim, Mountaineer, Soldier, Bear-Hunter, and Congressman, Defender of the Alamo.* Philadelphia: J. B. Lippincott, 1911.

Alphin, Elaine M. *Davy Crockett.* Minneapolis: Lerner Publishing Group, 2003.

Anderson, Paul. *The Davy Crockett Craze: A Look at the 1950's Phenomenon and Davy Crockett Collectibles.* Hillside, IL: R & G Productions, 1996.

Arpad, Joseph John. *David Crockett, An Original Legendary Eccentricity and Early American Character*, Ph.D. Diss, Duke University, 1969.

_____, ed. *A Narrative of the Life of David Crockett of the State of Tennessee.* New Haven, CT: College and University Press, 1972.

Baugh, Virgil. *Rendezvous at the Alamo: Highlights in the Lives of Bowie, Crockett & Travis.* New York: Pageant Press, 1960.

Beals, Frank. *Davy Crockett.* Evanston, IL: Row, Peterson and Co., 1941.

_____. *Real Adventures with Great American Pathfinders: Lewis and Clark, Davy Crockett, Daniel Boone.* San Francisco: H. Wagner Publishing Co., 1954.

Beecher, Elizabeth. *Walt Disney's Davy Crockett: King of the Wild Frontier.* New York: Simon and Schuster, 1955.

Bishop, Lee. *Davy Crockett: Frontier Fighter.* New York, Dell (American Explorer Series), 1983.

Blair, Walter. *Davy Crockett—Frontier Hero: The Truth as He Told It—The Legend as His Friends Built It.* New York: Coward-McCann, 1955.

Blassingame, Wyatt. *How Davy Crockett Got a Bearskin Coat.* Champaign, IL: Garrand Publishing Co., 1972.

Boylston, James and Allen J. Wiener. *David Crockett in Congress: The Rise and Fall of the Poor Man's Friend.* Houston, TX: Bright Sky Press, 2009.

Brown, Dee. *Wave High the Banner: A Novel Based on the Life of Davy Crockett.* Philadelphia: Macrae-Smith, 1942.

Burke, James Wakefield. *David Crockett, The Man Behind the Myth.* Austin: Eakin Press, 1984.

Burton, Ardis Edwards. *Legends of Davy Crockett.* Racine: WI: Whitman Publishing Co., 1955.

Coatsworth, Elizabeth Jane. *Old Whirlwind: A Story of Davy Crockett.* New York: Macmillan, 1953.

Chemerka, William R. *Fess Parker: TV's Frontier Hero.* Albany, GA: BearManor Media, 2011.

_____. *Alamo Anthology: From the Pages of The Alamo Journal.* Austin: Eakin Press, 2005.

_____. *The Davy Crockett Almanac and Book of Lists.* Austin: Eakin Press, 2000.

Chemerka, William R. and Allen J. Wiener. *Music of the Alamo: From 19th Century Ballads to Big-Screen Soundtracks.* Houston: Bright Sky Press, 2008.

Chutsky, Karen. *Young Davy Crockett: The Boy From Tennessee.* Lucerne Valley, CA: Grovesnor Square Press, 2014.

Clayton, Augustin Smith [attributed to David Crockett]. *The Life of Martin Van Buren.* Philadelphia: Robert Wright, 1835.

Clyde, Kit. *Davy Crockett's Vow, or, His Last Shot for Vengeance.* New York: Frank Tousey Publishers, 1886.

Cobia, Manley F. *Journey into the Land of Trials: The Story of Davy Crockett's Expedition to the Alamo.* Franklin, TN: Hillsboro Press, 2003.

Cody, William F. *Story of the Wild West and Camp-Fire Chats, by Buffalo Bill, (Hon. W. F. Cody): A Full and Complete History of the Renowned Pioneer*

Quartette, Boone, Crockett, Carson and Buffalo Bill. Philadelphia: Historical Publishing Co,. 1888.

Cohen, Caron Lee. *Sally Ann Thunder Ann Whirlwind Crockett.* New York: Greenwillow Books, 1985.

Collins, Phil. *The Alamo and Beyond: A Collector's Journey.* Buffalo Gap, TX: State House Press, 2012.

Corby, Jane. *The Story of Davy Crockett.* New York: Barse and Hopkins, 1922.

Crisp, James E. *Sleuthing the Alamo: Davy Crockett's Last Stand and Other Mysteries of the Texas Revolution.* New York: Oxford University Press, 2005.

Crockett, David. *A Narrative of the Life of David Crockett of the State of Tennessee.* Philadelphia: E. L. Carey & A. Hart, 1834.

_____ [and William Clark]. *An Account of Col. Crockett's Tour to the North and Down East.* Philadelphia: E. L. Carey and A. Hart, 1835.

Davis, Hazel. *Davy Crockett: Frontiersman and Scout.* New York: Random House, 1955.

Donovan, James. *The Blood of Heroes: The 13-Day Struggle for the Alamo—and the Sacrifice that Forged a Nation.* New York: Little, Brown and Co., 2012.

Dorson, Richard M. *Davy Crockett: American Comic Legend.* New York: Spiral Press, 1939.

Driggs, Howard R., and Sarah S. King. *Rise of the Lone Star: A Story of Texas Told by its Pioneers.* New York: Frederick A. Stokes Co., 1936.

Driskill, Frank A. *Davy Crockett: The Untold Story.* Austin: Eakin Press, 1981.

Eggleston, George Cary. *David Crockett.* New York: Dodd, Mead and Co., 1875.

Ellis, Edward S. *The Life of Colonel Crockett.* Philadelphia: Porter and Coates, 1884.

Evatt, Harriet. *Davy Crockett, Big Indian, and Little Bear.* Indianapolis: Bobbs-Merrill, 1955.

Farr, Naunerle C. *Davy Crockett/Daniel Boone.* West Haven, CT: Pendulum Press, 1979.

Feely, Thomas F., and Nancy E. Nagle. *Crockett's Last Stand: A Diorama.* Ridgefield Park, NJ: Historical Dioramas, Inc. 1995.

Folmsbee, Stanley J., and Anna Grace Catron. *The Early Career of David Crockett.* Knoxville: East Tennessee Historical Society Publications, 1956.

_____. *David Crockett: Congressman.* Knoxville: East Tennessee Historical Society Publications, 1957.

_____. *David Crockett in Texas.* Knoxville: East Tennessee Historical Society Publications, 1958.

Fontenay, Charles L. *Estes Kefauver: A Biography.* Knoxville: University of Tennessee Press, 1980.

Fontes, Ron and Justin Korman. *Davy Crockett Meets Death Hug.* New York: Disney Press, 1993.

_____. *Davy Crockett and the Highway Men.* New York: Disney Press, 1992.

Foreman, Gary L. *Crockett: The Gentleman from the Cane: A Comprehensive View of the Folkhero Americans Thought They Knew.* Dallas: Taylor Publishing Co., 1986.

Ford, Anne. *Davy Crockett: A See and Read Biography.* New York: G. P. Putnam's Sons, 1961.

Frank, Janet. *Davy Crockett and the Indians* [also as *Straight-shootin' Davy*]. Philadelphia: J. C. Winston, Co., 1955.

French, James Strange. *The Life and Adventures of Colonel David Crockett of West Tennessee.* New York: J. & J. Harper, 1833. [This was originally published anonymously, and later released as *Sketches and Eccentricities of Col. David Crockett, of West Tennessee.*]

Garland, Hamlin, *The Autobiography of David Crockett.* New York: Charles Scribner's Sons, 1923.

Grant, Bruce. *Davy Crockett: American Hero.* Chicago: Rand McNally, 1955.

Grant, Matthew G. *Davy Crockett, Frontier Adventurer.* Mankato, MN: Creative Education, Inc., 1973.

Groneman, Bill. *Defense of a Legend: Crockett and the de la Peña Diary.* Plano, TX: Republic of Texas Press, 1994.

_____. *Death of a Legend: The Myth and Mystery Surrounding the Death of Davy Crockett.* Plano, TX: Republic of Texas Press, 1999.

Groneman, William III. *David Crockett: Hero of the Common Man.* New York: Forge, 2005.

Hall, Roger A. *Performing the American Frontier, 1870-1906.* UK: Cambridge University Press, 2001.

Hanson, Dr. James A. *The Longhunter's Sketchbook.* Chadron, NE: The Fur Press, 1983.

Harrigan, Stephen. *The Gates of the Alamo.* New York: Alfred A. Knopf, 2000.

Hauck, Richard Boyd. *Crockett: A Bio-Biography.* Westport, CT: Greenwood Press, 1982.

Hazan, Barbara. *Davy Crockett: Indian Fighter.* New York: Pyramid Publishers Co., 1975.

Hazard, Harry [Joseph Edward Badger]. *The Bear Hunter; or Davy Crockett as a Spy.* New York: Beadles and Adams, 1876.

History of Morris County, New Jersey, 1739-1882. New York: W. W. Munsell, 1882.

Hogue, Albert Ross. *Davy Crockett and Others in Fentress County Who Have Given the County a Prominent Place in History.* Jamestown, TN, 1955.

Holbrook, Stewart H. *Davy Crockett: From the Backwoods of Tennessee to the Alamo.* New York: Random House, 1955.

Huthmacher, Ned Anthony. *One Domingo Morning: The Story of Alamo Joe.* New York: Vantage Press, 2003.

Hutton, Laurence. *Curiosities of the American Stage.* New York: Harper & Brothers, 1871.

Jackson, Jack. *The Alamo: An Epic Told From Both Sides.* Austin: Paisano Graphics Press, 2002.

Jeffries, Jeff. *Remember the Alamo! The Story of Davy Crockett.* London: The Children's Press, 1962.

Jones, Randell. *In The Footsteps of Davy Crockett.* Durham, NC: John F. Blair, 2005.

Judd, Cameron. *Crockett of Tennessee: A Novel Based on the Life and Times of David Crockett.* New York: Bantam Books, 1994.

Justice, Fred C. and Tom R. Smith, eds. *Who's Who in the Film World.* Los Angeles: Film World Publishing Company, 1914.

Kellogg, Steven. *Sally Ann Thunder Ann Whirlwind Crockett.* New York: HarperCollins, 1995.

Kelly, James C, and Frederick S. Voss. *Davy Crockett: Gentleman From The*

Cane—An Exhibit Commemorating Crockett's Life and Legend on the 200th Anniversary of his Birth. Washington, D.C.: National Portrait Gallery, 1986.

Kern, Russell S. *Marx Alamo Playsets and Toys of the Alamo & Davy Crockett Craze of the 50's, 60's & 70's.* Colorado Springs, CO: Atomic Enterprises, 2018.

Kilgore, Dan. *How Did Davy Die?* College Station, TX: Texas A&M University Press, 1978.

Kittredge, Belden. *The Truth About Casey Jones and other Fabulous American Heroes, including Johnny Appleseed, Davy Crockett, Roy Bean, and Mike Fink.* Girard, KS: Haldeman-Julius Publications, 1945.

Korman, Justine. *Davy Crockett at the Alamo.* New York: Disney Press, 1991.

_____. *Davy Crockett and the Creek Indians.* New York: Disney Press, 1991.

Lasalle, Charles E. [Ellis, Edward S.]. *The Texas Trailer, or Davy Crockett's Last Bear Hunt.* New York: Beadle and Adams, 1871.

Lawrence, James Duncan. *Davy Crockett and the Indian Secret.* New York: Books, Inc., 1955.

Lenvers, Leo. *Davy Crockett: Le Coureur Des Bois.* France: Fernand Nathan, 1984.

Le Sueur, Meridel. *Chanticleer of the Wilderness Road: The Story of Davy Crockett.* New York: Alfred A. Knopf, 1951.

Levy, Buddy. *The Real Life Adventures of Davy Crockett.* New York: G. P. Putnam's Sons, 2005.

Lind, Michael. *The Alamo: An Epic.* New York: Houghton Mifflin Company, 1997.

Lindley, Thomas Ricks. *Alamo Traces: New Evidence and New Conclusions.* Lanham, MD: Republic of Texas Press, 2003.

Littlejohn, Elbridge Gerry. *Texas History Stories; Houston, Austin, Crockett, La Salle.* Galveston, TX: E. G. Littlejohn, 1897.

Lofaro, Michael A., ed. *Davy Crockett: The Man, the Legend, the Legacy, 1786-1986.* Knoxville: University of Tennessee Press, 1985.

_____. *Davy Crockett's Riproarious Shemales and Sentimental Sisters: Women's Tall Tales from the Crockett Almanacs, 1835-1856.* Mechanicsburg, PA: Stackpole Books, 2001.

_____. *The Tall Tales of Davy Crockett; The Second Nashville Series of Crockett*

Almanacs, 1839-1841. Knoxville, TN, The University of Tennessee Press, 1987.

Lofaro, Michael A., and Joe Cummings, eds. *Crockett at Two Hundred: New Perspectives on the Man and the Myth*. Knoxville: University of Tennessee Press, 1989.

Long, Jeff. *Duel of Eagles: The Mexican and U.S. Fight for the Alamo*. New York: William Morrow and Co., 1990.

Lord, Walter. *A Time to Stand*. New York: Harper and Brothers, 1961.

McIntyre, John T. *In Texas with Davy Crockett*. Philadelphia: Penn Publishing Co., 1922.

McNeil, Everett. *In Texas With Davy Crockett; A Story of the Texas War for Independence*. New York: E. P. Dutton and Co., 1908.

Markey, Richard. *A Million Laughs: The Funny History of American Comedy*. Ivana Tinkle e-Books, 2015.

Mayer, Edwin Justus. *Sunrise in my Pocket; or, The Last Days of Davy Crockett, an American Saga*. New York: Julian Messner, 1941.

Meadowcraft, Enid Lamonte. *The Story of Davy Crockett*. New York: Grosset and Dunlap, 1952.

Meine, Franklin J. *The Crockett Almanacks: Nashville Series, 1835-1838*. Chicago: The Caxton Club, 1955.

Morphis, James A. *History of Texas from its Discovery and Settlement, with a Description of its Principal Cities and Counties, and the Agricultural, Mineral, and Material Resources of the State*. New York: United States Publishing Co., 1874.

Moseley, Elizabeth R. *Davy Crockett: Hero of the Wild Frontier*. Champaign, IL: Garrard Publishing Co., 1967.

Munroe, Kirk. *With Bowie and Crockett, or Fighting for the Lone-Star Flag*. New York: Charles Scribner's Sons, 1905.

Nunn, Marion Michael. *The Forgotten Pioneer: The Life of Davy Crockett*. New York: Vantage Press, 1954.

Parks, Aileen Wells. *Davy Crockett, Young Rifleman*. Indianapolis: Bobbs-Merrill Co., 1949.

Parrington, Vernon Louis. *Main Currents of American Thought.* New York: Harcourt Brace and Co., 1927.

Perry, Carmen, trans. and ed. *With Santa Anna in Texas: A Personal Narrative of the Revolution by José Enrique de la Peña.* College Station: TX: Texas A&M University Press, 1975.

Perry, Francis M. and Katherine Beebe. *Four American Pioneers: Daniel Boone, George Rogers Clark, David Crockett, Kit Carson; a Book for Young Americans.* New York: American Book Co., 1900.

Petersen, Gert. *David Crockett, The Volunteer Rifleman: An Account of his Life, while a Resident of Franklin County, 1812-1817.* Franklin County, TN: Franklin County Historical Society, 2007.

Phelan, James. *School History of Tennessee.* Philadelphia: E. H. Butler and Company, 1889.

Potter, Ruben. *The Fall of the Alamo: A Reminiscence of the Revolution in Texas.* San Antonio: Herald Steam Press, 1860.

Quackenbush, Robert. *Quit Pulling My Leg: A Story of Davy Crockett.* New York: Prentice-Hall Books for Young Readers, 1987.

Reiter, Harriet. *David Crockett.* Dansville, NY: F. A. Owen Publishing Co., 1905.

Ritchie, Robert C. and Paul Andrew Hutton, eds. *Frontier and Region: Essays in Honor of Martin Ridge.* San Marino, CA: Huntington Library Press, 1997.

Rourke, Constance. *Davy Crockett.* New York: Harcourt, 1934.

Sanford, William R., and Carl R. Green. *Davy Crockett: Defender of the Alamo.* Berkeley Heights, NJ: Enslow Publishers, 1996.

Santrey, Laurence. *Davy Crockett: Young Pioneer.* Mahwah, NJ: Troll, 1983.

Schaare, C. R. *The Life of Davy Crockett in Picture and Story.* New York: Cupples and Leon Co., 1935.

Shackford, James Atkins. *David Crockett: The Man and the Legend,* edited by John B. Shackford. Chapel Hill: University of North Carolina Press, 1956.

Shapiro, Irwin. *Davy Crockett's Keelboat Race.* New York: Simon and Schuster, 1955.

_____. *Davy Crockett: King of the Wild Frontier.* Simon and Schuster, 1955.

_____. *Yankee Thunder: The Legendary Life of Davy Crockett.* New York: J. Messner, Inc., 1944.

Shaw, Russel B. *Davy Crockett: Fabulous Frontier Fighter; The Life Story of an Amazing American Hero*. Gatlinburg, TN: Russel Shaw Guides, 1955.

Singer, A. L. *Davy Crockett and the Pirates at Cave-In Rock*. New York: Disney Press, 1991.

_____. *Davy Crockett and the King of the River*. New York: Disney Press, 1991.

Sistler, Byron and Samuel. *Tennesseans in the War of 1812*. Nashville: Byron Sistler and Associates, 1992.

Slide, Anthony. *The New Historical Dictionary of the American Film Industry*. New York: Routledge, 2013.

Sprague, William C. *Davy Crockett*. New York: The Macmillan Co., 1915.

Steele, William O. *Davy Crockett's Earthquake*. New York: Harcourt Brace, 1956.

Stephenson, Nathaniel W. *Texas and the Mexican War*. New Haven, CT: Yale University Press, 1921.

Sutton, Felix. *The Picture Story of Davy Crockett*. New York: Wonder Books, 1955.

Swann, Joseph. *The Early Life and Times of David Crockett in East Tennessee, 1786-1812*. Unpublished manuscript.

Taylor, Vincent Frank. 1955 children's book, *David Crockett: The Bravest of Them All Who Died at the Alamo*. San Antonio: Naylor Co., 1955.

Thompson, Bob. *Born on a Mountaintop: On the Road with Davy Crockett and the Ghosts of the Wild Frontier*. New York: Crown Trade Group, 2012.

Thompson, David. *Blood Hunt*. New York: Leisure Books, 1997.

_____. *Blood Rage*. New York: Leisure Books, 1997.

_____. *Cannibal Country*. New York: Leisure Books, 1998.

_____. *Comanche*. New York: Leisure Books, 1998.

_____. *Homecoming*. New York: Leisure Books, 1996.

_____. *Mississippi Mayhem*. New York: Leisure Books, 1997.

_____. *Sioux Slaughter*. New York: Leisure Books, 1997.

_____. *Texican Terror*. New York: Leisure Books, 1998.

Thompson, Ernest T. *The Fabulous Davy Crockett: His Life and Times in Gibson County, Tenn. Including Tall Tales and Anecdotes of the Western Wilds*. Rutherford, TN: Davy Crockett Memorial Association, 1956.

Tolliver, Arthur Tolliver. *The Wild Adventures of Davy Crockett: Based Mainly on the Writings of the Hero of the Alamo.* Girard, KS: Haldeman-Julius Publishers, 1944.

Tousey, Sanford. *Hero of the Alamo.* Chicago: Albert Whitman and Co., 1948.

Trotman, Felicity, and Shirley Greenway, eds. *Davy Crockett.* Milwaukee: Raintree Children's Books, 1985.

Turner, Frederick Jackson. *The Frontier in American History.* Mineola, NY: Dover Publications, Inc., 1996.

Wade, Mary Dodson. *David Crockett—Sure He Was Right.* Austin: Eakin Press, 1992.

_____. *David Crockett: Hero and Legend.* Houston: Bright Sky Press, 2009.

Wallis, Michael. *David Crockett: The Lion of the West.* New York: W. W. Norton and Co., 2011.

Warren, Charles Dudley. *Killb'ar, the Guide; or, Davy Crockett's Crooked Trail.* New York: Beadles and Adams, 1882.

Willett, Edward. *Davy Crockett's Boy Hunter.* Cleveland: Arthur Westbrook Co., 1908.

Wilson, Nat. *Davy Crockett: Danger From the Mountain.* New York: Triple Nickel Book, 1955.

Zaboly, Gary S. *An Altar For Their Sons: The Alamo and the Texas Revolution in Contemporary Newspaper Accounts.* Buffalo Gap, TX: State House Press, 2011.

Zucker, David, Paul A. Hutton, and Robert N. LoCash. *Crockett.* Unpublished film scripts, July and September,1993; January, June, July, November, 1994.

Newspapers
Age, The [ME]
Albany Argus [NY]
Albany Journal [NY]
American Advocate [Hallowell, ME]
American Daily Advertiser [PA]
Anaconda Standard [Anaconda, MT]
Arkansas Gazette [Little Rock, AR]
Austin Chronicle

Beaumont Journal [TX]
Bolivar Bulletin [Bolivar, TN]
Boston Bee
Boston Daily Advertiser
Boston Evening Transcript
Boston Morning Post
Boston Semi-Weekly Atlas
Breckenridge News [Hardinsburg, KY]
Charlotte News
Charleston Courier
Chattanooga Sunday Times
Chicago Daily Tribune
Chicago Sun-Times
Cincinnati Commercial Tribune
Cincinnati Post
Columbus Daily Enquirer [GA]
Commonwealth [Frankfort, KY]
Daily Crescent [New Orleans]
Daily Graphic [New York]
Daily Illinois Journal [Springfield, IL]
Daily Intelligencer [Seattle, WA]
Daily Nonpareil [Council Bluffs, IA]
Daily Pennsylvanian [Philadelphia, PA]
Daily National Intelligencer [D.C.]
Daily Record [Morristown, NJ]
Daily Telegram [Adrian, Michigan]
Dallas Morning News
Democratic Press [Ravenna, OH]
Dollar Newspaper [Philadelphia]
Downing Gazette [Portland, ME]
El Heraldo de Brownsville [Brownsville, TX]
Emporium and True American [Trenton, NJ]
Evansville Press [IL]
Evening Leader [Grand Rapids, MI]
Evening Tribune [San Diego]
Farmer's Cabinet [NH]
Fort Worth Star-Telegram

Gloucester Democrat [MA]
Gloucester Telegraph [MA]
Hartford Times [CT]
Hood County News [TX]
Idaho Statesman [Boise, ID]
Independent Gazette [Concord, NH]
Independent Hour [NJ]
Indiana State Sentinel [Indianapolis, IN]
Jackson Citizen Patriot [MI]
Jackson Gazette [TN]
Jamestown Journal [NY]
Kansas City Star [MO]
Knoxville Journal
Knoxville News-Sentinel
Knoxville Register
Lancaster Daily Examiner [PA]
Lexington Intelligencer [MO]
Lexington Leader [KY]
Little Rock Gazette
Louisiana Advertiser [NewOrleans, LA]
Massachusetts Ploughman and New England Journal of Agriculture [Boston, MA]
Massachusetts Spy [Worcester, MA]
Memphis Daily Advance
Miami Herald
Mississippi Free Trader and Natchez Gazette
Monroe Democrat [NY]
Morning Herald [Wilmington, DE]
Morristown Daily Gazette and Mail [TN]
Nashville Whig
New Era [PA]
New-Hampshire Patriot and State Gazette [Concord, NH]
New York Commercial Advertiser
New York Evening-Post
New York Mirror
New York Sun
New York Times
Niles' Weekly Register [Baltimore, MD]

A Popular Culture and Historical Calendar

Omaha World-Herald
Oxford Intelligencer [MS]
Pacific Commercial Advertiser [Honolulu, HI]
Polynesian [Honolulu, HI]
Raftsman's Journal [Clearfield, PA]
Raleigh Star [NC]
Rhode Island Republican [Newport, RI]
Sacramento Bee
Sacramento Daily Union
Salem Observer [MA]
San Antonio Express
San Francisco Bulletin
San Francisco Evening Post
Seattle Times
Sentinel of Freedom [NJ]
Shiner Gazette [TX]
Southern Statesman [TN]
Springfield Republican [MA]
Stamford Sentinel [CT]
Tacoma News
Times-Picayune [LA]
Trenton Times [NJ]
Trinity Advocate [Palestine, TX]
Urbana Record [OH]
USA Today
Utah Enquirer [Utah Co., UT]
Vermont Advocate [Chelsea, VT]
Vermont Chronicle [Bellows Falls, VT]
Vermont Phoenix [Brattleboro, VT]
Wall Street Journal
Wessington Springs Herald [Wessington, SD]
Western Aurora And Farmers and Mechanics Advocate [OH]
Wheeling Register [WV]
White Cloud Kansas Chief [KS]
Worcester Daily Spy [MA]
Yorkville, Enquirer [York, SC]

Periodicals
Alamo Journal, The
Billboard
Celebrations
Cincinnati Mirror and Western Gazette of Literature and Science
Cockeyed
Coronet
Crockett Chronicle, The
Disneyland Line
Entertainment Weekly
Film Index, The
Frontier Times
Galaxy of Comicalities
Go Ahead
Life
Look
Magazine of American History
Mentor, The
Moving Picture World
New England Magazine
New Monthly Magazine [Harper's]
Parade
Roundup
Tennessee Town & Country
Texas Magazine, The
Texas Monthly
True West
TV Guide

Collections and Archives
Neil Abelsma Collection
The Alamo
William R. Chemerka Collection
Phil Collins Collection
Paul DeVito Collection
Smithsonian Institution: American History Museum
Murray Weissmann Collection
David Zucker Collection

Index of Key Names

Abbott, John S. C., 77
Adams, Charles M., 267
Adams, John Q., 20, 23, 24, 226
Adler, David A., 171
Akin, Todd, 184
Alcorn, John, 260
Alexander, Adam, 20-22, 25, 200n, 215, 243
Allen, Charles Fletcher, 92,
Allen, Woody, 196
Alphin, Elaine M., 180
Anderson, Paul, 172
Armstrong, Zella, 101
Arnold, Guy, 155, 264
Arnold, William, 22
Arpad, Joseph, 61n, 146
Ash, John, 269
Atkinson, Wm. H. S., 270
Austin, Stephen, 102, 257
Autry, Gene, 116
Autry, Micajah, 181

Badger, Joseph Edward (see Harry Hazard), 77
Baker, Mark, 243
Baker, Sally, 53, 192
Ballou, Maturin Murray, 71
Barbera, Joseph, 150, 159
Bardette, Trevor, 115, 250
Barnard, J. H., 251
Barney, Mary, 218
Barrat, Robert, 104, 111, 208, 233

Barrett, William A., 125
Barrymore, Lionel, 87
Baugh, Virgil, 142
Beale, Charles T., 76
Beals, Frank, 105, 115
Bean, Robert, 8
Bearden, Jeff, 193
Beebe, Katherine, 85
Beecher, Elizabeth, 128
Bell, John, 74
Bender, J., 125
Benge, Geoff, 187
Benge, Janet, 187
Benton, Thomas Hart, 108, 133
Bernard, William Bayle, 57n
Berry, Noah, 111
Biddle, Nicholas, 41, 269
Binkley, William C., 213
Binney, Horace, 217
Bishop, Lee, 152
Blackburn, James, 213
Blackburn, Tom, 116, 117, 120, 135, 144, 149, 168, 216, 250
Blair, Robert, 24
Blair, Walter, 127, 218
Blanc, Mel, 133
Blassingame, Wyatt, 148
Blue, Uriah, 13
Blum, Chris, 159
Bode, Robert, 145
Boldt, Michael, 169
Bond, Thomas R., 233

309

Boone, Daniel, 58n, 90, 97, 101
Booth, Edwin, 224
Booth, John Wilkes, 224
Borgnine, Ernest, 133
Bosworth, Hobart, 90, 227
Bowie, James, 49, 50, 52, 113, 132, 151, 220, 225, 230, 231, 246, 252
Bowie, Rezin, 72
Boyer, Charles, 169
Boylston, James R., 58n, 185, 202n
Bradburn, Juan, 52, 242
Bradford, Henry, 249
Braun, Wilbur (aka Alice Chadwicke), 133
Brennan, Stephen, 187
Bromberg, David, 162
Brooks, Bailey, 207
Brooks, John Sowers, 182, 202n
Brown, Dee, 106
Brown, Harry, 215
Brown, L. D., 70
Browning, W. E., 93
Brunes, Karen (aka Tom Hill), 136
Bruns, George, 116, 120, 128, 135, 144, 168, 216
Bryan, John, 235
Burch, S., 241
Burgess, John A., 71
Burgin, Abner, 46, 48, 192, 266
Burke, James Wakefield, 153
Burr, Aaron, 23, 24
Burton, Ardis Edwards, 127
Bush, George W., 179
Butler, William, 19
Bygraves, Max, 135, 216

Cage, Nicholas, 162
Caldwell, James, 5
Calhoun, John C., 31, 83
Callaghan, C. W., 261
Canady, Charles, 6
Canady, John, 6, 54n, 237
Candelaria, Madam, 201n, 223
Cannon, Newton, 10

Carey, Edward L., 33, 34, 44, 64, 207, 208, 210, 211, 214, 216, 219, 222, 248, 269
Carey, Macdonald, 115
Carroll, William, 227, 248, 257
Carson, Cindy, 133, 134, 242
Carson, Kit, 66, 101
Caruthers, William Alexander, 57n, 67
Cash, Johnny, 158, 264
Cassidy, Hopalong, 116
Caywood, Danny, 179
Chadwicke, Alice (see Wilbur Braun), 133
Chandler, Lane, 102, 256
Chapman, Helen, 195
Chapman, John Gadsby, 37, 96, 100, 172, 240, 260, 262
Cheek, Jesse, 4
Chemerka, William R., 175, 184, 189
Chesney, Gary, 192
Chilton, Thomas, 33, 264
Christiansen, Jim, 131
Churms, Mark, 172
Chutsky, Karen, 189
Clark, James, 200n, 208
Clark, William, 44, 58n, 64, 208, 228, 269
Clarke, Matthew St. Claire, 31
Clay, Edward, 64
Clay, Henry, 30, 31
Clayton, Augustin Smith, 44
Cleaves, Frank, 37
Cleveland, Grover, 205n
Cloud, Daniel, 213
Coatsworth, Elizabeth Jane, 115
Cody, William F., 81, 101
Coffee, John, 10, 258, 260
Cohen, Caron Lee, 152
Cohen, Louis, 122
Cole, John, 3
Collins, Phil, 184, 188, 189
Connally, John, 156
Connally, Merrill, 156, 159, 219, 245, 246
Conrad, Robert T., 66
Constable, Richard, 39, 242

Cooper, Gary, 199n
Coppini, Pompeo, 104
Corbett, James J., 87, 199n
Corby, Jane, 96
Cordy, Annie, 136
Courtney, Peter, 199n
Costner, Kevin, 160, 161
Craig, William, 66
Crary, Isaac Edwin, 215
Crawford, Cheryl, 105
Crawford, Mel, 128
Crisp, James E., 169-171, 183
Crockett, Ashley Wilson, 58n, 97, 200n, 226, 231, 234-236, 258
Crockett, David: childhood 1-5; young adulthood and first marriage, 6-8; Creek War, 8-14; second marriage, 14-16; local and state public service, 16-20; congress, 20-46; Texas 46-52
Crockett, David (grandson), 231
Crockett, David (no relation), 171, 190
Crockett, Dorcas Matilda, 93
Crockett, Elizabeth Patton, 16, 22, 44, 46, 60n, 212, 223, 234, 242, 247, 252, 255, 256
Crockett, Geo. F., 252
Crockett, John, 1, 2, 4, 5, 53n, 259
Crockett, John Bell, 271
Crockett, John Wesley, 7, 60n, 66, 67, 70, 82, 204, 209, 210, 215, 231, 243, 264
Crockett, Margaret, 8, 48, 49, 60n, 178, 209, 264
Crockett, Matilda, 16, 46, 93, 236, 242, 247
Crockett, Olivia Elvira, 93, 97
Crockett, Polly (see also Mary Polly Finley), 7, 8, 234, 238, 264
Crockett, Rebecca, 1, 53n, 259
Crockett, Rebecca Elvira, 16, 222, 252, 270
Crockett, Robert Hamilton, 75, 82, 197, 198n, 207, 224, 249

Crockett, Robert Patton, 16, 58n, 93, 97, 182, 202n, 234, 236, 255-257
Crockett, William, 7, 209, 264
Cronkite, Walter, 148
Cruise, Tom, 160-162
Crump, E. H., 109
Cummings, Joe, 159

Darwin, Robert, 60
Davidson, James, 249
Davis, Erma, 220
Davis, Hazel, 127
Davis, James D., 47
Davis, Jefferson, 74, 83
Davis, Mac, 157, 259
Davis, Warren Ransom, 212
Davis, William C., 173
Dempsey, Jack, 99
Derr, Mark, 165, 166
de la Peña, José Enrique, 51, 52, 154, 169, 177
DeRose, Anthony Lewis, 73
Dewey, George, 85
Dickinson, Almaron, 51, 213, 220, 238
Dickinson, Susanna, 51, 213, 220, 238
Dillon, Allen, 191
Dillon, Wade, 190
DiMaggio, Joe, 102
Disney, Roy E., 162
Disney, Walt, 108, 114, 116, 118, 120, 121, 124, 130, 132, 137, 139, 140, 232, 248
Dixon, Jacob, 226
Dodd, Jimmie, 130
Doggett, Thomas, 248
Dolson, George, 170
Donovan, James, 188
Dooley, Eliot, 162
Dorson, Richard M., 104, 221
Douglas, Paul, 111
Douglass, A. H., 253
Driskill, Frank, 150
Dumas, Alex, J., 76

Dumas, Jim, 76
Dunigan, Tim, 157, 158, 209, 238, 239, 248, 264, 269
Dunn, George, 228
Dunn, Harry, 247

Easley, William, 255
Ebsen, Buddy, 117, 121, 125, 128, 146, 182, 229
Ederle, Gertrude, 98, 102
Edmondson, J. R., 176
Edson, Merritt Austin, 125
Eggleston, George C., 78
Eisenhower, Dwight D., 114, 115, 130
Eisner, Michael, 162
Elder, Margaret, 7, 259
Elliott, Wild Bill, 106, 107, 244
Ellis, Edward S. (aka Charles E. Lasalle), 77, 80, 116, 142
Esparza, Enrique, 51, 232, 239
Esparza, José Gregorio, 49, 51, 52, 239
Estes, Joel, 109, 200n
Evans, Robert, 252
Evatt, Harriet, 127
Evernden, Margery, 162

Falls, Charles B., 114,
Fannin, James, 51, 66, 179
Farr, Naunerle, 150
Farnum, Dustin, 93-95
Favor, Hiram, 225
Feely, Thomas F., 169
Feeney, Kathy, 178
Ferguson, Mrs. Walter, 240
Fidler, Jimmie, 109
Finley, Mary Polly (see also Polly Crockett), 7, 208, 247-251
Fitzgerald, William, 29-31, 208, 239, 243
Flowers, Wiley, 60n, 178, 209
Floyd, William, 56n
Flynn, Errol, 87
Folmsbee, Stanley J., 140
Fondersmith, John, 195

Fontes, Ron, 164
Ford, Anne, 142
Ford, Francis, 235
Ford, Glenn, 115
Ford, John, 220
Ford, Tennessee Ernie, 120, 135, 210, 220-222, 224-227, 229, 232, 236, 239, 241-243, 245
Ford, William P., 83
Foreman, Gary L., 155, 167, 177, 194, 204n, 218, 243
Forsyth, John, 113, 218
Foster, Austin P., 262
Foster, Norman, 116, 260
Fowler, W. B., 184
Fox, Michael J., 261
Frank, Janet, 127
Franklin, Benjamin, 8, 34, 48, 60n, 61n, 227
French, Charles K., 90, 237
French, James Strange, 31, 63
French, R. E., 87
Frizell, Frank, 246
Fullerton, W. H., 48, 60n

Galbreath, Thomas, 2
Garland, Hamlin, 97
Geary, Bud, 101
George, Gil, 128
Gibson, Dorothy, 242
Gibson, John H., 10, 11, 257, 258
Gibson, Mel, 160, 161
Glaspie, Francis, 8, 55n
Gillespie, A. E., 82
Gobel, George, 126, 219
Godines, Henry, 176
Gordon, Ibbie, 215, 216
Gore, Al, 165
Gorham, Benjamin, 217
Gowan, Charles E., 56n
Graham, Sheila, 104, 105, 109, 200n
Grange, Red, 98
Grant, Bruce, 127

Grant, Matthew, 149
Grant, Ulysses S., 74
Gray, John, 4
Gregory XVI, 224
Green, Carl, 171
Greene, Nathaniel, 8
Greenway, Shirley, 155
Greenwood, Jerome, 145
Griffith, Elijah, 5, 237
Griffith, James, 138, 241
Groneman, William (Bill), 168-171, 174, 183, 187
Grubbs, Gary, 158
Gummersall, Devon, 178
Gwynne, Fred, 147

Hack, William, 238
Hackett, James, 28, 32, 44, 57n, 65, 93, 228, 262, 265
Haldy, Emma E., 191
Haley, Bill & his Comets, 120
Hamer, Rusty, 254
Hamilton, Alexander, 8, 24
Hamilton, William, 194
Hanna, William, 150, 159
Hancock, John Lee, 181, 276
Hanson, James A., 152
Harding, Chester, 37, 58n, 130, 186, 231, 248
Harper, Herbert L., 155
Harrigan, Stephen, 176
Harrison, William B., 49, 209, 213
Hanks, Tom, 160, 161
Hart, Abraham, 33, 34, 44, 64, 207, 208, 210, 211, 214, 216, 219, 222, 248, 269
Harte, Betty, 90
Harvey, Laurence, 142
Hauck, Richard Boyd, 152
Hawkins, John, 2
Hayden, Jeffrey, 179
Hayes, Bill, 119, 134, 135, 172, 192, 216, 217, 220-222, 224-227, 229, 236, 239, 241-243, 268, 269

Hayes, Rutherford B., 205n
Hays, H. R., 101
Hazard, Harry (aka Joseph Edward Badger), 77
Herman, David, 227
Herron, France Edward, 130
Hickok, Wild Bill, 81
Hill, Tom (see Karen Brunes), 136
Hinchley, Lu, 54n
Hinchman, Gus Maxwell, 36, 229
Hinckley, David, 248
Hinnant, John, 60n
Hodgins, Earl, 102
Hogan, Pat, 158
Hogue, Albert Ross, 128
Holbrook, Stewart H., 127
Holderness, Mary Elizabeth Crockett, 39
Hood, Sir Thomas, 59
Hope, Bob, 140, 222
Hopper, DeWolfe, 100
Hopper, Hedda, 109, 248
Horsely, Lee, 233
Houston, Sam, 48, 52, 60n, 83, 104, 138, 174, 190, 213, 217, 220, 226, 233, 235, 241, 258
Howard, Ron, 133
Howell, Joseph B., 71
Hubbard, Henry, 217
Huberman, Brian, 166
Huddle, William Henry, 81
Hull, John, 254
Hungerford, Mary Jane, 200n
Hunnicutt, Arthur, 132, 142, 157, 159, 247
Hunter, J. Marvin, 103
Huntsman, Adam, 44, 66, 217, 244, 245, 248, 250-252, 254, 255
Hurst, Jack, 249
Huston, Walter, 104
Hutchings, Andrew J., 261
Huthmacher, Ned, 180
Hutton, Paul Andrew, 154, 160, 173

Iger, Bob, 240

Jackson, Andrew, 11-14, 19-21, 23-25, 27, 29, 30, 33, 41, 64, 97, 118, 149, 174, 207, 209-212, 214, 217, 220, 238, 248, 254, 256, 261, 262, 270
Jackson, Jack, 176
Jackson, Thomas "Stonewall", 74, 83
Jacob, John J., 246
Jacobs, John L., 55n
Jagger, Mick, 168
Jamborsky, William Eric, 159
James, Dick, 135
Jarvis, Lana Rae, 192
Jeffries, James, 87, 88, 199n, 210
Jeffries, Jeff, 142
Jenkins, Bill, 171
Jervis, John B., 30
Joe, 51
Joel, Billy, 159
John, Frances, 165
Johnson, Jack, 199n
Jones, Atlas, 29
Jones, Calvin, 250
Jones, Casey, 187
Jones, Francis, 10, 254, 256
Jones, Isaac, 48, 253
Jones, Jesse, 16
Jones, Margo, 108
Jones, Randell, 183
Johnston, Marianne, 175
Judd, Cameron, 168
Justice, Jeff, 237

Kahn, E. J., 253
Kanawah, David, 156
Kefauver, Estes, 109, 114, 115, 200n
Keith, Brian, 155, 156, 212
Kellogg, Steven, 169
Kelly, James C., 60n, 154
Kelly, William A., 234
Kendell, George W., 246
Kennedy, John [see John Canady], 6

Kennedy, Robert F., 244
Kern, Russell S., 196
Kerrigan, J. Warren, 98
Kilgore, Dan, 149, 150, 159
Kimball, Captain, 52, 242
King, Margaret J., 153
Kingston, Winifred, 93
Kirby, Jack, 131
Kitchen, Benjamin, 4
Kittredge, Belden, 108
Knauff, George P., 67
Korman, Justine, 164
Kramer, Miriam, 108

Lafayette, Marquis de, 20
Lancaster, Burt, 133
Landers, Lou, 111
Landis, Cullen, 98, 247
Lasalle, Charles E. (see Edward S. Ellis), 77
Lawrence, James Duncan, 127
Lawrence, Richard, 212
Le May, Alan, 109
Le Sueur, Meridel, 113
Lea, Pryor, 25, 215, 222
Lee, Robert E., 74
Legg, Adrian, 168
Lenvers, Leo, 152
Levy, Buddy, 183
Lincoln, Abraham, 74, 83, 102, 105
Lind, Michael, 173
Lindbergh, Charles A., 98
Lindley, Thomas Ricks, 170, 179
Lipton, Dean, 150
Littlejohn, Elbridge Gerry, 83
Lloyd, Frank, 132
LoCash, Robert, 160
Loesser, Frank, 111
Lofaro, Michael A., 152, 156, 159
Lolabrigida, Gina, 130
Lonergan, Lester, 87, 269
Long, Jeff, 162
Lord, Walter, 142

McAllister, C., 247
McCardle, Henry Arthur, 86
McCardle, Jim, 131
McCartney, Paul, 151
McCrae, Joel, 104, 105, 138
McCullough, Walter, 87
McCurry, Tim, 53
McEnery, Dave, 201n, 215
McIntyre, John T., 96
McKay, Sean, 204n
McKernan, Frank, 92
McKinney, Charles, 174
McLean, G. W., 210
McLean, John, 270
McLemore, John C., 260
McMillen, Davison, 210
McNeil, Everett, 89
Madison, James, 8, 9, 55n
Malanowski, Tony, 179
Malone, Ted, 209
Mamoulian, Rouben, 111
Markey, Rich, 195
Marsh, Jesse, 131
Marsh, Norman, 113
Martin, Michael J., 178
Marx, Groucho, 196
Mason, Robert, 207
Massey, Raymond, 105, 108
Massey, Tim, 198n
Mayer, Edwin Justus, 104, 111, 178
Mayo, Edwin, 265
Mayo, Frank, 78-80, 86, 88, 90, 93, 96, 97, 99, 105, 108, 133, 210, 222, 230, 232, 233, 238, 239, 250, 255, 257, 258, 260, 265, 269
Meadowcraft, Enid Lamonte, 114
Meine, Franklin J., 124
Méliès, Georges, 91
Melton, Kent, 182
Mendez, Antonio Tobias, 191
Milhouse, John Philip, 100
Milland, Ray, 109
Minor, Mike, 146

Montgomery, George, 111, 112, 205n, 208
Montgomery, Richard, 54n
Moore, William, 14
Morgan, Daniel, 8
Morgan, Dennis, 105
Morgan, John Hunt, 75, 76
Morris, Doug, 227
Morrow, Temple Houston, 258
Morton, James G., 87
Moseley, Elizabeth R., 162
Mossie, John C., 30, 37, 65, 222
Mott, Samuel, 210
Mott, Valentine, 72
Munroe, Kirk, 88
Murdock, Frank, 79, 86, 88, 90, 93, 97, 99, 105, 108, 133, 210, 222, 269
Myers, Adam, 4, 5, 224
Myers, Henry, 5
Myers, Ray, 92, 237

Nagle, Nancy E., 169
Nava, John, 90
Neagle, John, 129, 247
Newsome, Albert, 37
Nielsen, Leslie, 207, 221
Nixon, Richard M., 114, 115, 130, 159
Noble, Jim, 186
Nunn, Marion Michael, 115
Obama, Barack, 190
O'Conner, Walter, 205n
O'Daniel, W. Lee, 235
Onderdonk, Robert Jenkins, 86
O'Keefe, Neil, 113
O'Reilly, Bill, 190
Olsson, Ty, 191
Osgood, Samuel Stillman, 37, 58n

Page, Kevin, 181
Page, Robert C., 179
Parker, Chubby, 99, 259
Parker, Fess, 63, 90, 114, 116, 117, 120, 121, 125, 126, 128, 130, 133, 140, 141, 145, 146, 152, 155, 157-

160, 162, 166, 167, 175, 180-182, 184, 186, 187, 189, 194, 195, 199n, 202n, 205n, 211, 212, 218, 219-227, 229, 232, 235-237, 239, 241-244, 246-249, 252, 254, 256, 260, 261, 263, 270
Parks, Eileen Wells, 111
Parrington, Vernon Lewis, 98
Parson, Louella O., 105
Partain, Thomas, 237
Parton, Dolly, 269
Patton, Elijah, 253
Patton, Elizabeth (see also Elizabeth Crockett), 15, 56n, 253
Patton, George, 15
Patton, James, 253
Patton, Margaret Ann, 15
Patton, Robert, 222
Patton, William, 46, 48, 213, 266
Paulding, James Kirke, 28, 31, 63, 68, 73, 75, 79, 133, 270
Peale, Rembrandt, 26, 82, 195
Perrin, Jack, 237
Perry, Carmen, 149
Perry, Francis M., 85
Person, T. H., 215
Petersen, Gert, 184
Pettibone, Major, 198n
Phelan, James, 97
Poindexter, George, 218
Poindexter, Hugh, 101
Polk, James Knox, 23, 24, 83, 210, 211, 215
Porter, W. B., 65
Potter, Ruben, 73, 74, 80
Putnam, Henry, 81
Pyle, Ernie, 226

Quackenbush, Robert, 156
Quill, Dan, 268

Raine-Foreman, Caroline, 204n
Rainone, Joe, 59n

Rathbone, Perry, 129
Reiter, Harrie, 88
Remine, N. B., 198n
Reno, Kelly, 258
Retan, Walter, 166
Revere, Paul, 102
Rice, Thomas D., 35
Richards, Keith, 168
Rickenbacker, Davie, 195
Ridgeway, William Alexander, 239
Ritchie, Sharon, 127
Rivero, Julian, 102
Rix, Andy, 251
Roberts, Harry Borden, 155
Robertson, Dale, 114
Robbins, David (aka David Thompson), 172
Robbins, Tim, 160, 162
Rogers, Roy, 116
Rogers, Will, 196
Roosevelt, Franklin D., 101, 259
Roosevelt, Theodore, 85, 89, 102, 203n, 257
Ross, Thom, 173, 218
Rourke, Constance, 100
Rusk, Thomas, 49
Russell, Captain, 211
Russell, George, 10
Ruth, Babe, 99, 102
Ruth, Daniel, 157
Ryan, Irene, 146

Sanford, William, 171
Santa Anna, Antonio Lopéz de, 46, 49, 51, 52, 69, 80, 88, 92, 100-102, 108, 110, 148, 156, 166, 180, 212, 213, 230
Santrey, Laurence, 152
Savage, John, 178
Scates, S. E., 97
Schaare, C. R., 101
Schneider, John, 168, 226
Schoenke, Bob, 113

Schumann, Walter, 120, 220
Sears, A. D., 91, 257, 264
Seat, Robert, 220
Sedley, Harry, 87, 213
Seelye, John, 159
Segal, Peter, 221
Seguín, Juan, 49, 52, 246
Sensenig, Andrew, 238
Shackford, James Atkins, 139
Shackford, John B., 139
Schanzer, Rosalyn, 176
Shapiro, Irwin, 108, 128
Shaw, Artie, 111
Shaw, Russel B., 127
Shegogue, James Hamilton, 37
Shepard, Morris, 235
Sherman, William T., 74
Shoop, James, 191
Shostak, Dean, 177, 184, 215, 253
Shoumatoff, Alex, 173
Siler, John, 2, 3
Simmons, Hank, 99, 230
Simons, Justin S., 178
Simpson, J. B., 122
Sinclair, Prewitt, 66
Singer, A. L., 164
Singer, Serge, 136
Sitting Bull, 136
Smart, Billy, 136
Smith, Margaret Vance, 54n
Smith, Richard, 208
Smith, Richard Penn, 64, 76, 268
Smith, Seba, 30
Smith, T. F., 70
Snow, Seth R., 232
Snowden, Archibald Loudon, 205n
Snowden, Caroline Smith, 205n
Solik, Matt, 192
Spielberg, Steven, 174, 221, 248, 258
Sprague, William C., 93
Spreckles, A. B., 85
Standish, Myles, 68
Steele, William O., 139

Stephenson, Nathaniel, 96
Stephenson, Robert, 30
Sterne, Gordon, 232
Stevenson, Adlai, 114, 259
Stewart, Bartholomew G., 243
Stewart, Tom, 109
Stoddard, Haila, 109
Stone, Irving, 130
Stone, John Augustus, 28
Stonecypher, Roscoe, 126
Strong, Benjamin Rush, 82
Strong, Ken, 178
Sumner, Amy, 6
Sutton, Felix, 128

Taliaferro, Ernie, 172
Taylor, Alf, 198n, 249
Taylor, Mrs. E. M., 262
Taylor, R. E. B., 230
Taylor, Vincent Frank, 127
Terrel, James, 215
Thomas, Andy, 60n
Thomas, Augustus, 87
Thomas, Danny, 254
Thomason, John W., 213
Thompson, Bob, 188
Thompson, David, 172
Thompson, Ernest T., 133
Thompson, Philip, 66
Thornton, Billy Bob, 133, 181, 190, 202n, 225
Thurmond, John Houston, 100, 201n
Timanus, Rod, 174
Tinkle, Lindsay, 46, 48, 266
Tocqueville, Alexis de, 44, 45
Tolliver, Arthur, 108
Totten, James L., 214, 268
Townsend, Tom, 156
Tousey, Frank, 81
Tousey, Sandford, 109
Tracy, Spencer, 105, 133
Travis, William Barret, 49, 50, 52, 60n, 104, 113, 142, 173, 213, 217, 220, 230, 231, 240, 246, 252

Trell, Max, 113
Trollope, Frances, 28
Trotman, Felicity, 155
Truman, Harry S., 114
Trumball, Lyman, 70
Tunney, Gene, 99
Turner, Frederick Jackson, 53n, 83
Twain, Mark, 196

Uglebjerg, Preben, 136

Van Buren, Martin, 68, 83, 97, 218
Van Patten, Vince, 148, 267
Vaughn, Eleanor, 93
Vestal, H. B., 128
Villa, Pancho, 94
Von Schmidt, Eric, 153
Voss, Frederick S., 60n

Wade, Mary Dodson, 164, 185
Wahlgreen, Frances, 54n
Wainwright, Peter, 205n
Wainwright, Stuyvesant, 205n
Wallace, Allen, 54n
Wallis, Michael, 187
Warren, Charles Dudley, 80
Warren, Steve, 172
Washington, George, 8, 229
Waters, Sterling, 102
Wayne, John, 109, 113, 140, 142, 143, 157, 159, 202n, 205n, 220, 223, 231, 237, 248, 258, 260, 263
Webb, Noel, 169
Webster, Daniel, 31, 263
Webster, Laman, 245
Weil, Robert, 161, 241
Wells, E. L., 249
Weissmann, Murray, 177
Weissmuller, Johnny, 109, 248

Wharton, Clarence, 101
White, Hugh, 244
White, Kathleen, 196
White, William C., 67, 213, 214
Wickliffe, Mr., 215
Wickware, Scott, 225
Wiener, Alan J., 58n, 171, 184, 185, 202n
Wilde, Richard Henry, 217
Willett, Edward, 89
Williams, John, 20
Williams, Patty, 126, 127
Williamson, R. M., 51
Wilson, Abraham, 5, 6
Wilson, Kendrick, 263
Wilson, Mary, 144
Wilson, Nat, 127
Wilson, Ned, 150, 264
Winch, Frank, 96
Winchester, James R., 209
Winchester, Marcus, 22
Winders, Bruce, 186, 187
Wiseman, Mac, 120
Wood, David L., 68
Wood, K. R., 178, 184, 193, 215
Wright, David, 68, 174
Wynne, Jack, 189

Yastrzemski, Carl, 203n
Yohn, Frederick Coffay, 92
York, Alvin, 94, 128, 269
York, Jeff, 129, 211
Young, Fred, 162
Young, Paul, 153
Young, Richard, 258

Zaboly, Gary, 199n, 203n
Zucker, David, 160-162, 164, 165, 172, 196, 197, 221, 225, 241, 246

The author. Image created by Charles Martin Brazil.

OTHER BEARMANOR MEDIA BOOKS WRITTEN BY WILLIAM R. CHEMERKA

General Joseph Warren Revere: The Gothic Saga of Paul Revere's Grandson
Joseph Warren Revere served in the U. S. Navy; circumnavigated the globe; raised the first American flag in Sonoma, California during the Mexican War; battled pirates, sharks, and Indians; searched for gold; had a scandalous affair; served in the Union Army during the Civil War and received a court-martial for his actions during the Battle of Chancellorsville. And then he began the fight of his life.

Rock & Roll Recollections: A Journalist's 50-Year Diary

A revealing and interesting compilation of interview, conversations, and anecdotes about a diverse lineup of classic rock, pop, and soul performers, including the Beach Boys, Phil Collins, the Who, Van Halen, Meatloaf, the Ramones, Judas Priest, Danny and the Juniors, Stevie Ray Vaughan, ZZ Top, and more.

The Battle of Bunker Hill: A Novella based upon the Docudrama

An exciting story of the first major military conflict of the American Revolution and how two fathers and two sons left their respective farms to defend the heights overlooking Boston in 1775. Based on the 2009 Light a Candle Films production *The Battle of Bunker Hill*, produced and directed by Tony Malanowski.

Fess Parker: TV's Frontier Hero

The authorized biography of the Texan who served in World War II, and later became television's Davy Crockett in the 1950s, and Daniel Boone in the 1960s. After he ended his TV, film, and recording career in the 1970s, Parker became a successful businessman, hotel builder, and vintner in California. He was named a Disney Legend in 1991. The biography includes never-before-published photographs of Parker.

Gunga Din: From Kipling's Poem to Hollywood's Action-Adventure Classic

A comprehensive examination of the memorable 1939 RKO film directed by George Stevens about three British sergeants and the determined water carrier who served in India's northwest frontier in the late 19th century. The book is filled with images, including some that have never been published before.

www.ingramcontent.com/pod-product-compliance
Lightning Source LLC
Chambersburg PA
CBHW071955220426
43662CB00009B/1141